Political Volatility in
the United States

Voting, Elections, and the Political Process

Series Editors: Shauna Reilly and Stacy Ulbig

Receptive to studies in the American and comparative settings, the *Voting, Elections, and the Political Process* series examines the broadly defined electoral process. The series seeks scholarly monographs and edited volumes that investigate the ways in which voters, candidates, elected officials, parties, interest groups, the media, and others interact in the context of electoral politics. Works with a focus on individual attitudes and behavior, institutional and contextual influences, and the legal aspects of the electoral process are welcome. This series accepts interdisciplinary work using a variety of methodological approaches.

Recent Titles

Political Volatility in the United States: How Racial and Religious Groups Win and Lose by Baodong Liu

At Your Convenience: America's Early Voting Revolution by Elliott B. Fullmer

The 2020 Presidential Election in the South edited by Scott E. Buchanan and DuBose Kapeluck

The Trifecta in Voting Barrier Causation: Economics, Politics, and Race by Shauna Reilly

An Unprecedented President and the Prospect for American Democracy by Arthur Paulson

The Resilient Voter: Stressful Polling Places and Voting Behavior by Shauna Reilly and Stacy Ulbig

Unconventional, Partisan, and Polarizing Rhetoric: How the 2016 Election Shaped the Way Candidates Strategize, Engage, and Communicate edited by Jeanine E. Kraybill

The 2016 Presidential Election: The Causes and Consequences of a Political Earthquake edited by Amnon Cavari, Richard J. Powell, and Kenneth R. Mayer

Political Volatility in the United States

How Racial and Religious Groups Win and Lose

Baodong Liu

LEXINGTON BOOKS
Lanham • Boulder • New York • London

Published by Lexington Books
An imprint of The Rowman & Littlefield Publishing Group, Inc.
4501 Forbes Boulevard, Suite 200, Lanham, Maryland 20706
www.rowman.com

86-90 Paul Street, London EC2A 4NE

British Library Cataloguing in Publication Information Available

Library of Congress Cataloging-in-Publication Data

Names: Liu, Baodong, 1965- author.
Title: Political volatility in the United States : how racial and religious groups win and lose / Baodong Liu.
Description: Lanham : Lexington Books, [2022] | Series: Voting, elections, and the political process | Includes bibliographical references and index.
Identifiers: LCCN 2021043600 (print) | LCCN 2021043601 (ebook) | ISBN 9781793651280 (cloth) | ISBN 9781793651303 (paperback) | ISBN 9781793651297 (ebook)
Subjects: LCSH: Political parties—United States—History. | Minorities—Political activity—United States. | Religion and politics—United States. | Group identity—Political aspects—United States. | Equality—United States. | Political sociology—United States. | United States—Politics and government.
Classification: LCC JK2265 .L58 2021 (print) | LCC JK2265 (ebook) | DDC 324.273—dc23/eng/20211001
LC record available at https://lccn.loc.gov/2021043600
LC ebook record available at https://lccn.loc.gov/2021043601

For Dick Engstrom

Contents

List of Figures and Tables

FIGURES

TABLES

Acknowledgments

Writing this book has taken a much longer time than working on any of my previous books. The urge to focus on political volatility, an important and yet strangely understudied topic, came to me during the first term of President Obama's administration. It was based on my realization of too many observers, among them some of the most prominent political scientists, jumping to a conclusion that electing Obama had heralded an era of post-racial politics. I strongly opposed this view in an earlier book of mine, *The Election of Barack Obama: How He Won*. But after that book was published in 2010, it became clear to me that it would be necessary to go further in discussing the intersections of race and religion in order to understand the source of volatility in American politics.

The election of Donald Trump in 2016 made it clear that to fully capture the structural reasons for his surprising win of the presidency in one of the most volatile political eras, one should put race and religion into considering the historical trajectory of American democracy. During the first two years of the Trump administration, I formulated and developed the atomic structure theory and its operating principles. The book manuscript was finally ready for blind peer review and revision at the time when the nation elected Joe Biden in 2020.

The COVID-19 pandemic, undoubtedly, underscored the urgency in completing this book. It also reminded me how precious life is and why we need our loved ones more than ever. In addition to my immediate family, including my wife, Lu, and my two children, Rebecca and Daniel, Dick Engstrom has long been a part of my closest circle of life. He was my dissertation advisor who shaped my professional life more profoundly than any other scholar, and he especially has a lasting influence on my thinking about racial relations, as manifested in this book. Moreover, the impact of Dick and his wife, Carol, on every member of my family is beyond the traditional expectations of a mentoring relationship. This book is dedicated to him.

I also would like to thank Les Roka who not only read and edited the manuscript but also offered theoretical insights and verified political facts. Without Les, this book certainly would not have been fully developed to its current form. Mary Banks, my assistant, provided timely data-collection assistance. Mark Button and Brent Steele at the Department of Political Science of The University of Utah facilitated the completion of the book in many of their capacities as chair. Edmund Fong, the chair of the Ethnic Studies Program at The University of Utah, granted me a one-course reduction in 2018 to finish and submit the original version of the book proposal. Edmund also read a part of my proposal and introduction and gave his astute suggestions. Michael Dichio, a fellow political scientist, was generous in offering many of his great ideas to logically connect my atomic structure theory to the American political development literature. I have been blessed with many productive conversations with brilliant colleagues, such as Desmond King, David Wilson, Sharon Austin-Wright, D'Andra Orey, Laura Olson, Hakan Yavuz, Steven Lobell, Steven Johnston, Chris Hsiung, Jia Lu, Ming Wen, Colin Wu, Joseph Zhou, and Bob Darcy, among others. Many graduate and undergraduate students in my seminars about political volatility also played an unforgettable role in reinforcing my conviction in American democracy and its incredible resilience through numerous volatile episodes, past or future. Finally, special thanks goes to Joseph Parry, Monika Jagadeesh, and Sara Noakes at Lexington Books, and Shauna Reilly, the editor of Lexington's Voting, Elections, and the Political Process Series.

Introduction

The Roots of Political Volatility in the United States

When summer arrived in 2020, the United States had failed to "flatten the curve" in the numbers of COVID-19 cases, raising questions about how President Donald J. Trump's administration had managed the federal government's response to the worst pandemic in a century. Meanwhile, the murder of George Floyd, a 46-year-old Black man, in Minneapolis, Minnesota, on May 25, 2020, sparked mass demonstrations across the country against police brutality. Before the end of June, the Black Lives Matter (BLM) movement became the platform advocating for racial justice at a global scale. National polling conducted in July showed that President Trump trailed his Democratic challenger and former vice president, Joe Biden, by more than 10 percentage points. The groups that drove Biden's surge in polls in June and July of 2020 were seniors and white voters with college degrees (Wasserman, 2020).

On July 30 at 6:46 a.m. EDT, shortly after the report that the U.S. economy had suffered its biggest quarterly contraction ever, President Trump sent out the following message on Twitter calling for the 2020 presidential election to be delayed: "With Universal Mail-In Voting (not Absentee Voting, which is good), 2020 will be the most INACCURATE & FRAUDULENT Election in history. It will be a great embarrassment to the USA. Delay the Election until people can properly, securely and safely vote???"

Trump's tweet surprised even his own allies, drawing criticism from the Republican leaders in Congress as well as conservative organizations such as the Federalist Society, whose co-founder Steve Calabresi (2020) called for the impeachment of President Trump. His characterization of "the most inaccurate and fraudulent election" and his unsubstantiated accusations of corruption and fraud in "Democratic-run" cities and states prior to the actual voting itself brought back memories of the history of race relations and the

1

struggles of African Americans for legal protection of their voting rights. It was the 1867 *Military Reconstruction Act* and the *Fifteenth Amendment* ratified in 1870 that required southern states to grant the access of Black males to voting. "The elimination of black suffrage was made possible," not only through Jim Crow laws, remarked political scientist Chandler Davidson in his chronicle of U.S. voting rights history, but also by "northern indifference to the plight of southern blacks after the Hayes-Tilden Compromise in 1877" (which resolved the disputed 1876 presidential election and effectively ended the Reconstruction Era with U.S. troops pulling out of the former Confederate states). Furthermore, the Supreme Court struck down several provisions of the Enforcement Act of 1870 and the Force Act of 1871, "permitting southern states to rewrite their constitutions to exclude blacks by devices such as literacy and good character test and the poll tax" (Davidson, 1994, 21). By the turn of the twentieth century, in the eleven states of the former Confederacy the Black vote had already been diluted or completely nullified (Kousser, 1999; Davidson and Grofman, 1994).

Amplified fear among Black voters in the summer of 2020—which coincided with the passing of John Lewis, legendary voting rights leader—about being disenfranchised invited compelling questions about the stability of the democracy and the near-term trajectory of U.S. history. Trump came to power after the nation had elected its first Black president who served two terms. Many Black voters, at first, did not believe that the American electorate was ready to elect a Black president when Barack Obama announced his candidacy for president in Springfield, Illinois, on February 10, 2007. Thirteen Black presidential candidates had tried and failed to win the highest office. But within a year Obama drew record crowds nearly everywhere he went in his 2008 campaign. David Wright, during the evening news program of ABC News, described the mood of the nation on February 19, 2008, in this way: "People's hope has been raised so high: Young people hoping that Obama can redeem politics from sheer partisanship; Blacks hoping that they can finally achieve Martin Luther King's Dream; White people hoping that he can redeem America from the sin of slavery and segregation."

Obama won the election with 53 percent of the votes in 2008. Moreover, he was able to build an unprecedented multiracial coalition to win the presidency. Exit polls conducted on election day showed that whites cast 74 percent of the total votes in the 2008 general election. More than 38 million white votes were cast for Obama, which constituted 61 percent of Obama's total votes (Liu, 2010; West, 2010). The historic white support for Obama appeared to support the claim that America had entered the so-called post-racial era. Political scientists Ceaser, Busch, and Pitney wrote in 2009 that the election of Obama "showed how far race relations had progressed" and that "this result [of Obama's election] leaves open the possibility that, like the question of Catholicism after the 1960 election (where John Kennedy's religious affiliation was considered), race will diminish as an issue in national electoral politics in the future" (28).

The unexpected success of Trump in winning the 2016 presidential election shocked Democratic voters as well as observers of U.S. presidential elections who earlier had claimed the arrival of a post-racial era in U.S. politics. The rapid political changes since Trump's election also proved how premature that claim turned out to be. Not only has racial tension grown dramatically, the daily political reality itself seems more unpredictable than ever. Take Portland, Oregon, for example. In the summer of 2008 and just a week before Obama was officially nominated by the Democratic Party, his supporters gathered in his final campaign rally and the passionate crowd quickly grew to about 75,000 people. Only twelve years later, however, Portland become the site where the Trump administration sent federal agents wearing camouflage uniforms to confront Black Lives Matter protestors, to project the image of a "law and order" president, most notably Portland, Oregon, where agents were sent to control the streets around the federal courthouse in mid- and late July 2020 (Barrett et al., 2020). The tremendous shift from Obama's election and post-racial hopes to the rapid rise of Trump and worsening racial relations illuminates a question central to this book: Why did such a volatile swing occur within such a short time?

POLITICAL VOLATILITY

The political changes during the Obama and Trump administrations and the potential impacts of these changes will certainly be debated among scholars for many years to come. This book puts the political volatility of the 2008–2020 period in broader historical contexts explaining how social groups, especially racial and religious ones, have interacted with each other and have variously won and lost politically. When rapid political changes occur, social groups are unsure about how the next federal administration will affect the direction of existing policies and whatever progress already made in their favor (at least, from the perspective of the affected social group) will be sustained in the new term.

Uncertainty reigns in volatile political times, but the clearest effect of this volatility, in the short run, is its immediate impact on rapid changes in human emotions. Chief among these emotions is fear. The fear of losing, in particular, has led to the unprecedented polarization between the left and the right, diminishing the incentive to compromise. As Lilliana Mason put it, "As multiple groups line up behind one party or the other, they all win or lose together. The humiliation of loss is amplified" (Mason, 2018, 23).

Political volatility has also worried many observers of American politics about the future of a viable democratic republic and its constitutional practices. Perhaps Thomas Friedman, a columnist for *The New York Times*, articulated most effectively the anxiety many observers of American democracy had with respect to the Trump White House. After examining President Trump's efforts to block the investigation of Special Counsel Robert Mueller regarding possible Russian interference in the 2016 presidential election, Friedman concluded: "That [possible obstruction of justice] must not be tolerated. This is code red. The biggest threat to the integrity of our democracy today is in the Oval Office" (Friedman, 2018).

In the eyes of the political left and Never-Trump-moderate Republicans, the president's persistent efforts to halt the investigation along with many controversial policy positions on issues ranging from immigration, racial justice, and environmental protection to healthcare insurance costs and access, taxes, among others, have turned the country backward. LeBron James, one of the NBA's most prominent star athletes, remarked:

> We are at a time when the most powerful position in the world has the opportunity to bring us close together as a people and inspire youth and put youth at ease by saying it's OK for me to walk down the street and not be judged by the color of my skin or because of my race . . . And [Trump] doesn't even care. (Schilken, 2017)

But, for his core supporters, Trump represented the best hope for the country, a point that reinforced their unwavering loyalty. The stark differences between Trump's opponents and supporters raise the difficult question about the possibilities of finding consensus on how the country should move forward. Is there any common ground to pursue a more just and more equal society for all, which would be acceptable to all Americans, regardless of their support or criticism of the president, whomever that person might be?

Americans always will have different opinions on justice because "good people" are always divided by politics and religion, a remark couched by the moral psychologist Jonathan Haidt in *The Righteous Mind,* a book written during the second term of Obama's presidency but also well before anyone would have suggested that Trump would be a formidable contender for the presidency (Haidt, 2012). The differences between the left and the right, as defined in the United States, have its roots, according to Haidt, in how human minds are "prewired" and then "revised" by the environments they encounter in shaping their worldviews. Perhaps, it might be better not to demand consensus, especially on the issue of racial and religious justice and equality, to the dismay of others who see a corrective path, but also worry that a particular approach might inadvertently disenfranchise or aggrieve some Americans.

Haidt's view on the fundamental differences and their unresolvable conflicts between the left and the right, as he acknowledged, was influenced by intuitionism. Espoused by David Hume, the Enlightenment philosopher from Scotland, this philosophical school of thought that emphasized the central role of human emotions has been forcefully challenged by various American political philosophers including John Rawls who suggested that agreement or "social contract" is possible among rational political actors.

To be sure, there have been endless, inconclusive debates among philosophers and social psychologists about how achieving full social justice is possible in the first place, given the historically rooted differences between Americans. As an effort to resolve our differences, more than forty years ago Rawls, an American philosopher in the liberal tradition, proposed a principle of justice based on his belief in the human capability to engage in conscientious reflection and moral reason. His principle started with the ideal of equality, as affected by the condition of a "veil of ignorance," which is observed among all parties and stakeholders in the initial phase of forming a social contract. That is, no one knows in advance any advantages or disadvantages that would manifest themselves when proposing an acceptable principle of justice to emulate and follow. All of the parties and stakeholders to a social contract are willing to agree on the broad term of equality when they do not know which party or stakeholder actually will be positioned as the most advantaged. However, all of the engaged parties would recognize, once the veil is pulled away, that no real (or politically feasible) sense of equality would be possible in the ensuing realities, because there always will be parties and stakeholders who will enjoy more advantages (for example, just because many reward individuals for higher education levels especially when they attend elite institutions) and pay comparatively lower cost for finding the path to success (for example, just because they are born into privileged circumstances). Based on the inevitable social reality, Rawls then proposed a fairness principle, which essentially requires that social and economic inequalities "are just only if they result in compensating benefits for everyone, and in particular for the least advantaged members of society" (Rawls, 1971, 14–15). Though this book is not a direct response to the philosophical debate between the schools of thought put forth by Hume and Rawls, it does address not only why these differences came to exist but also why they matter in American politics. This book discusses how members of religious and racial groups in the United States always have maintained solid allegiances within their respective groups and how their differences led to a history of political volatility in the United States, which is not exclusive to the current time.

Political volatility in this book refers to the unexpected and/or unpredictable changes in the political statuses of social groups, reflected by their gains (or losses) in rights, legal protections, and political representations. The main aim is to explain why and under what conditions political volatility may take place for racial and religious groups in America. If political volatility does happen in a certain historical context, what then becomes the range of possible changes in these groups' political statuses (if no one is sure what exact change(s) may be expected).

To carry forward a holistic study of complex group relations in the United States, I take an interdisciplinary approach based on the collective forces called the atomic structure (introduced in chapter 2). This book is, first of all, inspired by the modern social psychological literature about how human affect and cognition work in human grouping, and what is the foundation of in-group favoritism and human groupings. As David Hume (1978) in his eighteenth-century *A Treatise of Human Nature*, reminded us, all human passions have a common root in "self," and whether or not attraction can take place between humans is related to how they can be associated through "resemblance" (see, in particular, Part II, Section I of his Treatise). Taking into account the magnitude of in-group favoritism or bias, this book puts forth the argument that, even in this particular volatile period of American politics, it still is politically feasible and practical to reduce levels of inequality among social groups over time. Distinguishing from the rational choice theory of Rawls and his opponents in the traditions of utilitarianism and intuitionism, this book suggests that the reason for the possibility of political progress directed toward strengthening the climate for equality between and among social groups is because of the collective forces that go beyond the premises of rationalists such as Rawls and his peers who express their own political counterpoints to his philosophical premises. These collective forces comprise the atomic structure of politics, as explained in this book. Furthermore, the intersections of modern psychology and neuroscience have deepened our understanding of how our unique political affections are intertwined with our perceptions of external threats. To account for group-level phenomena, however, one has to go beyond the micro-level analysis of individuals.

This book also is inspired by sociologists who explored how societies evolve and develop what Nicholas Christakis (2019) labels as the social suites. Groups also can be positioned in a society structurally, as suggested by Herbert Blumer (1958), and there is a core group that initiates and defines the relative positions of potentially all groups in a society. As Rogers Smith (2015) argues in his recent comparative study (*Political Peoplehood*), how a society determines the memberships of the core against those of peripheries is formulated not only socially and politically but also culturally through storytelling, scholarly texts, visual arts and folk songs, among other media, genres, and categories. Finally, to combine the micro-level analysis of individuals and macro-level examination of groups and their relationship positions within a society, a theoretical proposition can be advanced by analyzing the historical data to assess its validity and relevance.

This book borrows heavily from the American political development literature on how the two racial alliances and political groupings, or the two racial orders, as coined in the original work of King and Smith (2005), have shaped and are reorienting the trajectory of American democracy. There always has been an antagonistic ideological rivalry between the egalitarians and white supremacists (referred to as traditionalists in this book). The color-blind and race-conscious institutional alliances also are documented in King and Smith's more recent work (2011). But, King and Smith focused their analysis mainly on elites who occupy political institutions.

While one can agree on the importance of elites in the history of American political development, the atomic structure presented in this book also leads the readers back to considering the importance of grassroots voters (Nackenoff, 2014). This book emphasizes that it is through competitive elections that major political developments occur, and groups either gain or lose their status, rights, legal protections, and political representations. Because of the paramount objective to win competitive elections, a pair of rival alliances has been formed not only based on the ideological differences between them but also because of strategic decisions of racial and religious groups to be on the winning side in the political game. These strategic alliances sometimes do help minorities raise their group status, especially when electoral volatility spikes to higher than standardly predicted levels.

This book aims to provide a systemic model for understanding how competing "orders" grounded in white supremacy and egalitarianism have collided, contested, and endured across American history. To continue, it explains why these orders persist and reach peaks of volatility, as well as how a specific order achieves prominence at least temporarily over another. Hence, where Smith and King (and the American political development literature generally) give primarily historical accounts that narrate the ebb and flow between these two orders, this book expands the analysis, which is rooted in strategic imperatives and pressures, opportunities and threats on collective action.

CHAPTER OUTLINE

This book comprises two parts. In part I (chapters 1–8), it develops and explains the five axioms or principles (as represented by the ADVICE acronym) which introduces the atomic structure for consideration. Then, in part II (chapters 9–13), the book applies these principles in case studies to explain the atomic structure within the context of political volatility throughout U.S. history, especially since the Civil Rights era.

Chapter 1 introduces a puzzle about political volatility and social groups as framed within the 2012 presidential campaign. The basic concept of the atomic structure and its five principles as represented by the acronym ADVICE are introduced in chapter 2. The chapter then addresses how political volatility extends beyond racial and religious minority groups and the implications for White Anglo-Saxon Protestant (WASP) political dominance and how that position has waned considerably in recent generations.

Chapter 3 summarizes the relevant research on rationality and perceptions and whether or not the clues from the existing research can clarify our ability to solve the puzzle presented in chapter 1. In rejecting the possibility that rational choice theory alone is enough to explain the way that voters collectively select their candidates, I consider the role that political perceptions and habits may play in their decision-making process. The social psychology theory which proposes that various factors (such as social demographics and party identification) influence voter's decisions sequentially is introduced as an alternate explanation to rational choice. But, that too is insufficient to describe comprehensively what has occurred. This chapter points out the intellectual challenge of evaluation—particularly in the face of multiple threats and negative information, which become more common in periods of intense political volatility. The chapter dives into the complexities of voter evaluation process, eventually concluding that the weight of risks has far more pull on the ultimate decision than the potential appeal of rewards.

In chapters 4 and 5, the origins of multiple threats along with what become concrete and abstract threats are discussed. Several chapters introduce the principles and corresponding historical events in American politics that are integral to the atomic structure theory. In chapters 6, 7, and 8, the five axioms or principles which inform the theory of atomic group structure, as represented in the ADVICE acronym, are presented. Numerous historical events are discussed in chapter 6, and readers will note the ongoing references to the case of the 2012 presidential election with challenger Mitt Romney (white but a member of The Church of Jesus Christ of Latter-day Saints) and the incumbent Barack Obama (Protestant but Black). As the first instance of a U.S. presidential election in which neither major candidate could claim status as a member of the historically dominant WASPs group in its full traditional description, this election is instrumental for how the atomic structure theory is postulated.

Data collected from the 2012 elections demonstrate how the complexity of weighing multiple threats can play out in the voters' decision-making process. Based on the 2012 data, it is clear that white Protestants voted against Romney in large numbers due to his out-group status as a religious minority during the primary. Yet, in the general election, white Protestants supported Romney in droves against his Black Protestant opponent, Obama. Clearly, not all threats are perceived as equal.

The attraction-similarity principle (which represents the A in ADVICE) is introduced to explain how dominant groups assess the degree of threat from out-groups. When determining positionality, the dominant group is accepted as the norm with all minorities holding some degree of otherness. This leads to the second principle introduced in the book: the distance principle (which represents the D in ADVICE), explaining how members of the dominant groups perceive the degree of threat that minority groups pose, as based on their degree of difference. For instance, the pure WASP identity status covers the ideal, white Protestant with origins in northwestern Europe (such as Germans) as preferable to white Catholic southeastern Europeans (such as Italians). While these characteristics can be effective in determining the abstract threat that a minority group poses, the abstract threat itself does not necessarily lead to a specific response from the dominant group.

Chapter 7 takes up this challenge of predicting the dominant group's response to particular levels of threat and concludes that the response to a threat is based on various factors—only one of which is the degree of threat present. Instead of predicting the dominant group's response to a minority group at a given time, the significance of the threat is actually related to the number of possible responses that the dominant group may provide. The more threatening a group is, the greater range of possible responses it could solicit from the dominant group, and therefore the degree of political volatility also grows to which the minority group is likely to experience. This is labeled as the volatility principle, the third principle (which represents the V in ADVICE).

In chapter 8, I continue to dissect the factors that produce a dominant group's response to a minority group. This time, rather than looking at intergroup relations, I examine the way that the internal organizations of the dominant group can influence the broader political context. In explaining the interworking of a dominant group, I identify the fourth and fifth principles of the book. The fourth is the internal-threat principle (which represents the I in ADVICE), indicating the dominant group has divided into two competing political coalitions, only one of which will be allied with minority groups. The purpose of this division is to maintain dominant group leadership within both major political factions. The fifth principle is the competitive-election principle (which represents the C and E in ADVICE). That is, whichever political coalition is currently winning has the opportunity to determine the temporary status of a minority group. Ultimately, this chapter presents an argument for the common structure of internal conflict within the dominant core of the political system—that is, the atomic structure. This concept is integral to the case studies presented in part II.

The second part of this book applies the theory of atomic structure to the modern political context. I examine the past several election cycles with an eye toward ever-shifting race relationships in American politics. In chapter 9, after thoroughly constructing the atomic structure theory, I show how the theory is useful when trying to make sense of U.S. political changes. In particular, this chapter focuses on using the theory to explain the changing status of the historically dominant WASP group. Citing the 1920s as the most recent peak of WASP power, I examine several competing theories commonly used to explain the decline that followed.

There are two main schools of thought in this area. The first posits the decline of WASPs as the result of internal conflict. While many particular theories exist in this realm, Eric Kaufmann's theory of liberal progressivism comes closest to being complete. By contrast, the other school of thought envisions the WASP decline in power as an issue of boundary control rather than as a total demise. Here, scholars such as Theodore Wright describe the decline as an issue of necessary assimilation and integration of minority groups due primarily to changing demographics. In chapter 10, instead of adopting one of these two theories, I pull ideas from each to support my more unified theory of atomic structure. Incorporating the five principles introduced in the first part of the book, this chapter explains the WASP decline, thereby setting the stage to solve the puzzle presented in chapter 1.

The end of WASP domination ushered in profound political changes and the reconfiguration of the atomic structure. The new core now contains all whites with a European origin. Chapter 11 zeroes in on racial divisions in post-1965 American politics. I examine the way that race has interacted with and helped to shape the modern Democratic and Republican parties. According to the internal-threat principle, the concrete threat minorities pose to the two dominant group coalitions differs significantly and is fundamental to divergences and splits occurring within the white electorate. Additionally, the competitive-election principle suggests that the experiences and positions of the minority groups are largely determined by the winning coalition.

As a result, the minority groups are highly relevant to the internal conflict of the new core of the atomic structure. According to the empirical data analyzed in chapter 11, minority groups in the majority of numbers consistently have been aligned with the Democratic Party since 1965, yet whites also remain absolutely critical to the success of the Democratic Party. There has not yet been a point when Democrats could win a presidential election with less than 60 percent of their total votes coming from whites. As race has been central to American politics, I describe the process of deracialization that has gradually redefined political rhetoric, especially by the Democratic leadership to build multiracial coalitions. Overall, the atomic political structure has made it challenging for minority leaders, notably Obama, to navigate American politics.

They have been forced to balance the risk of posing a threat to whites while trying to address the need to make substantive change in policy making.

Chapter 12 returns to the 2012 election, allowing us to complete solving the puzzle of chapter 1. While Obama did not win a majority of white voters, this voting bloc was still critical to his victory as an incumbent. The two candidates, in an unprecedented representation, provided the perfect opportunity to test the validity of the atomic structure. How would white voters, especially WASPs, respond to multiple minority candidates without a candidate of their own? This chapter examines the patterns that existed among white voters who supported Romney and the voters who changed their voting preferences between the GOP primaries and the general election. Using the existing theories about group relations, this chapter tests four hypotheses including the strategic voting hypothesis that I derived from the ADVICE principles encompassing the atomic structure. The empirical results support the theory proposed in this book.

Chapter 13 looks to the current political environment and the 2016 election cycle. It starts by describing the changing threat environment that set the stage for Trump's ascendance and what was to come in the election. There were concerns that race relations had worsened as Obama neared the end of his presidency. The Black Lives Matter movement was gaining steam while white support for Obama was waning. When Trump entered the campaign, the racial tensions were compounded and exacerbated. The threat that not only African Americans but Mexican Americans and Muslims also posed to white supremacy became clear in Trump's campaign. This history again fits well within the proposed atomic structure model. Rhetoric of an anti-immigrant and anti-minority nature was born out of concrete and abstract threats perceived of several minority groups, especially Mexicans and Muslims. Playing on the fear that the threat of these minority groups provoked, one of the dominant group coalitions secured their victory.

The conclusion briefly restates the theory and invites readers to digest and interpret the trajectory of American democracy in their own experiences, within the context of political volatility that is the springboard for this theory. There is space for optimism, and it is not foolish to hope for a more just American society. It only is foolish to believe that achieving progress is an easy, linear, and fast process.

THE IMPORTANCE OF DIFFERENCES BETWEEN GROUPS AND WITHIN ONE GROUP

Many previous studies of racial politics have focused either on intergroup differences or intragroup divergence, and they lead expectedly to different conclusions. For example, the end of WASP dominance in the U.S. politics has been explained as a result of intergroup struggles which forced WASPs to concede their political power over time (see, e.g., Wright, 2004). But, for scholars of intragroup divergence, WASP decline occurred because of ideological debates within the WASP cultural elites (Kaufmann, 2004). The importance of studying both intergroup and intragroup differences highlights three points central to this book.

First, individuals of a group do see themselves belonging to a social group, whether or not the group identity is defined by race, religion, or something else, and their political, economic, and social status is affected by their group identity. Michael Dawson (1994) described this as a phenomenon of linked fate, as he explained how African American political opinions and behaviors coalesced into a coherent social group. But, at the same time, not all members of a social group may agree on the approach they should take to maintain or change their group status. Differences entail deep political implications. For example, during the Civil Rights Movement, divergences within both whites (e.g., liberals versus conservatives) and African Americans (e.g., Martin Luther King Jr. versus Malcolm X concerning integration or separation) generated debates about prioritizing political objectives and needs (King and Smith, 2005; Lichtman, 2008). Regarding Asian Americans, opinions are divided about whether or not affirmative action programs and the perceptions of a "model minority" have been helpful or harmful to protecting Asian American interests (Liu, 2018; Zhou, 2009; Chua and Rubenfeld, 2014).

Second, political changes occur as differences between groups and divergences within a group upend the political equilibrium and leads to a new political coalition that is competitive in elections (Riker, 1962). For example, slavery not only contributed to racial inequality between whites and Blacks but also divided white communities in the latter half of the nineteenth century (Kaufmann, 2004). Abraham Lincoln's Republican coalition won the 1860 election and eventually ended slavery after a brutal war. Thus, to understand political changes, one has to examine both intergroup differences as well as intragroup divergence.

Finally, modern nation states are seldom monolithic and static, and demographic changes amplify tensions in societies as well as political systems (Schmidt et al., 2009; Hero, 2007). The United States, in particular, has always been a society of multiple groups. At its founding, African Americans, for instance, were about 20 percent of the population when the Constitution was ratified. Thus, groups constantly searched for the most effective approach in dealing with each other, particularly as they often have faced multiple threats simultaneously. For example, the white majority has been compelled to face perceptions of multiple threats from Blacks, Hispanics, Asians, and Native Americans throughout American history. Minority groups, for the same reason, also face perceptions of multiple threats from whites and from each other. Inside the white majority, religious differences between and among Protestants, Catholics, and Latter-day Saints also have led to political confrontations. In short, groups adapt to evolving environments, and their political strategies change accordingly (Tate, 2014).

Of course, studying multiple groups simultaneously is a complex task. This book borrows insights from several disciplines of the social sciences. The rational choice theory in political science, for instance, suggests that understanding individuals as rational agents is critical to building a theory of group (partisan) behavior (Downs, 1957). If group identity is critical to how an individual will be treated in a political system, then it is reasonable to assume that individuals will vote accordingly to maximize their group interests. But, social psychological research also shows that making decisions to maximize politically favorable circumstances is difficult at the grassroots levels for communities of people, if possible at all (Lau and Redlawsk, 2006; Bartels, 2008).

Individuals are rational, but they also are more likely to turn away from risks. Negative information, such as the perceptions of external threats from an out-group, often gets more attention in individuals' cognitive and evaluative processes than the benefit of activities, which would generate concrete rewards. This book examines how groups collectively respond politically to risks and threats they perceive not individually, but wholly as a group.

One more difficulty in studying multiple groups simultaneously is that all the groups under study must be placed in the same theoretical framework. For example, suppose a society has three groups (A, B, and C), then a sound theory should be capable of explaining the relationships between A and B, A and C, and B and C, at the same time. This theory should also explain how these complex relationships may cause divergences within a group, especially within the dominant group which has the power to change public policies. Unfortunately, many existing studies focus on political experiences from a limiting uniracial or biracial perspectives (e.g., Dawson, 1994; Barreto, 2010).

To build a richer theory concerning multiple groups, this book borrows extensively from sociological theories, especially the group position theory developed by Herbert Blumer (1958). By introducing the atomic group structure, this book then sets out to explain not only the historical experiences of minority groups—including German Americans, white Catholics, Latter-day Saints, Blacks, Hispanics, Asians, and Native Americans—but also the experiences of the nation's originally dominant group, namely, WASPs. Therefore, the book not only explains why social groups endure and sustain their positions through governmental actions and policies but also how group positions have evolved throughout history, in particular the historical changes leading to the end of WASP dominant group status (Blumer, 1958).

Throughout the chapters, readers will see numerous examples comparing and contrasting group experiences to reveal similarities and differences among them, as situated across the long timeline of U.S. history. The book is developed from considerations of qualitative and quantitative data. While historical events (for example, the 1838–1839 removal of Cherokees) are examined based on public speeches, government documents, and secondary data, contemporary issues (for example, racial divides on immigration policies and the 2016 campaign) are analyzed through surveys, polling and voting trends, which are tested for statistical significance.

In sum, by positing a unified theory concerning multiple groups, this book contributes to scholarship in political science and American studies by explaining why political changes affecting social groups have occurred. These political changes can be both positive (e.g., Reconstruction in the post-bellum era) and negative (e.g., Jim Crow laws after Reconstruction). One clear benefit of studying political volatility is that it helps to address the normative debate on social justice and group inequality. For example, should inequality be a necessary evil for a just society? Why does it occur in the first place? For Edmund Burke, inequality serves the role of motivating individuals to work harder. Rawls acknowledged that his theory would be challenged by two most formidable schools of thought on social justice: utilitarianism and intuitionism. Utilitarianism proposes a principle based on maximization of benefits, especially happiness, while intuitionism does not believe that it is even possible for people from different positions to form a consensus on a moral principle in the first place. Passions always take over the rationality, said intuitionists such as David Hume. The best way out of the dilemma, according to some scholars, is pluralism. The empirical analysis of group inequality presented in this book provides evidence for the theoretical claims proposed by pluralist scholars such as Miller, Walzer, and Inazu (see Miller, 1999; Walzer, 1984; Inazu, 2016).

A better understanding of these political changes is not only useful in grasping the trajectory of social group relations in U.S. history but also invites readers to a timely investigation of American democracy and its resilient potential to deliver ultimately upon genuine promises of freedom and equality.

Part I

INTRODUCING THE THEORY AND PRINCIPLES OF THE ATOMIC STRUCTURE

Chapter 1

Political Volatility and Social Groups

A Puzzle

Let us start with a puzzle, which will be solved in part II of this book. William Congreve, an English playwright and poet of the Restoration period once remarked, "Fear comes from uncertainty. When we are absolutely certain, whether of our worth or worthlessness, we are almost impervious to fear." After another deadly mass shooting in El Paso, Texas, on August 3, 2019, resulting in twenty-two deaths and twenty-four injuries, uncertainty about stopping the spread of gun violence had become the norm for many Americans, and fear occupied the minds of people from one particular community in this particular incident—Hispanic Americans. Less than two weeks after the shooting, *USA Today* (Hawthorne, 2019) reported:

> Dads are telling their daughters, "Por favor, cuidase, mija," pleading with them to be careful at work, keep quiet, have an exit plan. School is starting and along with it, some mothers are worrying if they should let their children speak Spanish at school, let them walk to class alone. Friends are telling their amigas, the ones who speak Spanish with an accent, the ones who are darker, who are both immigrant and Latino: Be aware of your surroundings.

Among many uncertainties, one thing the Hispanic community knew for sure was that Patrick Crusius, 21, from Allen in the Dallas metropolitan area was a white nationalist who published his anti-immigrant manifesto (with an emphasis on Hispanic immigrant) only twenty-seven minutes prior to the shooting.

Fear is not a monopoly. It was not only experienced by the Hispanic community, after the El Paso mass shooting, many whites also were fearful about the future of their own community as well. Far away from El Paso, Marysville, Michigan, was the site of a public forum less than three weeks after the Texas shooting in August 2019. Jean Cramer, a white candidate for the City Council election that November, commented that she would keep "Marysville a white community as much as possible." Cramer is from St. Clair County, about eighty-eight miles northeast of Detroit, an area seen as a key swing region that helped elect Trump in 2016. When pressed by a reporter from *The Times Herald* in Port Huron about her comment in the public forum on the issue of race, Cramer told the reporter that she was not "against blacks," but she also did believe that married couples "need to be the same race" (Associated Press, 2019).

During the Trump presidency, the fear of whites was not limited toward Blacks and Hispanics, two minorities that had experienced hundreds of years of racial antagonism and white resentment. In Alabama, the Republican Party called for its congressional delegation "to proceed with the expulsion process in accordance to Article 1, Section 5 of the U.S. Constitution to expel Rep. Ilhan Omar from the United States House of Representatives" (Hayes, 2019). Congresswoman Ilhan Omar then was a freshman lawmaker and one of the first two Muslim women ever elected to the U.S. House of Representatives, in 2018.

To understand the racial and religious tensions that spread during the Trump era, one should return to an earlier political environment that fostered the conditions for volatile racial relations. Just four years before the election of Trump, it was a different kind of fear that dominated the airwaves and the presidential campaign. In the 2012 Republican primary elections, the voters faced the growing probabilities of nominating the first-ever religious minority candidate, Mitt Romney, to be the party's candidate for president. The fear about his nomination was widespread, and the intensity of it was amplified by leaders of white evangelical denominations. Surprisingly, the fear did not cost Romney's nomination. In fact white evangelical voters comprised his strongest base among all voters in the 2012 general election. Let us continue with laying out the puzzle with some additional background.

THE CHOSEN ONE

"If you vote for Mitt Romney, you are voting for Satan!" the Florida-based televangelist Bill Keller wrote the religiously charged sentence for his daily devotion on May 10, 2007. The devotion was sent the next day to his 2.4 million email followers more than five years before Romney secured the Republican nomination for president in 2012. Keller explained his warning in this way (WND, 2007):

> Romney is an unashamed and proud member of the Mormon cult founded by a murdering polygamist pedophile named Joseph Smith nearly 200 years ago. The teachings of the Mormon cult are doctrinally and theologically in complete

opposition to the Absolute Truth of God's Word. There is no common ground. If Mormonism is true, then the Christian faith is a complete lie. There has never been any question from the moment Smith's cult began that it was a work of Satan and those who follow their false teachings will die and spend eternity in hell.

In addition to the email list through which he received more than 40,000 replies daily, Keller's influence as a Christian leader was bolstered by his daily television broadcast called Live Prayer TV and his popular website, LivePrayer.com (Scherer, 2007). Romney's religious problem, which political scientist David Campbell and his colleagues (Campbell et al., 2014, 2012) labeled "the Stained Glass Ceiling," turned out to be an insurmountable obstacle to his presidential aspirations in 2008. Romney withdrew from the Republican nomination contest on February 7, 2008, before the end of Republican primaries which chose U.S. Senator John McCain as the winner to face Obama in the general election.

Romney's failure in the 2008 Republican primaries puzzled Campbell and his colleagues (2012), for they believed that the dominance of Protestantism had been substantially challenged and reduced since the successful campaign of John F. Kennedy, a white Catholic, in the 1960 presidential election. Previous studies had shown that religious affiliation in recent decades had become less important while strength of religious commitment played a more critical role in voter's decisions. Moreover, "stronger commitment has become associated with Republican voters and weaker commitment with Democratic voters" (278). The fact that the Latter-day Saints (i.e., members of The Church of Jesus Christ of Latter-day Saints) are highly conservative and strongly Republican would have made Romney a valuable, competitive choice for the Republican Party. However, Campbell et al. (2012) found that the 2008 presidential voters "were concerned specifically with Romney's religious affiliation, not simply with the fact that he is religious" and the "concern over Romney's Mormonism dwarfed concerns about the religious backgrounds of Hillary Clinton and Mike Huckabee" (277).

Before the start of the 2012 campaign, Romney's religious problem returned to the headlines. Attending the Values Voter Summit in October, 2011, Robert Jeffress, a senior pastor at First Baptist Church in Dallas, mentioned the word "cult" in referring to Romney's religion in front of reporters. His comment about Romney's religion drew strong reactions from both pro-Romney and anti-Romney camps. During an interview with Fox News, Jeffress asserted that LDS church members had "never been considered a part of mainstream Christianity," and "Mormonism was invented 1,800 years after Jesus Christ and the founding of Christianity, and it has its own founder, Joseph Smith, its own set of doctrines and its own book, the *Book of Mormon*. And that, by definition, is a theological cult" (Fox News, 2011).

A majority of Protestant voters echoed Jeffress' strong words against Romney's religion when they voted in the 2012 Republican primaries. Romney's Protestant support was steady and lower than 50 percent across all fifty states. The reason why Romney never received majority Protestant support throughout the 2012 GOP primaries was because the Protestant votes were divided among several candidates. His Catholic opponent, Rick Santorum, remained competitive in the Protestant electorate. Santorum, a former U.S. senator from Pennsylvania, had been defeated even in his own state as an incumbent for re-election and had minimum, if any, national name recognition early in the primaries. However, he became popular among Protestants and even beat Romney in some of the later primaries. Romney was never the true preference of Protestant voters in the primaries whose ballot choices favored more Santorum, even when Romney was almost certain to win the nomination late in the primary season.

Despite the forceful challenges from his main rivals, such as Santorum and Newt Gingrich, Romney endured the long primary season and finally clinched the Republican presidential nomination on May 29, 2012. In addition to his powerful ground organization and superior financial backing, non-religious voters kept Romney in the race and eventually allowed him to win. Immediately after the 2012 primaries, Romney's lack of support from religious Republicans, especially the Protestants, raised concerns about his chance of winning the general election. For one thing, the Protestants, especially the born-again religious right, had been an integral part of GOP victories in recent presidential elections (Wilcox and Robinson, 2011). The election outcomes of the primaries had shown that the religious groups did respond to Protestant leaders' view about the concerns of electing a president associated with the Church of Jesus Christ of Latter-day Saints. Nearly seven out of ten Republican, born-again Protestants voted against Romney consistently throughout the primaries. Without the backing of this critical voting bloc, the Republican candidate's chance in beating a Democratic incumbent in the general election would be improbable.

"No matter how it turns out, the 2012 presidential election will have made history," wrote Brad Knickerbocker, a staff writer of *Christian Science Monitor*, in the summer of 2012. Knickerbocker pointed out that none of the major party candidates in 2012 for president or vice president were WASP (White, Anglo-Saxon Protestant). Knickerbocker wrote the article after Romney had just announced his choice for running mate—Paul Ryan, a Catholic congressman from Wisconsin.

Three of the four candidates were white in 2012. "Mr. Romney is Mormon, Mr. Ryan and Vice President Joe Biden are Roman Catholic," said Knickerbocker, and President Obama is "a man of mixed race" and "most obviously is not a WASP." The disappearance of WASPs from both parties' presidential tickets was noticed not only by Christian writers such as Knickerbocker, but also religion scholars such as Thomas Whitley, who wrote on the Associated Baptist Press news blog: "For the first time in our country's history the Republican Party is set to nominate a presidential ticket that does not include a Protestant . . . And in a strange turn of events that is sure to have many WASPs scratching their heads, President Obama will be the only Protestant on either party's ticket." This "strange" turn of events certainly came true because Obama was not only the Democratic candidate but also Black. All of a sudden, Republicans, especially the WASPs, would have to make a choice between a white religious minority and a Black Protestant as president. Would they vote for Romney—the ultimate threat to their Christian belief, as Bill Keller reminded, and "a vote for Satan?"

On November 6, 2012, Romney came up short. He won 47.2 percent of the popular votes, almost 4 percent less than President Obama's showing. Asked by CNN's Gloria Borger about whom to blame, Romney responded by blaming the timing of Hurricane Sandy, "I wish the hurricane [which hit New Jersey and part of New England prior to the election] hadn't have happened when it did because it gave the president a chance to be presidential and to be out showing sympathy for folks. That's one of the advantages of incumbency" (Easley, 2013). Romney went on to mention that several other factors might have helped him win the election, if timing was on his side.

White evangelical antagonism against the belief system of Romney's faith was never mentioned as a reason for his defeat. Romney's post-election silence on the vote of the religious right was not because of him avoiding any future controversies surrounding his faith. The reason was, instead, that it turned out that there was not any white Protestant antagonism against his church in the general election at all. The survey data from the American National Election Studies (ANES) indicated that white Protestants actually were, by far, the strongest supporters for Romney in the 2012 general election. White mainline Protestants (many of whom were WASPs) gave more than 60 percent of the votes to Romney, which was the highest among all groups with the only exception from another non-mainline white Protestants/ Christians (i.e., the religious right such as evangelical born-again Protestants). The religious-right white Protestants provided a stunning 71 percent of their votes to Romney. In comparison, Catholics, regardless of race, provided modest and less than majority support for Romney, while African Americans, regardless of their religious affiliation, offered the minimum level of support for Romney. Only about 5.7 percent of the Black born-again Protestants cast their votes for Romney, which is 65 percent less than his white Protestant support from the same religious group.

The dramatic turnaround of the white Protestant vote for Romney in the general election made their backlash against his religion in the primaries only about six months previously look almost like ancient history. It is safe to say that white Protestants not only failed to form the main obstacle to Romney's presidential aspiration, which evangelist Bill Keller passionately called for in 2007, but also kept him in the race in the first place, and made the 2012 general election much more competitive than otherwise it might have been.

What were the driving forces behind this change of heart on the part of white Protestants?

To answer this query, a quick intuitive answer could come from the nature of the general election. Unlike in the primaries which involved candidates from the same political party, in the general election, Romney, a Republican nominee ran against Obama, a Democrat. Perhaps white Protestants voted for Romney because these white Protestants shared the same political party with Romney. Thus, their vote was a vote for the party, not the candidate. It is also worth noting that only 37 percent of the white mainline Protestants and less than 39 percent of other white Protestants/Christians identified as Republicans. Romney's vote from these two white groups were as high as 60.7 percent and 71.3 percent, respectively.

These numbers lead to the puzzle's most compelling questions. Clearly, there were many non-Republican white Protestants who also voted for Romney in the general election. Though party identification is an important part of voters' decision-making process, it is still not resolved as to why this party identification factor was so important to these voters that it superseded all other considerations. It still does not answer the question why for the white Protestant Republicans who voted against Romney in the primaries the religious threat they perceived in the primaries was all of a sudden not important any longer in the November election. Conceivably, if Romney's faith was a threat to the true nature of Christianity, as forcefully argued by Robert Jeffress at the Values Voter Summit in October 2011, this threat then should not have disappeared this quickly.

Regardless of the extent to which white Protestants cast votes against Romney in the primaries for their concern of a religious threat, this concern certainly faded to secondary importance in the general election in which Obama, notably a Protestant, shared the same religious affiliation with white Protestants. But Obama's Protestantism did not matter to these white Protestant voters. Perhaps the genuine nature of Obama's religious faith was always questioned by some white Protestants who were influenced or even persuaded by the accusation that Obama was actually a Muslim (Grieve, 2010). Or, perhaps the threat that Obama brought to these white Protestants was much more serious than the religious threat from Romney's Church. If so, what was the threat that Obama embodied for these white Protestant voters? Was it because of his race (as a Black threat) or because of the party he represented (as a Democratic threat)? Or both? Or, something else?

To begin answering these questions, we introduce the theory of the atomic structure in politics in chapter 2.

Chapter 2

An Overview of the Atomic Structure

The term atomic structure in this book refers to the positional arrangements of racial and religious groups in America and incorporates the relationships between and among these groups shaped by external and internal social tensions. The definition obviously emphasizes the enduring feature of the political structure itself, which is made possible through the positions and arrangements of the groups. Simply, groups are located in the structure, and their positions are stable, at least in the short term. More specifically, the core of the atomic structure is occupied by the dominant group, and the peripheries are minority groups. The dominant group at the core initiates and defines the relationships among groups. The members of the core also debate, negotiate, and decide, at least for the time being, the direction and trajectory of political changes within the structure through competitive elections.

The most important result of the atomic structure is the system's durability. But, durability also does not mean that the atomic structure is a static, closed, hierarchical, and caste-like system. Due to the positional nature which occurs within the structure, there have always been tensions between and among groups. The structure at any given point of time reacts to relevant contemporary tensions. Adjustments are made to adapt to new environmental factors that increase tensions to the point that only competitive elections can settle the differences within the atomic structure's core. The tension within the core leads to two political alliances, which promote different, and often opposing, views on how to treat the groups located in the peripheries of the atomic structure.

Overall, adjustments of atomic structure have meant expanded legal protections, rights, and political representations for the peripheral groups. These adjustments explain why there has been progress for equality at the group levels in U.S. history. However, adjustments by the atomic structure's core dominant group also can mean taking away such rights, legal protections, and political representations from the minority groups who reside in the atomic structure's periphery. These adjustments spark political volatility. These changes, however, do not occur in linear fashion, which subsequently makes it difficult to predict when and how political volatility will occur and what impact it will have.

ADVICE: THE ATOMIC STRUCTURE AND ITS OPERATING PRINCIPLES

I use the word "atomic" to not only emphasize its structural nature (again, mainly through positional arrangements of groups) but also to address the compositional entities concerning the major racial and religious groups. Recall a basic lesson from an introductory chemistry class which explains the two components of the nucleus at the core of an atom. The protons are positively charged while neutrons are electrically neutral in the chemical atom.

In order to establish a nation, there must be a core of a political system. From the founding of the American Republic, that core was initiated and formulated by the most dominant group of the time, the white Anglo-Saxon Protestants (WASPs) who, through story-telling and political rhetoric, pursued a particular manifestation of "peoplehood" in their own image (Smith, 2015). This core, however, also showed inner differences about how to treat other smaller, politically weaker and disenfranchised groups, primarily Native Americans, Blacks, Catholics, other religious groups who experienced persecution, and, later, immigrants from Europe, Central and Latin America, Asia, and elsewhere in the world. Their differences, just like protons and neutrons, sparked tension and competition inside the core. The political fate of the minority groups, like electrons in the chemical atom, has been not only a result of their own struggle for equality but also a function of how the two electoral coalitions were initiated and became (un)balanced inside the political core. The electoral competition between the two opposing sides of the core led to the ups and downs of temporary group statuses as well as volatility of the whole system. The atomic structure, therefore, reacts to relentlessly evolving political environments and the emergence of fresh issues in the realms of political campaigns and governance.

The most significant reconfiguration of the atomic structure in the history of American political development came with the end of WASP domination, amplified by the political events, debates, and discourses of the 1960s. These reconfigurations led to laws, regulations, and policies that enlighten and transform society as consequences.

Through examples taken from the nation's history and political events, this book also probes the micro-level foundation, which made this group-level structure possible in the first place. In this regard, we must examine fundamental principles governing human behavior. With respect to the atomic structure, there are five principles that operate simultaneously to govern how the atomic structure works at a given time and throughout history. They are:

1. *A*ttraction, or in-group favoritism based on similarity of in-group members
2. *D*istance, or perception of threat from distant external groups
3. *V*olatility of group statuses due to various political responses to different threats
4. *I*nternal threats inside the core
5. *C*ompetitive *E*lections, the strategy to win and determine, for a particular time, the relevant group statuses.

These five axioms comprise the *ADVICE* principles. They will be discussed within the context of political changes in forthcoming chapters.

Throughout U.S. history the dominant group (the WASPs) certainly attempted to adopt and implement public policies to institutionalize racial or ethnic inequality to gain political advantages over minority groups. Examples of such institutional domination include the practice of slavery imposed on African Americans, forced relocation of Native Americans, exclusionary immigration laws, such as the 1882 *Chinese Exclusion Act*, the 1924 *National Origin Act* against Southern and Eastern Europeans and Jews, and recent attempts to block the access of minorities and immigrants to the ballot box.

But, in history, the predominating group of WASPs also periodically has passed and enacted omnibus legislation to enfranchise and protect the rights of minority groups. Examples of such equality-oriented legislation include the Thirteenth, Fourteenth, and Fifteenth Amendments to the U.S. Constitution, the *Civil Rights Act of 1964* and *Voting Rights Act of 1965*, all of which were passed by a majority-white Congress. Of course, this is not to ignore or discount the enormous impact of the other alliance to press their case vigorously in public protests and coordinated movements emphasizing nonviolence. These tensions certainly encompass the atomic structure of politics.

This book recommends the reader to consider the larger portrait of American development, especially the ongoing configuration and reconfiguration of the core and the peripheries within the atomic structure of American politics. Throughout the history of American constitutional democracy, racial and religious groups' temporary statuses, especially their legal protections and political representations, have tended to be volatilely affected. But their positional statuses (i.e., core or particular periphery) also indicate enduring patterns of surprisingly consistent magnitude. One then can see how a system-level shock produces a drastic change in the atomic structure itself. Thus far, the end of WASP domination, which started in the 1960s and continues to expand visibly and unmistakably, has led to the most far-reaching political consequences in the American experiment as a democratic republic, a point that becomes clear later in the book.

To fully capture the essence of the atomic structure of politics, one should not treat the American system as simply a hierarchical, static, caste-like, and closed system. Instead, it is a resiliently dynamic system capable of producing volatility, absorbing its impact, and generating progress that strengthens the collective objective of group equality over time. A greater demonstration of equality does not suggest, however, that there always is a monotonic increase in equality (Kersch, 2004). For example, religious and racial minority groups often are treated worse after the time in which they just have gained more rights and benefits from the political system.

This book helps explain the fundamental reason for the existence of inequality between and among social groups and the positive political changes in the long run to reduce such inequality. This book addresses political changes and intergroup relationships in U.S. politics. Throughout the text, there is a particular focus on the power relationships between the historically dominant group and various religious and racial minority groups (Catholics, Latter-day Saints, Muslims, Jews, Native Americans, African Americans, Hispanics, and Asian Americans) that have ebbed and flowed over the years. The book offers an analysis of historical and contemporary political volatility in the United States by building on previous theories of political change to produce a more complete picture of how and why political change occurs in U.S. politics.

A DEEPER LOOK AT ROMNEY'S RELIGION

With the basic outlines of the atomic structure theory and principles now identified, let us return briefly to the puzzle introduced in chapter 1 and add a few more significant pieces to it.

As Romney's two attempts to make it to the top of the nation's political ladder failed, his church certainly had endured its widest contemporary experience of political scrutiny and test. Some feared the rise of "Mormonism" (a term widely used in national media coverage of Romney's two presidential campaigns, but it is also descriptor that The Church of Jesus Christ of Latter-day Saints has recently encouraged its members and the public to avoid, along with popularized terms such as Mormons and LDS). There also were white Protestants, who embraced Romney, regarding him as the church's most visible member and a source of pride for his faith community. In this sense, the change of heart on the part of the traditionally dominant group (i.e., white Protestants) toward a religious minority group could and did happen so quickly in U.S. politics. However, this was not the first time that such a dramatic and somewhat unpredictable change took place in U.S. history.

Established in 1830 by Joseph Smith in western New York, from its beginning, The Church of Jesus Christ of Latter-day Saints always had been politically controversial. Members claimed they were Christians who believed that salvation was only possible through Jesus Christ. However, the nascent faith also introduced several doctrines that conflicted with the fundamentals of American Protestantism. The theological differences included, as political scientists Wald and Calhoun-Brown (2011) summarized, "the origin of God, the doctrine of the Trinity, the role of works in salvation, the nature of man, original sin, baptism of the dead, sacred temple rights, and the long-repudiated practice of polygamy."

Specifically, the church's members believed there were ancient Israelite prophets in the Americas who "foretold the coming of the Messiah and that Christ himself came to minister to those who were waiting for him in the New World after his resurrection and ascension" (Wald and Calhoun-Brown, 2011, 299). Moreover, the *Book of Mormon* was regarded as scripture, in addition to *The Bible*. Perhaps, the most controversial doctrine was its assertion "that prophetic revelation did not end with the Bible but continues to this day through the president of the LDS church" (Wald and Calhoun-Brown, 2011, 299).

The theological differences already framed the religious minority as a threat to mainstream Protestants. The devoted members of the original church also posed a political threat to their original home in the state of New York and other frontier states, Ohio and Missouri, because of the growing numbers of converts from the United States and western Europe, and because of their political cohesiveness as a voting bloc. They were persecuted through violence and pushed out from one state to another, especially in Gallatin, Davies County, Missouri where the so-called Mormon War of 1838 took place between Latter-day Saints and angry Missourians. Missouri militia units imprisoned Joseph Smith and other leaders for six months, and eventually pushed church members out of the state during the 1838–1839 winter.

However, by the time the church settled in Nauvoo, Illinois, in the spring of 1839, the political fate of the Latter-day Saints improved. They convinced the Illinois state legislature to grant a city charter that gave them sufficient powers to operate essentially as a city-state. Smith and his followers "were overconfident that the city charter protected them legally and politically. Over the next few years, they did not hesitate to push their newly gained powers to the limit to establish a safe haven for their religion. Furthermore, they used their new political clout as a voting bloc to play the Whigs and the Democrats against each other in local and state elections" (Foster, 2008, 58–59).

The improved political environment renewed the confidence of the church and its leaders. Their missionary work also proved to be successful in Europe as more converts, including Romney's ancestors (Miles Archibald Romney and his wife Elizabeth from Great Britain), grew the population and economy of the City of Nauvoo to rival cities including Chicago. Church representatives negotiated with Sam Houston, the president of the newly independent Republic of Texas, to relocate to Texas as a special legion to defend its southern frontier against Mexico. In 1842 a church newspaper article proudly announced that "Nauvoo, then, is the nucleus of a glorious dominion of liberty, peace, and plenty; it is an organization of that government of which there shall be no end" (Foster, 2008, 59). Joseph Smith announced his candidacy for U.S. president in 1844 to expand the theological and organizational foundation for a political "kingdom of God." These bold political moves made this religious community a greater political threat, and violence quickly spread. Smith and his brother were assassinated in June 1844, and the church was forced to cross the Mississippi River and move west toward the Great Basin.

Yet the church's short-lived political honeymoon in Nauvoo, Illinois, demonstrated that the political experiences of minority groups could change—sometimes for better, sometimes for worse—throughout U.S. history. What explains changes in the American minority groups' political experiences? Why were they treated sometimes as political equals, but other times as the worst enemies? One thematic thread of political science research suggests that the political behavior of the dominant group toward a minority group depends on the perception of threat that the minority group instills in the dominant group.

V. O. Key (1949), for example, in his classic study of Southern politics argued that white hostility toward Blacks in the 1940s' South was directly related to the level of Black concentration in the counties where these whites lived. The higher the level of Black concentration, the higher the level of white perception of Black threat to their political domination; thus, the higher the level of white aggression toward Blacks. "It is the whites of the black belts who have the deepest and most immediate concern about the maintenance of white supremacy," said Key (1949, 5).

Key's study captured an important social psychological impulse of human behavior. Humans react strongly to perceptions of danger. An enhanced fear about an imminent threat can cause them to react strongly in attempting to reduce the threat anxiety. If this fear is shared by members of a political group, one can reasonably expect that the group's collective response reveals a common trait. The insights of Key, one of the shrewdest political scientists of his time, still echoes in the contemporary social and behavioral sciences. This is especially true for scholars who studied white Southerners' political response not only to liberal politics, such as Black-led urban programs, and elections in cities, such as New Orleans and Atlanta, but also radical right-wing political mobilization, such as the 1991 gubernatorial campaign of David Duke, an avowed KKK activist and state legislator, in Louisiana (Giles and Buckner, 1993; Glaser, 1994; Longoria, 1999; Taylor, 1998; Swain, 2002). As that campaign showed, white hostility toward Blacks was found directly related to Black presence in the white communities.

Key's finding, as based on the 1940s' South, nevertheless, did have its limits. While it is certainly reasonable to suggest that a higher level of perception of threat can lead to enhanced threat anxiety, it is obviously not true that threat anxiety always translates to group aggression toward minorities. As we have already seen, white Protestants voted as a strong bloc against Romney in the 2012 GOP primaries, but they became his strongest supporters only months later in the general election. If their primary vote was driven by the threat anxiety concerning a religious minority-group takeover, this threat anxiety should have been ramped to a new high, as Romney's probability of winning the presidency as the first Latter-day Saints candidate increased substantially in the general election. Clearly, white response to minority threat is much more complex than Key's proposition of a linear positive relationship between minority threat and majority political backlash.

Groups, especially dominant ones, change their political strategies toward minority groups continuously. For example, throughout U.S. history, the dominant group (WASPs, or later, whites, and as seen in chapters in part II of this book) had tried to institutionalize racial or ethnic inequality to gain political advantages over minority groups. Examples of such institutional domination were outlined earlier in the Introduction.

An important yet understudied phenomenon of U.S politics concerning group relations is that the political status of minority groups can be highly and frequently volatile. By volatility, I suggest that the political status of a minority group, though not completely random, can have any of the following characteristics:

1. There was no guarantee that the minority political protection would always be enhanced over time. More favorable periods would be followed by cycles of backlash against the minority that just had received an enhanced political status. One example of this instance were the Jim Crow laws targeting Black citizens immediately after the period of Republican-led Reconstruction in the South.
2. Politicians and opinion leaders repeatedly have changed their minds about minority groups. An example of this change of mind can be found

in two dramatically different decisions (*Cherokee Nation v. Georgia* of 1831 and *Worcester v. Georgia* of 1832) handed down during the Supreme Court tenure of U.S. Chief Justice, John Marshall, regarding the removal of Cherokee Indians.

3. The dominant group members, as a whole, had changed their minds about a minority group. An example concerned Chinese immigrants who were welcomed as a valuable labor supply and who functioned as strike breakers in the 1850s. But, then the1882 Exclusion Act prohibited the Chinese from immigrating to the United States.

4. When group positions of minorities were unstable, the respective group political status, as based on the laws, changed as well. An example of this is the experience of white Catholics between 1815 and 1855. They were welcomed by WASPs as the new immigrant labor in the first two decades of the nineteenth century, but the Know-Nothing Party, which dominated state legislatures throughout New England, enacted laws to require residency periods of twenty-one years for new immigrants to qualify for the right to vote.

5. Dominant group behavior toward minorities also has changed rapidly within a short time. An example is the *1848 Guadalupe Hidalgo Treaty*, which allowed Mexicans to choose their citizenship and protect their property rights. Their property rights, however, quickly evaporated after the treaty and Mexicans had to go to U.S. courts to seek protections and their legal fight often failed in the WASP-dominant judiciary.

POLITICAL VOLATILITY BEYOND THE RACIAL AND RELIGIOUS MINORITIES

On the surface, the characteristics and examples about the political volatility surrounding minority groups mentioned above invite readers to imagine that a natural corollary could be to refer to long-term hegemony by WASPs in U.S. history. After all, the experience of minority volatility seems to suggest that minority rights, even when provided by the actions of WASPs, should not override the WASPs' own group interest. But, American historical and political developments have not sustained the corollary concept of a WASP hegemony. On the contrary, the political status of WASPs undoubtedly is much weaker today than it has been in the past.

The demise of WASP domination certainly has not occurred as a result of WASPs' own negligence. In this regard, my proposed thesis runs clearly against those provided by scholars such as Amy Chua and Jed Rubenfeld (2014). Chua and Rubenfeld argue that the success of a group in U.S. history must have "the triple packages"—the senses of superiority, insecurity, and impulse control. Chua and Rubenfeld (2014) explain, in particular, why WASPs have lost their dominant position: "Success softens; it erodes insecurity. Meanwhile modern principles of equality tend to undercut group superiority complexes. And with its freedom-loving, get-it-now culture, America undercuts impulse control too. WASP economic dominance in the United States declined under the weight of all these pressures" (20).

My analysis of political history concerning WASPs shows a different finding. Much of the political volatility minority groups have experienced has been largely due to the responses of WASPs toward various threats they perceived from minority groups. Through educational, cultural, and especially political means, WASPs always had enjoyed their position of superiority, and they were constantly alerted to potential political threats, and it was WASPs that throughout history have emphasized the values of impulse control. But, they still could not (and will be unable) reverse the decline of their political power. This book presents a solution to the puzzle we have discussed in the first two chapters by using the atomic structure theory.

Chapter 3

Rationality and Perceptions

Political Habits and Responses

Throughout the 2012 presidential campaign, Romney attempted to focus on President Obama's policy record, especially about the recovery from the Great Recession of 2008, which he deemed as a failure. Romney believed that he would be judged by voters based on his differences from Obama, particularly from his own impressive credentials as a successful strategist in achieving economic rebounds rather than an emphasis on his religion. Faced with attacks from evangelical leaders such as Robert Jeffress, Romney calmly reminded voters that they "should remember that decency and civility are values, too," he said. "Poisonous language doesn't advance our cause. It's never softened a single heart or changed a single mind. The blessings of faith carry the responsibility of civil and respectful debate" (Fox News, 2011).

Nevertheless, negative campaigns labeling and delegitimizing Romney's religion as a cult continued as the news media sustained their interest in highlighting the controversial history of his Latter-day Saints faith in their coverage. This was true for not only liberal media such as *Huffington Post*, but also conservative powerhouses such as *Fox News*, which finally tempered the discussion of Romney's religious identity after he secured the nomination.

A *Washington Post* report, for example, summarized various events throughout Romney's primary campaign and concluded, "As Romney's political star has risen, so has interest in Mormonism. That creates complications for the campaign, but it also presents opportunities and potential pitfalls for the church" (Horowitz, 2012). Likewise, Jodi Kantor, a *New York Times* presidential campaign reporter, echoed this: "Just as Ronald Reagan deployed acting skills on the trail and Barack Obama relied on the language of community organizing, Mitt Romney bears the marks of the theology and culture of the Church of Jesus Christ of Latter-day Saints" (Kantor, 2012).

Politico, one of the most widely followed digital news media content pro-
ducers of political coverage, published an article about Romney's religious
obstacle: "Deep into his second run for president, Romney's Mormonism
remains one of his great mysteries—and obstacles—in many voters' minds.
The Senate has more Mormons than Episcopalians or Lutherans, but polls
consistently show that Romney's religion has remained a factor" (Dovere,
2012).

The article linked Romney's religious obstacle to political acceptance, by
citing the "white horse prophecy," which "predicts that after the banks fail and
when the Constitution is nearing collapse, Mormons flush with wealth—the
White Horse, in the prophecy's metaphor—will rise and lead America back
to greatness." Romney's connection with the alleged White Horse prophecy
of his faith harkens to his ancestry. His fraternal great-grandfather Miles Park
Romney was dispatched by Brigham Young, the church's second president,
to build the city of St. George in Utah and to "defeat a new congressional
effort to enforce an antipolygamy law" (Kranish and Helman, 2012, 40). A
son of George Romney, who was a three-term governor of Michigan and U.S.
secretary of housing and urban development in the Nixon Administration,
Mitt Romney was envisioned by some during the campaign as the "chosen
one" for the hope of fulfilling a prophecy.

As a successful business leader, Mitt Romney was called upon to rescue the
scandal stricken 2002 Winter Olympics Committee that not only embarrassed
the International Olympic Committee but also brought unexpected negative
perceptions to the state of Utah and the church (Kranish and Helman, 2012,
204–223). Romney's ability to turn the 2002 Winter Olympics into a success,
in addition to his credentials as a Republican governor elected in the liberal
state of Massachusetts and as the co-founder and chief executive officer of
Bain Capital, made him a widely appealing national politician. He also was
seen as an ideal Republican candidate to beat President Obama whose reelec-
tion bid was troubled by the nation's stubborn economic problems. Before
Romney's 2008 campaign, nine candidates from his church, including Joseph
Smith and Romney's father, had run unsuccessfully as a presidential candidate. Romney naturally became the first member of the church with a realistic
chance to win a presidential bid.

For some of the faithful, the white horse prophecy was on the verge of
materializing in 2012. In 2019, as President Trump faced impeachment, the
Salt Lake Acting Company, in its annual musical comedy review of Utah
and national politics, *Saturday's Voyeur*, featured a song and dance about a
reluctant Romney coming in on a white horse to save the country from the
president and the constitutional crisis surrounding his impending impeachment. And, when Romney, as a U.S. senator representing Utah, cast the sole
GOP vote to convict the president in 2019 and in 2021, some media pundits

and reporters once again invoked the Romney connection to the white horse prophecy. In 2020, Romney also emerged as the first U.S. Senate Republican to push for massive relief for millions of Americans whose livelihoods essentially came to an abrupt ground stop due to the rapidly unfolding COVID-19 pandemic.

Latter-day Saints have long believed their faith will be the final hope for America. Brigham Young said, in 1854, "Will the Constitution be destroyed? No, it will be held inviolate by this people" and Young further cited Joseph Smith: "The time will come when the destiny of the nation will hang upon a single thread. At that critical juncture, this people will step forward and save it from the threatened destruction" (Foster, 2008, 52). Amplifying this promise was the white horse prophecy, allegedly told by Joseph Smith to his followers in 1843: "I love the [U.S.] constitution; it was made by the inspiration of God; and it will be preserved and saved by the efforts of the White Horse . . . The White Horse will find the mountains full of miners and they will become rich . . . there will be peace and love only in the Rocky Mountains" (Foster, 2008, 53–54). Apparently, the white horse imagery was intended to refer to the Apostle St. John's prophecy, as recorded in Revelations 6:1-8, but for the church, it was appropriated to confirm the Latter-day Saints' unique role in saving the nation from calamity.

The white horse prophecy, while shared widely in the church community, did not lead necessarily to good public relations ink for Romney. Even in 2007, when asked by *The Salt Lake Tribune* about whether or not he was personally influenced by the prophecy, Romney responded by explaining that he never heard it from the church and it was never at the heart of his belief. Indeed, "leaders of the Church refused to accord it status as a valid revelation" (Foster, 2008, 57) despite "copies of these [white horse] accounts are archived in the LDS Church Historian's Office" (Foster, 2008, 52). There were also other explanations offered about the white horse prophecy. For example, Foster pointed out that "Some who accept the prophecy as valid have interpreted the 'White Horse' as a single individual who would step forward to preserve the Union, but the text clearly shows that the White Horse (assuming the prophecy to be genuine) represents the Mormons as a whole" (see Foster, 2008, 57). Obviously this explanation would not reduce the perception of Mormon threat to the WASPs as the real chosen.

Regardless of whether or not the white horse prophecy was directly foretold by Joseph Smith, it was, after all, a religious issue. Why did it capture so much national attention in the heat of a presidential campaign in 2012? Arguably this prophecy ran afoul of the highly cherished belief of WASPs themselves that they were really the chosen people for God's plan (a call of white Christian nationalism to which we will come back to in chapters 12 and 13). Furthermore, the idea of a white horse to save the U.S. Constitution and its symbolic representation in Romney's presidential campaign imposed a potential threat to WASP's own political identity and pride. In the minds of a majority of Christian voters, this prophecy could also be the evidence that Romney's religion is heretical or apostasy and should be prevented from expanding, not to mention that a Latter-day Saint conceivably could win the presidential election. The prophecy, when articulated in this way, could confirm the perception of a religious threat to the nation's traditionally dominant religion—Protestantism.

Romney's cautious response to the prophecy acknowledged the potential damage such a prophecy might inflict upon his presidential campaign. From this perspective, one can see how minority groups might face an uphill battle as they try to move to the top of the nation's political hierarchy. Meanwhile, for minority groups, how they can reduce, if not completely remove, the perception of their group's threat to the powerful majority becomes a tall political order, even if no intent to pose such a threat ever exists. To a large extent, the political experience of minority groups depends significantly upon how the majority decides to respond politically to the perception of minority threats.

Conversely, why should majority voters, such as WASPs, be concerned with a minority threat, symbolized by the white horse prophecy, given the relatively small size of the Latter-day Saint community, which constitutes only about 2 percent of the U.S. population? What kind of a political threat can it actually take? More puzzling is, as I already introduced in previous chapters, why such a threat, if it does exist, caused white Protestants to vote against Romney in the primaries, but not in the general election in 2012? To answer these questions, one must solve two problems theoretically. The first is the rationality behind the majority group's decision-making process. The second is to find the underlying factors that may lead to the perception of minority group threat to the majority.

RATIONALITY AND ITS LIMITS

To account for human decisions at the group level toward external threats, we first examine the research about rational choice, which has been a major part of many studies in American political science, but also one of the most misunderstood particularly by those who oppose this school of thought. The primary assumption suggests that political actors make their decisions rationally. Put simply, rationality is about using the most efficient way to achieve one's goal, whatever that might be. However, only using this definition for rationality may lead to a "tautological conclusion" because one always could claim all human behaviors are rational, as they are aimed toward specified goals, and likely in the eyes of the decision makers, the returned benefits of their behavior outweigh the costs (Downs, 1957, 6).

Downs contributed extensively to this concept in *An Economic Theory of Democracy,* which defined the concept of rationality based on how individuals make political decisions in order to maximize their "utility income." In other words, one can focus on how political decisions can engender maximum economic benefits with minimum costs to the political actor. Though not all decisions, being political or economic, are rational in this sense, according to Downs, one can expect "a rational man to outperform an irrational man, *ceteris paribus,* because random factors cancel and efficiency triumphs over inefficiency" (6).

The rational choice model seems to explain satisfactorily why the white majority group sometimes might feel threatened by a minority group and how the majority reacts to such a perception of threat. William Julius Wilson (1980) in his award-winning book, *The Declining Significance of Race,* surveyed the history of racial relations from the angle of economic development. He discovered that racial antagonism and white political oppression often occur after white economic interests were perceived to be threatened by Blacks. For example, in the post-bellum era, there were waves of large-scale Black migration from the rural South to the urban North. Blacks entered the labor force in the North, sometimes as strikebreakers, and their entrance "exacerbated not only the economic and social anxieties of the white working class but also their racial antagonism" (Wilson, 1980, 73).

But, rationality based on maximization of utility income cannot explain satisfactorily why white Protestants were politically motivated to vote against Romney in the 2012 Republican primaries, and then they changed their mind to vote for him in the general election. For one, neither Romney nor the colleagues representing his faith or the Latter-day Saints Church formed any substantial economic threat to the utility income of majority white voters. What then is the limit of rational choice theory? A rational choice theorist may reply by saying that the white Protestants, who voted against Romney in the 2012 GOP primaries, were simply irrational. Two problems follow from this response. First, why did the irrationality of voters portray a systematic pattern, as it was the white Protestant group that persistently opposed Romney for five months in the GOP primaries and then systematically changed their vote choice in the general election? Second, if the irrationality was distributed among voters in a systematic way, it appears that there likely were other systematic factors in play. Thus, rational choice theory should account for these other factors (whatever they are), even if rationality explains in part the reasons for how white Protestants decided which candidates to support.

It should be noted that in the past three decades, the empirical tests of the rational choice theory, as suggested by Green and Shapiro (1994), have turned out to be uncertain and sometimes almost impossible or contrary to what the theory suggested could be predicted. For example, if voters make their decision entirely on their utility income, then it is not rational at all for them to even cast a vote, because any single vote has practically no chance to swing the election outcome one way or another. And, casting a vote in the United States does generate costs (at least the time spent on voting is a cost in the sense of utility income, as seen in Green and Shapiro, 1994).

Furthermore, if one analyzes American voters based on their group identities, it has been shown in subsequent studies that groups often do not act rationally for their group interests. Larry Bartel's (2008) research, for instance, found that white working-class voters did not rely on the utility maximization principle, as suggested by rational choice theory, to vote for the party that would actually protect their long-term economic interests to the greatest degree. Instead, they chose the Republican Party who, according to Bartel, contributed much more to the income gap between the working class and the rich than to the economic improvement of the poor. Clearly, to explain group behavior more robustly than the narrow domain of rational choice, one has to go beyond rational choice theory and analyze why rational choice has its limit.

POLITICAL DECISION BASED
ON PERCEPTION AND HABIT

If any individual's vote does not matter, why does anybody vote? As Green and Shapiro (1994) aptly put it, this simple and yet profound question, as a paradox, has shadowed the rational choice theory for decades. To dig into the paradox, the social psychology school of thought, as an alternative theory, provides an intuitively sound answer to the question that cannot be solved by rational choice theory.

Based on the social psychology theory, we can simply answer the question by saying "a voter casts a vote because of her social and psychological tendency. At least it's a habit based on some prior or current perception. Maybe sometimes the habit leads to the maximization of utility income, maybe not." This line of thinking does save scholars from the unnecessary assertion of voters always making political decisions based on rationality, as defined by Downs (1959) and other rational choice theorists. However, what causes individuals to form a habit and from where do their perceptions arise?

To answer this question, one must start with the discussion of *The American Voter*, from 1960, arguably one of the most influential political science books published in America. The book's influence is demonstrated not only by a new theory formulated as a powerful alternative to rational choice but also as a result of the research institution established and housed at The University of Michigan in Ann Arbor, which has amassed one of the most comprehensive longitudinal datasets available in modern social science research history.

To the supporters of this school of thought, the most powerful feature of *The American Voter* is that it presents a more realistic picture of common people and average voters than what is required by rational choice theory. The average voters depicted in *The American Voter* are not scholars, philosophers, politicians, or elites. But their behavior also matters to elites. Ever since its original publication, in order to test and corroborate the theory originally developed by Angus Campbell and his colleagues, scholars have often used the National Election Studies (NES) as a primary source of empirical data. The NES is a survey conducted before and after each presidential election to gauge variables that influence voting behavior. The nationally selected random samples allow scholars to test their theories.

The social psychological approach developed in *The American Voter* sought to understand factors that affect voter turnout and choice. One way to see how the theory of *The American Voter* works is to imagine a "funnel of causality," which includes the various factors put through a "funnel-like" sequence of time, namely, moving from socio-demographics, to party identification, and then onto issues and candidates (see Lewis-Beck, 2009, 22–23, for a summary of the funnel). This means that each factor plays a role in influencing how an individual might decide their votes in a sequential process. But, as we already know, as the date for voting draws near, candidates and issues become more important in the voter's decision-making process. Meanwhile, social demographics and party identification also play a long-term profound role for voters. In *The American Voter*, researchers placed party identification at the center of the whole theoretical construct—the Michigan Model, as it is commonly labeled in political science research. To understand this, the best way is to imagine a "cognitive map," using Ray Hyman's concise phrase. This cognitive map is subjective, real only to the person who possesses it. For the funnel of causality to work, family normally is treated as a primary agent of socialization that feeds information and education to their children. The parents' political party identification eventually becomes the perceptual screen for the children to keep for a long time, lasting into their adulthood. Thus, the funnel has an internal filter that removes unnecessary and sometimes detailed information while keeping the bits the voter actually activates in their decision-making process.

Voting for a political party, as based on the Michigan Model, eventually becomes a habit. Families also are important for the model's party identification formulation. According to the 1992 NES data, "in families where both parents conveyed a consistent partisanship, close to three in four offspring adopted the parental party (including Independent learners)" (see

Lewis-Beck, 2009, 139). Using social psychology to explain why this likely is the case, the typical American voter shows limited interest in grasping a broad range of issues and is only affected by issues that are salient to them. In campaigns, issues only play a limited role in determining the voting decision of many individuals. This is because the electorate is generally disengaged and uses its preferred problem-solving approach to compensate for not having time, for example, to pay attention more closely on the process of deciding whom to support in an election. Moreover, unlike elites, grassroots voters do not always demonstrate coherent ideological positions to rely on, which effectively means that social demographics, and especially, political parties, are powerful devices for helping voters streamline and simplify their decision-making process (Lewis-Beck, 2009, 426).

The Michigan Model seemingly explains one of the most enduring legacies of American politics—the two-party system. Voters opt for their parties as a habit, and they rarely change their party loyalty. But, one implication of this theory is that the voters' habit and their perceptual screen may leave a lot of room for politicians to play a role in manipulating the political process for the advantage of the elites. After all, in the Michigan Model, voters do not appear to be as rational as predicted by the rational choice model put forth by Downs. But are voters then seen as subjects easy to manipulate? If the answer is yes, then politicians can use various tactics, including framing political issues as threats to certain voters, for gaining on their opponents when it comes to persuading voters to change their loyalties to a particular candidate.

More recent studies in social psychology have opened insights into the inner workings of the human mind's decision-making process. The short answer to the above questions is that voters differ from each other. Neither Downs' rational choice nor the Michigan Model's original theory making can explain all of the variance, or even voters themselves when it comes to identifying the dynamics that influence their decision strategies. There are many perceptual tools, not just party identification, that voters rely on (and trust) to make their voting decision manageable.

VOTING AND INFORMATION SEARCH

Voting is a political decision which involves a process. Richard Lau and David Redlawsk (2011), in their book *How Voters Decide,* traced the nuances of this process to explain how an individual might evaluate the choices they have available in deciding how to vote. The evaluation component of decision making, according to their study, encompasses a complex cognitive process. A correct decision, which Lau and Redlawsk argue, can be found within the perspective of rational choice, as illustrated by Anthony Downs, William Riker, and other scholars who subscribe to this theoretical view.

Lau and Redlawsk also found that American voters do poorly in selecting candidates who best represent their priorities and values. Voters often lack the necessary informational framework to decide how to vote, at least correctly in the context that matters most to them. The key intervening variable involves the information search that leads to their decision. Unfortunately, the search can be more limited than what humans expect—a potentially startling self-discovery. Humans are "designed" in a way that does not always allow them to launch information searches successfully (see Lau and Redlawsk, 2011, 23). One problem is the limit of human short-term memory (STM), which does not have sufficient length or bandwidth always handy, and long-term memory (LTM), which can contain a lot of information, but also only a limited amount is accessible at any given time. These physiological limitations therefore could make an individual's information search occasionally unsystematic and incoherent.

Fortunately, voters are not powerless, in spite of their limited cognitive capabilities for this function. The most important finding of Lau and Redlawsk (2011) is how humans develop cognitive tools to deal with the limitations by simplifying and narrowing the information needed for decision making. For voting evaluation these tools can range from using what's actually available in memory to stereotypes, schemes, party identification, and ideology, among other factors.

To filter, distill, and edit the information that they already have searched for, voters also use habit, familiarity, affect referral, endorsement, viability, and other perceptual schemes. Lau and Redlawsk (2011) suggested four approaches to how voters might make their decision. One is "rational," which relies heavily on the voter's use of memory and analytical skills. The second is "confirmatory," as often suggested by the Michigan Model, which is based on primarily past experience. The third is fast and frugal, which allows voters to streamline and make their decision quickly. The fourth is described as semi-automatically intuitive, which becomes important as a task becomes more difficult. Thus, voters could be differentiated according to which of these four approaches they use (Lau and Redlawsk, 2011, 45).

THREAT AND INFORMATION SEARCH

Lau and Redlawsk also delve into what might happen when a voter perceives a threat from an out-group. First, as they suggested, both content and process of information search matter. In terms of content of information, we can classify the content of information into positive and negative information.

Positive information is the content that "benefits" the searchers (i.e., the pros), and negative information is the content that "threatens" the searchers (i.e., the cons). The rational choice model normally would demand voters to "calculate" the difference between the pros and cons. But the perception of threat also may overwhelm the voters so much that a thorough, accurate calculation of benefits versus costs is psychologically impractical. Voters are especially concerned with the "negative information" that is perceived to threaten their well-being, prestige, status, and power. In this way, the study of political threat is about how voters minimize the potential negatives of their lives through political actions, such as voting, rather than relying entirely upon utility maximization, as indicated by the rational choice model.

For example, the negative information search, such as one based on media reports leading to the awareness of a white horse prophecy in the Latter-day Saints Church (regardless of whether or not the media coverage produces any conclusive evidence or not), is vital to voters. This is not only because a voter's real utility income can be affected by how much cost each benefit will incur, but also because of the way voters react when they come upon information they see as potentially threatening their well-being, status, power, and survival. The negative information, especially when it is presented as an imminent threat, can trigger physiological reactions as well, a point to be discussed shortly. The perception of a threat also can have a long-term effect on memory. This is especially apparent when voters frequently rely on stereotypes, affect referrals, and other cognitive and affective means to deal with threats they perceive as frequent and consistent.

Negative information also can sustain the information search process. A strong perception of threat will likely occupy the voter's memory for a long time. As suggested by Lau and Redlawsk (2011), a deeper information search produces long-term memory. Moreover, the sequence of information search is also important because the earlier impression influences how later stages will play out in a voter's mind. A perception of threat will prolong the information search, unless a solution to a threat and the anxiety it causes is found. An example comes from an empirical study (Young Kim and Kelly Garrett, 2012), which was conducted during the February 2008 Democratic Party primary debate held in Ohio with Hillary Clinton and Barack Obama. Using an internet connection and a web browser, a total of 280 participants evaluated the two candidates before and after the debate. The respondents reported in real time their impressions of the candidates at regular intervals during the debate and listed what they remembered about the candidates after the debate. Furthermore, participants could watch the debate in a natural social setting which provided "a more realistic picture of how individuals assess candidates in everyday life" (354).

Kim and Garrett were interested in how respondents processed information as they watched the real-time debate between Clinton and Obama and whether the participants would use different information-processing methods for Clinton and Obama. The researchers discovered that respondents evaluated Obama with much more memory-based information processing, whereas their evaluation of Clinton was more related to the information presented at the time of debate, the online tally method.

What is the difference between online tally (which the respondents used for evaluating Clinton) and the memory-based information processing (used for evaluating Obama)? First, the timing of forming opinion or evaluation statement is different: online tally occurs at the moment of the respondent being exposed to information, while memory-based occurs at the time of judgment (therefore, at the end). Second, the role of long-term memory differs in the two methods: online tally does not use it at all while the memory-based model assumes retrieving relevant information from long-term memory. Third, concerning how information is processed, online tally assumes a series of evaluative impressions formed at the time of information exposure. The memory-based model, on the other hand, assumes that long-term memory must be incorporated into the working memory to process information. Fourth, the level of difficulty varies in that online tally is more effortless whereas the memory-based counterpart requires a deeper level of information search. Finally, the results of information processing differ as well: online tally assumes an affective integrator, while the memory-based model assumes "a sampling, or averaging" from working memory to produce a judgment.

The findings challenged previous studies suggesting that voters either use online tally or memory-based information processing, Kim and Garrett proved that voters may use both methods simultaneously, which became known as the dual process model. Voters, therefore, are flexible, agile, and nimble in processing information. They use online tally and memory-based search simultaneously, and both methods have independent effects on decision making.

Kim and Garrett's finding that Clinton's candidacy compelled voters to use online tally, or the "affective integrator," to quickly update and form an opinion on her is quite understandable. She was a well-known but polarizing politician with rich political experience and a long public life dating to the administration of her husband, President Bill Clinton, in the 1990s. On the other hand, voters clearly perceived Obama, an unknown and potentially "threatening" candidate, differently. Despite the fact that most voters in February 2008, when this empirical study was conducted, had no clear knowledge of Obama's previous political career, these voters nevertheless went deep into their own memory to try to "finalize" their evaluation of his candidacy.

This strongly suggests that Obama's candidacy triggered a strong level of anxiety and voters needed to link his candidacy to other political experiences to which they could relate. Later, we also will see this deeper level of search of memory often is related to memory about the political group to which Obama belonged. A judgment can only be made after a new political figure is evaluated based on the perception of threat that their group brings to ordinary voters. For example, Wilson and Davis (2011) summarized the discussion about the motivations for racial resentment and "the subtle framing of Obama as a person who receives 'special treatment' from the media" (128).

PERCEPTION OF THREAT AND BIOLOGY

Political scientists Peter Hatemi and Rose McDermott (2011) argue that many political preferences, such as vote choice, can be studied in terms of biology. For example, the use of long-term memory when a threat is present in a voter's information search process has biological roots. Humans are more likely to be alerted when they perceive that they are in danger than when they are in a peaceful, secure state. Threat anxiety, research shows, causes humans to react biologically. In short, the humans' universal need to deal effectively with threats is at the center of evolutionary information processing, adaptation, and strategizing. The following examples show how threat anxiety may appear when the threat content is racial in nature.

Kevin Smith and John Hibbing (2011) used their data encompassing psychological and physiological dimensions to study political attitudes and behaviors. They studied how humans react to external threats by examining patterns in how they blink their eyes. Because it is a known fact that human eyes blink harder "if startled during an aversive stimulus" and less "during a pleasant stimuli," Smith and Hibbing examined whether their lab participants, who were white, would display different eyeblink patterns when faced with various racial images representing whites and Blacks (234). The white participants were asked questions such as whether or not "blacks should be given preference in hiring and promotion" because of past histories of discrimination. They discovered that "race-conscious policy attitudes can be indexed physiologically—that is, that these sorts of attitudes have, at a minimum, biological markers and perhaps even a biological basis" (241). The perception of racial threat can increase the rate of blinking in the eyes as well as other muscle movements, for example.

There also are findings that "white subjects who involuntarily frowned while viewing images of black applicants were more likely to recommend whites for a scholarship" (Smith and Hibbing, 2011, 235). Using new technology, such as the clinical assessment SCAN tool, neuroscience scholars also found that amygdala, a small almond-shaped region in the human brain, is the place where "the processing of fear" takes place. Amygdala is also discovered as the area for "racial processing." Moreover, "as individuals become more familiar with foreigners [of different race], amygdala activity diminishes" (Schreiber, 2011, 284–285).

The perception of threat can also be examined based on the biological effect it may have on the recipient of a threat once its content is actualized. Importantly, what will the recipient perceive if the threat becomes reality? In this vein, Coren Apicella and David Cesarini (2011) engaged in an innovative study of male participants who watched the 2008 presidential election outcome live on television. Their empirical finding revealed that "the stronger a subject was attached to the party of the losing candidate, the greater his relative testosterone decline" (269). Apicella and Cesarini conclude that the physiological effects might dampen or constrain confidence levels in those who saw their candidate lose while those who backed a winning candidate will become more confident and engage in subsequent political debates or support other campaigns.

CONCLUSION

As we noted in the puzzle introduced earlier in the book, the religious threat surrounding an alleged white horse prophecy led to an important question about what motivated the white majority, especially those white Protestants, to react to both of Romney's presidential campaigns. We first investigated the theory of rational choice to try to find a clue. The rational choice theory emphasized the means used to reach the goal. The use of the means that maximizes mainly economic well-being, in the words of Downs referring to "utility income," can be described as rational (Downs, 1957). For Downs, voters are rational if they choose the political parties and their electoral representatives, as based on the principle of utility maximization. However, this explanation appears to contradict the decisions of white Protestants in the 2012 GOP presidential primaries. These voters seemed to be more concerned with the fear of electing Romney (thereby, giving unprecedented power to the church of his Latter-day Saints faith than picking the candidate who could give them the maximum benefits).

Writing in the early sixteenth century, Niccolo Machiavelli advised his *Prince*: "Here the question arises: is it better to be loved than feared, or vice versa? I don't doubt that every prince would like to be both; but since it is hard to accommodate these qualities, if you have to make a choice, to be feared is much safer than to be loved" (Machiavelli, 1977 edition, 47). *The Prince*, for Machiavelli, should know how to threaten his subject in a way that takes advantages of human nature, which is more motivated in politics by fear rather than by love. Machiavelli explained: "People are less concerned with offending a man who makes himself loved than one who makes himself feared: the reason is that love is a link of obligation which men, because they are rotten, will break any time they think doing so serves their advantage; but fear involves dread of punishment, from which they can never escape" (48).

Machiavelli's observation of human nature seems to align with some of the empirical evidence presented in modern social science. In sum, the reviews of the social psychology literature and political biology both point to clearer direction for understanding political threat. First, a threat can engender a strong perceptual impact on the recipient of the threat (i.e., the threatened). Second, this perception of threat has a deep relationship with not only the emotional aspect of human cognition but also the information processing that involves the long-term memory function of the individual who is threatened. Third, the perception of threat also has its biological roots and can influence how human psychophysiology (and even the human brain) works. Clearly, the research on the connection of threat and biology is still developing. But, empirical evidence from modern social science suggests that the level of difficulty in the information search process, and especially negative information, can have a great impact on how voters ultimately make their choices in elections.

As Rose McDermott (2011) states, the main question for political scientists is "why do some people confronted with a threat choose to fight, while others confronted with the same threat choose to retreat?" (247). The social psychology literature and political biology have introduced the discourse in useful form, but we also still need a sound comprehensive theory. Based on the understanding of the research reviewed so far, I will propose five axioms for the atomic structure theoretical model in the following chapters, which will focus on the formation of perception of multiple threats and possible political responses to complex political threat environments.

Chapter 4

The Origins of Multiple Threats

In the previous chapter, we discussed why political actors tend to respond more frequently to threats than to reward politicians who could offer them economic benefits. Economic benefits, or what rational choice theorist Anthony Downs (1957) called utility incomes, apparently are particularly important to all voters regardless of their backgrounds. But, it also is critical to note that calculating costs and benefits associated with each political act engenders too much uncertainty for ordinary voters, who may not have the capacity, time, or focus to process information that is complex and multidimensional. On the other hand, the perception of an external threat imposes a much greater immediate impact on the voter's information search process. The exposure to negative information (i.e., the threat to a voter's well-being, survival, status, or power) can motivate the voter to search deep into their long-term memory (which reinforces the perception of threat) and might cause them to respond according to biological stimuli until an acceptable solution is found to respond to the perceived threat.

In this chapter and the next, the condition under which multiple threats are perceived is discussed, as a fundamental building block in the atomic structure theory of American politics that is central to this book. First, we must understand sources of threats and why they lead to perceptions of multiple threats in the first place. The reason for paying attention to multiple threats is obvious. Recall our discussion of political threat was inspired by the change of votes among white Protestants in the 2012 presidential election. Clearly, if voters are concerned with a political threat, the fact that white Protestants moved from an anti-Romney position in the primaries to becoming the strongest Romney supporters in the general election was related to the changed political environment. Recall from chapter 1 that many media commentators observed that the 2012 general election was the nation's first-ever general election without a WASP candidate. Thus, the first thing that whites were likely to notice was the obvious difference between themselves and the two major candidates. Obama is a Protestant, but he is Black, while Romney is white, yet a Latter-day Saint.

OTHERNESS AS THE SOURCE OF MULTIPLE THREATS

The first step for discovering the origins of multiple threats is to examine voter preferences. We knew that white Protestants (WPs hereafter) preferred Romney to Obama, as shown by their actual vote in the 2012 general election. But, we also need to ask whom WPs would have voted for, if in addition to Obama and Romney another candidate would have been available for WPs to support. This additional candidate could have been their true first choice. As discussed later in part II of the book, I will explain why we call the first choice a congruent candidate, as we know that Romney would be their second choice, and Obama the third.

Jeffress, the Southern Baptist pastor who had called Romney's faith a cult prior to the 2012 Republican primaries, was asked by *Fox News* whom he would vote for if Romney was not his first choice. Jeffress' response offered a clue about the potential preference of a typical WP. His answer was the then Texas Governor Rick Perry. Jeffress was also asked whom he would vote for in the general election, if Perry was defeated in the Republican primaries. Jeffress responded that he "prefers Romney to Obama in the White House." He went on to explain:

> The reason I would probably select Mitt Romney over Barack Obama is, I do think being an evangelical, or Christian, is important, but it's not the only criteria by which we select a leader. I personally would rather have a non-Christian like Mitt Romney who embraces [biblical] principles than Barack Obama. (Fox News, 2011)

Jeffress did not elaborate how Romney embraced the same Protestant principles which Obama did not share, in his own perception. He mentioned religion but said that it is not the only criterion for him to select a leader. Using principles as the basis to form a voting decision would lead to the category of rational voters in Lau and Redlawsk's (2012) typology of voters, the most demanding task in terms of complexity of the information search and cognitive ability required. Regardless, Jeffress' choices were clear: He preferred Perry over Romney, and Romney to Obama. Perry was a popular Texas governor who was raised as a Methodist and went to the same church as former President George W. Bush. Though not a Baptist, for WPs, Perry is a Protestant who shares more common religious beliefs than does Romney. Thus, it is, in fact, fairly straightforward to lay down a matrix comparing the three president candidates from the perspective of WPs, such as Jeffress, as shown in table 4.1.

Table 4.1 indicates that the number of shared identities turns out to be a good predictor of Jeffress' preference for presidential candidates. Obama was the least preferred, or put differently, he was the candidate whom WPs such as Jeffress wanted to defeat, because he shared only one identification with WPs. Moreover, as introduced in chapter 1, Obama's Christian identification was challenged by many Protestants throughout his presidential campaign (this "misperception" of Obama's true religious identity may come handy for the cognitive challenge imposed on those white Protestant voters who cared about their religion, as we will see shortly). On the opposite side, Perry shared the largest number of identifying factors with WPs, and he was WPs' most favored candidate for president before the primaries were completed. This cognitive mechanism seems to be naive, but as Lau and Redlawski (2006) revealed, voters often choose the most accessible, easiest path to make their voting decision.

Rick Perry's candidacy in the 2012 GOP primaries did not last long, and his campaign quickly turned into a public relations disaster, largely as a result of his own mistakes manifested by his poor debate performance and a blip of memory loss when asked to name key federal agencies.

As the 2012 GOP primaries drew to a close with Romney's delegate margin lead too large to challenge, Jeffress finally endorsed Romney on April 17, 2012. He told the Associated Press that he still did not believe Latter-day Saints are Christians. But "voters will have to choose between a Christian like President Barack Obama and a Mormon like Romney," and "the difference is that Obama embraces non-biblical principles while Romney embraces biblical principles like the sanctity of life and the sanctity of marriage" (Coleman, 2012). Obviously, though Jeffress did not dispute Obama's Protestant affiliation, he asserted that Obama did not embrace the "biblical principles" that a Protestant "should" embrace. Obama in the eye of Jeffress is someone who looked like belonging to "other" groups, but not the true WP group.

Table 4.1   White Protestant Voters and the Presidential Candidates, 2012

	Same party identification	Same racial identification	Same religious identification	Total # of shared identifications
Rick Perry	x	x	x	3
Mitt Romney	x	x		2
Pres Obama			x	1

Source: Created by the author.

The "principles" Jeffress alluded to made clear that in politics candidates are evaluated based on how they are similar to the ideas or identities about which voters care. In the research literature of social psychology, scholars use the term in-group to describe a social group to which a person psychologically identifies as a member. In comparison, the term out-group refers to a social group with which an individual does not identify.

Thus, both Obama and Romney symbolize out-groups, while Perry is a member of the in-group by which WPs can identify. If the classification of in-group versus out-group can be useful for the discussion of politics, one has to demonstrate two interrelated important political orientations for voters. First, voters prefer their in-group members when they face political choices. Second, a voter's preference might not only be a result of in-group favoritism but also hostility toward out-groups due to perceptions of external threats.

IN-GROUP FAVORITISM

In-group favoritism has been documented thoroughly in social science. In political science, for example, many studies have shown that Americans often cast their votes along racial lines. Indeed, "divided by color" describes voting patterns in numerous elections (Kinder and Sanders, 1996, 208–228; Dawson, 1994, 131–158; Engstrom, 1985, 13–41). The literature on racially polarized voting also shows that though some white voters have occasionally crossed racial lines to vote for minority candidates, white electoral support for Black candidates is often "short lived" (see, e.g., Liu and Vanderleeuw, 2007; Mollenkopf, 1997, 98–113).

In the 1990s, Mayor Wilson Goode and Mayor David Dinkins were defeated for re-election by their white opponents in Philadelphia and New York City, respectively. In Chicago, according to *The New York Times/WBBN-TV* poll, more than three-quarters of the whites who had voted for the Black candidate, Harold Washington in the 1983 mayoral election, voted for a white candidate, Richard M. Daley, over a Black candidate in 1989.

In New Orleans, Hurricane Katrina on August 23, 2005 not only flooded 80 percent of the city where many Black Americans had resided, especially in the city's east side neighborhoods, but also diluted the Black-majority voting strength in the city's racial makeup. Two months after Katrina, the city's white population even shortly surpassed its Black share at 46.9 percent and 46.4 percent, respectively. The rapid racial demographic change led to a dramatic change in racial voting patterns as well. In the 2006 mayoral election, 80 percent of the white residents voted for the white candidate Mitch Landrieu against Ray Nagin, the Black incumbent who had received 86 percent of white support only four years before (see Liu and Vanderleeuw,

2007). In 2010, Landrieu was elected as the first white mayor after Black mayors had been in charge of the City of New Orleans for thirty-two years.

Modern sociological studies also reveal the lasting effect of in-group favoritism. In workplace settings, for example, evaluators were shown to rate individuals more favorably on performance who shared similar identities based on gender and/or race (Greenwald and Pettigrew, 2014). In laboratory studies, scholars also found that subjects allocated more resources to members of their own groups than to members of out-groups (Billig and Tajfel, 1973).

Why is in-group membership a powerful predictor of individual favoritism and preferences? In his pioneering social psychological study, Byrne (1961) discovered that liking someone and attraction toward strangers were a result of similar attitudes. Byrne (1961) suggested that "any time that another person offers us validation by indicating that his percepts and concepts are congruent with ours, it constitutes a rewarding interaction and, hence, one element in forming a positive relationship" (713). Preferences given to in-group members also were found to enhance self-esteem for someone offering a favorable gesture (Greenwald and Pettigrew, 2014). Evolutionary biologists and psychologists suggest that in-group favoritism is an innate human trait during human grouping processes. In experimental studies, scholars discovered that children as young as 5 years old (some even as young as 3 or 5 months) "allocated more of a scarce resource (toy coins) to the kids [wearing the same T-shirt color] . . . reported more positive thoughts about them . . . they were better able to remember and recall positive actions of their in-group, encoding favorable information describing those of their own type" (Christakis, 2019, 4). In the next section, we turn to out-groups and the hostility they might experience.

OUT-GROUP HOSTILITY

Out-group hostility, whether in the United States, South Africa, Australia, or elsewhere, undoubtedly has led to widespread incidents stemming from tragic antagonism that always seem to be present in human history. Social and political groups can and do impose harsher treatments, as cruel as slavery or hidden racial or gender discrimination in the workplace, toward out-group members than they would contemplate with their in-group peers. Arguably, in-group favoritism feeds into out-group hostility. However, it is not enough to just assume this happens naturally, because it is almost unimaginable and obviously wrong to believe that out-group hostility such as slavery institutionalized by WASPs against African Americans transpired simply because WASPs favored their own group members. One can favor their own group, but the individual also does not have to treat out-group members harshly. In

U.S. history, for example, it was such an inhumane government policy to remove Indigenous Americans from the east to the west of Mississippi by force (e.g., the Trail of Tears) that it could not be reasonably explained by in-group favoritism alone (or even as a primary factor).

Neither the widespread practice of out-group hostility in world history nor the human spirit against oppression manifested in events, such as the American Civil Rights Movement, however, led to a unified understanding of how out-group hostility occurs. The discussion turns to the research on out-group hostility, as based on two threads to consider. In one thread, early social psychological studies, for example, were mainly concerned with the human predispositions and personality traits, such as the propensity to become authoritarian, which may cause individuals to become hostile to out-group members (Adorno et al., 1950).

What defines authoritarian thought? MacWilliams (2016) described it as: "Uniformity and order are authoritarian watch words. Authoritarians obey. They seek order. They follow authoritarian leaders. They eschew diversity, fear 'the other,' act aggressively toward others, and, once they have identified friend from foe, hold tight to their decision" (717). Hetherington and Weiler (2009) focused on the political impact of authoritarianism in the contemporary era. Their empirical analysis of American National Election Studies (NES) data demonstrated that the sorting of authoritarian predispositions already had intensified the polarization between the two main parties in the United States before Trump's candidacy in the 2016 election. Hetherington and Weiler argue that the two major political parties have sorted themselves "clearly along authoritarian/nonauthoritarian lines" with authoritarians moving toward the Republican Party and non-authoritarians toward the Democratic Party (Hetherington and Weiler, 2009, 158).

While authoritarians value authority, order, and conventions, they also may become extremely hostile toward out-groups. Many empirical studies have demonstrated that racism expressed by whites often has its roots in authoritarianism. Karen Stenner (2005), for example, found that white authoritarian respondents in social surveys were much more likely to blame Blacks for their comparatively lower position and social status than white non-authoritarians. The respondents who identified as white authoritarian believe in "the relative safety and comfort" to attack Blacks when the interviewers were also white (248). Furthermore, white authoritarians were much more likely to claim that whites themselves "had been discriminated against or disadvantaged for being white" (Stenner, 2005, 249).

Political scientists such as Key (1949), who was mentioned previously, paid more attention to how the geographic distribution of Blacks in the South might have caused various perceptions of Black threat to white dominance (also see Longoria, 1996, 885; Glaser, 1994, 21–41; Herring and Forbes,

1994, 431–445; Giles and Buckner, 1993, 702–713). One finding in some behavioral studies is that socioeconomic status may influence how white voters perceive threats from out-groups. Lower-class whites, it has been argued, are more likely to be hostile to Blacks and to form an anti-Black voting bloc (Pettigrew, 1972; Lipstiz, 1965, 103–109; Lipset, 1963, 87–126). This may be because "(t)he white working class is in more direct competition with blacks for jobs and admissions to schools, and in bad economic times, the working class is hurt more by unemployment and inflation" (Howell, 1994, 193). In contrast, Chandler Davidson (1972), based on his study of biracial politics in the Houston metropolitan area, argues that the "simple dichotomy of upper-class racial moderation vs lower-class prejudice is misleading . . . one's membership in a social class is only one of many factors that influence, in a complex manner, his attitude and behavior towards ethnic groups" (180).

Conversely, Davidson suggests that a biracial coalition between whites and Blacks should be based on the redistribution of income, opportunity, and power that certainly attract more lower-class whites. A biracial coalition may be "radical" in the sense that it "would constitute significant departures from the elitist liberalism of the 1950s and 1960s" (273-275). Nearly fifty years after Davidson's study in Houston was published, in 2021, Heather McGhee writes in her latest book *The Sum of Us: What Racism Costs Everyone and How We Can Prosper Together* that once white Americans move past looking at race relations through a zero-sum lens, they can unify on common interests, such as sustainable wages, universal health insurance, and secure retirement. We will come back to the question concerning the factors that may help build biracial coalitions for collective political actions in chapters 7 and 8. At the moment, let's focus on out-group hostility.

Out-group hostility may occur because of a lack of social interactions among groups. For example, from sociology, the social contact theory emphasizes how social interactions in workplaces and neighborhood, as well as community organizations may reduce racial prejudice and perception of minority group threat and enhance racial tolerance toward out-groups (Huckfeldt, 1986). Carsey, for example, reports that in the 1989 New York City mayoral election that brought Black candidate David Dinkins to victory, "the level of black voter density at the local level [i.e., precinct] positively influences the probability that a white voter in that locale will vote for a black candidate" (Carsey, 1995, 221, also see Bledsoe et al., 1995, 434–458).

In sum, these studies from different perspectives focus on the relationship between the potential perception of threat and the level of hostility that dominant group members may have against minorities. The body of scholarly research, though coming from different fields, suggests that not all dominant group members have the same level of out-group hostility. Thus, the connection between threat anxiety and out-group hostility seems to be quite evident. Scholars may disagree about what types of concrete threats— economic, social, or political—an individual may perceive and who among the dominant group may perceive such a threat. However, they agree that the more intense the perception of out-group threat (i.e., threat anxiety) is, the more likely it will amplify the hostility toward the threatening out-group.

Moving on to the second research thread of out-group hostility, some studies have looked beyond the "concrete" threat, as discussed previously. Instead of focusing on the types of individuals in a given group who are likely to feel threatened by out-groups, here the question is shifted to why a group may collectively be perceived as threatening to another group. For example, regarding racial groups "people necessarily come to identify themselves as belonging to a racial group; such identification is not spontaneous or inevitable but a result of experience" (Blumer, 1958, 3). Individuals do have numerous groups they can identify with, but their experience will lead them to identifying with specific groups. For Herbert Blumer (1958), all individuals of a racial group, especially the dominant group, identify with their racial group because of the "positions" their groups occupy within political and social systems. Hence, in whatever way personal positions may be identified (rich or poor, educated at higher levels or not, etc.), individuals of a racial group "all are led, by virtue of sharing the sense of group position, to similar individual positions" (5). Furthermore, according to Blumer (1958):

An analysis of how the sense of group position is formed should start with a clear recognition that it is an historical product. It is set originally by conditions of initial contact. Prestige, power, possession of skill, numbers, original self-conception, aims, designs and opportunities are a few of the factors that may fashion the original sense of group position . . . However variable its particular career, the sense of group position is clearly formed by a running process in which the dominant racial group is led to define and redefine the subordinate racial group and the relations between them. (5)

Two propositions are important here, which need to be elaborated upon in understanding the position and interactions of groups within the atomic structure of politics. First, all individual members of a group are collectively "located" on the spectrum of power, prestige, and allocation of resources. Therefore, an individual may be poor, but that person also may feel a sense of the dominant power from the whole group. The individual's racial prejudice, thus, might occur intentionally or unintentionally to make the person feel "superior." More importantly, the sense of dominant group position also leads members of the dominant group to feel that "the subordinate race is intrinsically different and alien" (Blumer, 1958, 4). In short, the collective identity, as a result of human grouping, has shaped the social psychology along the dichotomous sense of "we," "us," "superior" versus "they," "other," and "alien," and "inferior."

Second, group positions were defined and redefined by the dominant group. Thus, members of the dominant group naturally develop a feeling of "proprietary claim to certain areas of privilege and advantage" and "fear or apprehension that the subordinate racial group is threatening, or will threaten, the position of the dominant group" (Blumer, 1958, 4). The wage for being in the dominant position leads to acknowledging persistent perceptions of subordinate group threats to the "rightful" claim of power and prestige of the dominant group (see, for example, Orey et al., 2011 on how white hostility was manifested through their support for racial referenda in the Deep South).

In sum, different from the earlier thread of research that focused on the concrete threat minority groups represent, this group position theory stresses the importance of the collective group positions and the "abstract threat" minority groups may engender. As Blumer (1958, 4) indicated, this sense of group position transcends the feeling which individuals in the dominant group might have by giving them a "common orientation" not otherwise found in their individual sentiments or views. Blumer adds that this specific type of definition in the dominant group is possible because of an abstract image of the subordinate minority group, which also represents a common orientation as perceived by the dominant group as a whole.

Blumer's group position theory has relevance for contemporary discussions about racial relations, particularly in results taken from many public opinion surveys. For instance, Kinder and his colleagues examined white racial attitudes based on longitudinal National Election Studies data, to show that white racial resentment still deeply affects how they perceive the image of racial minorities, especially Blacks. The so-named label of symbolic racism can be used to describe new "abstract, moralistic resentments" that are rooted in the belief that "blacks violate such traditional American [WASP] values as individualism and self- reliance, the work ethic, obedience, and discipline" (Kinder and Sears, 1981, 416; also see Kinder and Sanders, 1996).

Michael Dawson (1994), in his often-cited study of Black public opinion, found evidence of an impact of what he called "linked fate" which "measures the degree to which African Americans believe that their own self-interests are linked to the interests of the race" (77). For Dawson, "Crucial to the formation of social identity is the active process of comparing in-group and out-group members. The more differences that are perceived between in-group and the out-group on the salient social dimensions, the stronger the group identity of in-group members" (76).

Moreover, favoritism and preferences provided to members of the dominant group may occur because of trying either intentionally or unintentionally to conform to the social norm which traditionally has promoted socially acceptable higher status for the dominant group members. It is this conformity to the norm that also facilitates stereotype and prejudice at the expense of the minority group members. Empirical studies showed that this social norm even can have an impact on the behavior of marginal group members, who were found, for example, to tip more to taxi drivers and restaurant workers of the dominant group than to those of marginal groups (Gaertner and Bickman, 1971; Ayres et al., 2005; Lynn et al., 2008).

Perceptions of group positions and group threats also have been shown to predict anti-Semitism among Blacks. Moreover, contradictory white attitudes toward college admission standards have been found to correlate to their perceptions of an Asian threat (thereby, white hostility toward the use and the importance of grade point average [GPA] in college admission), and the perception of threats by Blacks (thereby, white support for the use of GPA for college admission, see Samson, 2013). In the next chapter, we discuss concrete and abstract threats.

Chapter 5

Concrete and Abstract Threats

Group Perceptions and Responses

Continuing from the previous chapter, there have been many social science studies attempting to explain why humans not only favor members of their society who share common identities with them (i.e., in-group favoritism) but also often are hostile to members of out-groups (i.e., out-group hostility). The research also has sought to gauge the level of hostility toward out-group members based on the external threat perceived by the dominant in-group.

External threats can be viewed in two forms: concrete or abstract. For example, in her recent study of voting access restrictions implemented since the election of Barack Obama in 2008, Shauna Reilly (2020) described the differences between "realistic threats and symbolic threats" (19). As Reilly indicated, realistic threats tend to take the "tangible form" such as threats to one's "economic or physical safety," while symbolic threats are perceived when the in-group culture perceives "existential dangers" (19).

I am using the terms of abstract (or symbolic) threat versus concrete (or realistic) threat in this book. Understanding these two forms of threat will be important to building the principles that inform the theory of the atomic structure in American politics.

Take a moment to examine table 5.1 to compare the main attributes of abstract and concrete threats. To understand these differences, one must pay attention first to the structure of a threat environment. For a threat to exist, three elements are necessary. The first is the threatener (i.e., the originator of a threat, or the source of the threat). The second is the threatened, that is, the recipient of threat. Finally, the content of a threat is about what is articulated, such as the consequence of the threat being realized. Other elements of a threat may also determine how a threat originated, was processed, and then ended. For example, the intent of the threatener may be of ultimate importance to the threatened. But, it also is not a necessary condition for a threat

Table 5.1   Abstract Threat and Concrete Threat, Compared

	Abstract Threat	Concrete Threat
Threatened	Whole dominant group	Part or whole dominant group
Threatener	Whole minority group	Part or whole minority group
Threat content	The superior position of dominant group	Economic, political, demographic, social
Impact of threat	Social norm	Elections and political parties
Speed of change	Slow	Fast

Source: Created by the author.

to exist, as a threat can be completely unintentional, as the next few chapters demonstrate. Also, it is the threatened who subjectively strongly feel the existence of such a threat.

Table 5.1 indicates that the first crucial difference between abstract and concrete threat is that an abstract threat is perceived by the whole dominant group while a concrete threat applies either to a subset of the dominant group or the whole group. This is exactly how Blumer (1958) discussed group relations and "the abstract images" (Blumer's words) the dominant group assigned to the subordinate groups. Being in the dominant position, the members of dominant group collectively can feel an external threat from a subordinate group.

A concrete threat, on the other hand, can be a specific threat that is perceived by those in the dominant group who are directly threatened. For these members of the dominant group, obviously, identifying who are the actual threateners from a subordinate group is an important task, and their responses to these specific threats take shape once they have identified the direct source of the threat. For example, Indigenous Americans who lived in the lands now part of the state of Georgia were considered a concrete threat to those WASPs who wanted to occupy more land in the rapidly developing economy of the South during the 1830s. This concrete threat was the main reason for the Indian Removal plan of the Andrew Jackson administration (see chapter 7 for more details). Chinese Americans also were considered the concrete threat to the white working class, especially Catholic immigrants, in the Chinese exclusion era that emerged in the 1870s and 1880s.

For an abstract threat to exist, all dominant-group members can sense, recognize, or be alerted (or informed) that their group dominance is threatened by a subordinate group. For a concrete threat to exist, the threat content can be economic, such as job security, or political, such as losing an electoral office. It also can be demographic, such as the growth of minorities in the community, or social, such as organizational changes.

Finally, the impact of an abstract threat is different from the impact of its concrete counterpart. Abstract threats have a greater effect on social norms while concrete threats influence elections and political parties. In addition, the change caused by concrete threats occurs more quickly than with abstract threats. The impacts of these two forms of threats will be discussed in forthcoming chapters. In this chapter, we now introduce a discussion about the abstract threat.

WASPS AND THE PROBLEM OF MULTIPLE GROUPS

Reiterating an earlier point, to start a discussion of group relations, one must pay attention to the dominant group who, according to Blumer (1958), defines and redefines the subordinate groups in a political system. Therefore, it starts by acknowledging the origin of WASPs in the United States.

When Captain Christopher Jones of the Mayflower ship sent his team of explorers to search for a suitable settlement site in North America on November 27, 1620, he did not anticipate the bitter winter awaiting him and his 102 Puritan passengers. Only 167 years later, as the Articles of Confederation were completed on September 17, 1787, and the new U.S. Constitution was adopted and signed, the offspring of the original Puritans and other White Anglo-Saxon Protestants (WASPs) constituted the undisputed dominant group among roughly 4 million people of the young Republic.

"Not all of the colonists, to be sure, were of English descent, but seven out of ten of the white population were of English blood and almost nine out of ten were British," Winthrop Hudson writes in *American Protestantism* (1961, 3). What was the bond that united these English and Protestant subgroups together? In addition to ethnicity, Hudson points to the theological roots—"the overwhelming majority of these churches stood within a single Reformation tradition" (17), and for the five English-speaking denominations—Congregationalists, Presbyterians, Baptists, Anglicans, and Quakers—who represented 85 percent of all the Protestant congregations at the time of the American Revolution. "It was the stamp of Geneva which left the deepest mark upon American Protestantism," Hudson continues. "The English-speaking churches were Calvinistic in background, and were reinforced in this respect by the German, Dutch, and French Reformed churches representing an additional 9 per cent of the total number of congregations" (Hudson, 1961, 23).

As dominant as they were, WASPs had other groups with which to interact. African Americans represented about one-fifth of the total population in the colonies. In addition to African Americans and Indigenous Americans, there were groups, respectively, of 1.4 percent Roman Catholic and 0.34 percent Jewish (Hudson, 1961, 4). Moreover, about 80,000 Black slaves were imported in the decade after the U.S. Constitution was ratified, and about 3,000 immigrants arrived from Europe per year, between 1793 and 1814.

To establish an orderly government, WASPs adopted many laws of conformity and in-group favoritism to assign power and resources. But, the fact that there were multiple subordinate groups presented a serious problem. If all out-groups had constituted threats to the domination of WASPs, as suggested by Blumer's abstract threat theory, then how should these multiple threats be prioritized? Furthermore, the white Catholic population increased exponentially in the first half of the nineteenth century. There also were newly formed domestic minority groups, such as the Latter-day Saints who organized in the 1830s, starting in the western half of the state of New York. Western expansion also enlarged the population not only through immigration but also through pacts such as the Guadalupe-Hidalgo Treaty of 1848, which placed Mexicans of the Southwest onto the new map of the United States.

As Blumer (1958) notes, the group positions within a society were initially defined and redefined by the dominant group—in this case, WASPs. But, with the share of subordinate groups ever increasing, the business of defining and redefining group positions could become a political inconvenience, to say the least. Consider a society with only two groups: one dominant and one subordinate. In this scenario the number of external threats (remember, we are discussing the abstract threat in Blumer's sense) is only two as the two groups form an external threat to each other.

But, if the number of groups increases to three, then the number of external threats will increase to six, and when the number of groups increase to four, the total number of external threats will further increase to twelve. There are a total of twelve bivariate threat relationships in an environment of only four groups. It is thus practically impossible to track the detailed threat relationship if one wants to study all possible external threats when the number of groups is increased to more than three.

One way to study multiple threats is to narrow the key threat relationships and ignore other possible threats between groups. For instance, to discuss the following four-group situation as presented in figure 5.1: G4 is threatening G2, G3, and G1, while G1 is a recipient of multiple threats from G4, G2, and G3. There are only five threat relationships we are concerned with in this figure for whatever purpose set for the study.

Figure 5.1 represents the strategic dynamic taken into consideration throughout this book. Certainly we can enlarge the number of groups further, which we will do below, but we also will focus on the external threats to the dominant group—in this figure, G1. This is because G1 is perceiving threats from all other groups, and G1 needs to formulate a strategy to deal with these multiple threats.

As revealed in figure 5.1, G4 is also of particular interest to us, as G4 is the source of threat for G2 and G3. Imagine that in figure 5.1, G1 is the dominant group (WASPs), and G4, G2, and G3 are minority groups representing

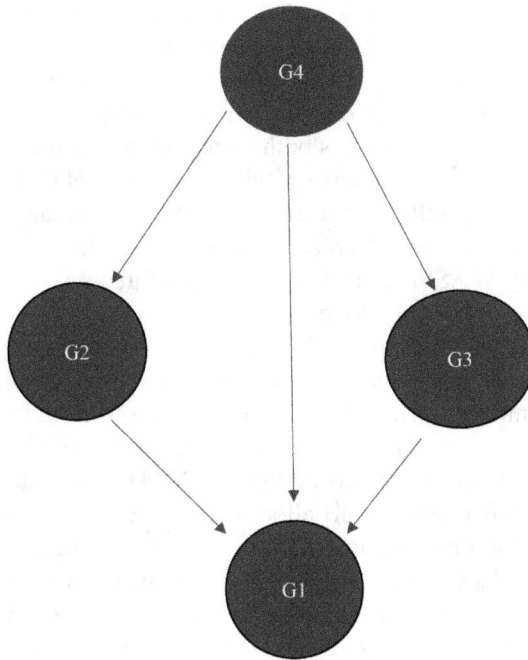

Figure 5.1 A Hypothetical Threat Environment Involving Four Groups. Created by the author with G1 denoting the dominant Group, and G2 through G4 denoting the subordinate groups.

Blacks, white Catholics, and Latter-day Saints, respectively. G4 (i.e., Blacks) is shown to be a threat not only to the dominant group, WASPs (G1), but also to other minority groups—white Catholics (G2) and Latter-day Saints (G3). The existence of multiple threats, such as what is shown in figure 5.1, is a key feature of group relations in the United States. Many previous studies ignored this key feature, focusing instead on the bivariate threat relationship. This commonality in previous studies explains why a unified theory has yet to emerge to comprehend and observe how complex threat relationships operate in American politics.

GROUP SIMILARITIES AND WASP
PERCEPTIONS OF MULTIPLE THREATS

Given the unending existence of multiple group threats from the beginning of the Republic, when the dominant WASPs institutionalized group positions, the abstract threat theory illustrated by Blumer (1958) and contemporary scholars (e.g., Kinder and Sanders, 1996) predicted that WASPs would use their political power to dominate all subordinate groups. This is a useful theory, but it also does not explain logically how WASPs institutionalized group inequality. Would WASPs, for example, treat Blacks the same way as they treated white Catholics, as both were defined as inferior groups? The abstract threat theory does not answer this clearly. It is at this point where we meet the problem of multiple threats and so we must return to the research about in-group favoritism, which actually provides relevant insights into the strategies used by WASPs to deal with multiple threats.

Recall that the dominant group is subject to the rule of in-group favoritism, which suggests that they prefer members of their own group, as far as allocating resources and payments are concerned. The reason is because of the attraction-similarity principle (which is discussed in the next chapter) in addition to self-esteem and social norms, which are maintained to favor the dominant group (Greenwald and Pettigrew, 2014). If the same logic holds, when the dominant group has to allocate some resources and payments to out-groups, the dominant group will seek the subordinate group that is most similar to itself. They would favor that group over others. This is because similarity is a measure of degree. On one extreme is the group that shares every social identity (i.e., the same in-group), and on the other extreme is the group that shares no social identity (i.e., complete strangers, aliens).

Figure 5.2 shows four groups. Assuming G1 is the dominant group, and G2 through G4 are all subordinate groups. We can look at the overlapping areas between G1 and the subordinate groups (i.e., the connecting joints in the areas) to identify the level of similarities between groups. Obviously, the preference for G1 would be G3 (the largest joint) to G2 (the smaller joint) to G4 with which there is no joint, and thus G4 is a distant group for G1.

This logic turned out to be powerful in predicting and explaining the way how WASPs see minority groups. Throughout U.S. history, WASPs have talked about minority groups in terms of how they are similar to WASPs and whether or not they could be equal or even mix with WASPs. Let's take a look at how Benjamin Franklin spoke about the Germans in Pennsylvania, as early as in 1751 (Kaufmann, 2004, 485):

Why should Pennsylvania, founded by the English, become a colony of Aliens, who will shortly be so numerous as to Germanize us instead of our Anglifying them, and will never adopt our Language or Custom, any more than they can acquire our Complexion . . . I am not for refusing entirely to admit them into our Colonies: all that seems to be necessary is to distribute them more equally, mix them with the English, establish English Schools where they are now to think settled . . . I say I am not against the Admission of Germans in general, for they

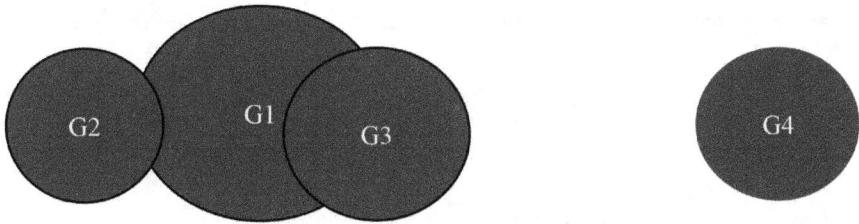

Figure 5.2 Similarities and Groups. Created by the author with G1 denoting the dominant Group, and G2 through G4 denoting the subordinate groups.

have their Virtues, their industry and frugality is exemplary; They are excellent
husbandmen and contribute greatly to the improvement of a Country.

Though Germans caused serious concern regarding the threat of Germanization,
the characteristics of Germans in the mind of Franklin were close enough to
WASPs to be mixed for the improvement of the new country.

As shown in table 5.2, Germans, like other Western European Protestants,
scored highest on the similarity measure, and thus led to minimum perceptions of external threats to WASPs. On the other end of the similarity measures are Blacks, who were constantly demonized by WASP intellectuals and
common man alike. Thomas Jefferson (1787) in his "Notes on the State of
Virginia" infamously remarked about Blacks and defended the practice of
slavery which was legally protected in his own state: "I advance it therefore
as a suspicion only, that the Blacks, whether originally a distinct race, or
made distinct by time and circumstances, are inferior to the whites in the
endowments both of body and mind . . . This unfortunate difference of color,
and perhaps of faculty, is a powerful obstacle to the emancipation of these
people." Jefferson based his anti-Black argument on how Blacks were "a
distinct race" and "inferior to whites."

Based on the similarity measures, white Catholics were less similar to
WASPs than white Protestants from other European countries, such as
Germany (see table 5.2), thus were more threatening than Germans and other
western European Protestant immigrants. White Catholics also believed Jesus
Christ as their Savior (thus a + in the religious column for Catholics in table
5.2), but the existence of Catholic Church also was a major theological threat
to WASPs. The influential *Masonic Review* reminded WASPs that "the battle
is on which will decide whether the Pope or American citizens will rule
America" (Kaufmann, 2004, 30).

Images of sexual sins were also brought against the Catholic Church. The
sensational and anti-Catholic novel, *Awful Disclosures*, written by Maria
Monk and published in 1836, became an instant best-seller. According

Table 5.2 Similarities and External Threat Concerning Minority Groups: The WASP Perspective

	Same Race	Geographic Proximity to Britain	Common Religion	Count of Similarities	Perception of External Threat
W. Europe Protestants	X	X	X	3	1
W. Europe Catholics	X	X	+	2+	2
SE Europe Catholics	X	+	+	1++	3
Latter-day Saints	X	+		1+	4
Mexicans	+		+	++	5
Indians, Asians, Blacks				0	6
(total)	(4+)	(2++)	(1+++)		

Source: Created by the author with X denoting the exact sameness, while + is used to show closeness, but not exact sameness.

to historian Richard Hofstadter, the book was "probably the most widely read contemporary book in the United States before *Uncle Tom's Cabin*." Moreover, "Religious commentators like Lyman Beecher warned that the new immigrants were instruments of papal design who had to be converted immediately through the growing American public school system" (24–25).

As the southern and eastern European immigrant population grew to levels of an obvious threat to WASPs, especially in urban America, the anti-Catholic rhetoric was heard loudly. "It is not best for America that her councils be dominated by semi-civilized foreign colonies in Boston, New York [and] Chicago," roared Kansas Republican Edward C. Little at the U.S. House of Representatives before the 1924 immigration policy debate (Kaufmann, 2004, 33). Carl C. Brigham of Princeton University in his "academic" explanation of why the Nordic Americans should be concerned with the Slav immigrants stated, "We must now frankly admit the undesirable results which ensure from a cross between the Nordic in this country with the Alpine Slav, with the degenerated hybrid Mediterranean, or with the negro, or from the promiscuous intermingling of all four types . . . The evidence is undeniable" (Brigham, 1923, 208). Clearly, here "the Alpine Slav" was regarded as "the degenerated hybrid," much different from the WASPs.

Furthermore, southern and eastern European immigrants differed from WASPs in terms of both geographic and ethnic origins of the groups (see + sign for the geographic proximity column in table 5.2). The words used to describe Mormonism—though completely a white religious group composed of white Americans and immigrants from Europe before the 1850s—were even worse than those for Catholics, as this new religion formed an even greater theological threat to Protestantism than did Catholicism. In addition to the religious difference, the sexual image of Latter-day Saints as polygamists and Joseph Smith as a "tyrant" were the major targets of the WASP attacks.

For example, in early 1840s, a local newspaper, the *Nauvoo Expositor*, in Nauvoo, Illinois, printed anti-Mormonism stories, announcing, "We are earnestly seeking to explode the vicious principles of Joseph Smith, and those who practice the same abominations and whoredoms" (Kranish and Helman, 2012). The violence between those on the newspaper side and the church led directly to the riot, the imprisonment of Joseph Smith, and the subsequent mob attack that killed Smith in the summer of 1844.

The words used to describe the "other" races such as Mexicans and Asians were even more hostile than those for white Catholics or Latter-day Saints. Their differences from whites were specifically emphasized. For example, a *New York Evening Post* editorial remarked about Mexicans in this way:

The Mexicans are Indians—Aboriginal Indians. Such Indians as Cortes conquered three thousand [three hundred] years ago, only rendered a little more mischievous by a bastard civilization. The infusion of European blood whatever it is, and that, too, infused in a highly illegitimate way, is not enough, as we see, to affect the character of the people . . . (Steinfield, 1970, 74)

The editorial explicitly warned that "the infusion of European blood" was not enough to "affect the character" of Mexicans, and they were closer to the "aboriginal" and "Indians." With respect to Mexicans, right before the *Treaty of Guadalupe Hidalgo*, U.S. Senator John C. Calhoun, during his address on the chamber floor, linked the problem of Mexicans to the future Caucasian race:

We have never dreamt of incorporating into our Union any but the Caucasian race—the free white race. To incorporate Mexico, would be the very first instance of kind, of incorporating an Indian race; for more than half of the Mexicans are Indians, and the other is composed chiefly of mixed tribes . . . The greatest misfortunes of Spanish America are to be traced to the fatal error of placing these colored races on an equality with the white race . . . (Steinfield, 1970, 75)

The mixed race and "the infusion of European blood" added some similarity with respect to WASPs, but for Calhoun, Mexicans could not be considered equal to the free white race (see the + sign for Mexicans in the first column of table 5.2), as they were closer to American Indians.

The differences between Asian immigrants and the white race were also the selling points for anti-Chinese legislation and anti-Asian sentiments in the second half of the nineteenth century and early twentieth century. For example, William Jennings Bryan, the presidential candidate and leading politician representing the populist wing of the Democratic Party at the time, vehemently opposed American imperialism in the Philippines. His explanations were grounded on the differences between the Asian race and the white race. He reminded the American people that "Are we to bring into the body politic eight or ten million Asiatics . . . so different from us in race and history that amalgamation is impossible?" Note that the emphasis was on whole Asian group "so different from us in race and history" when he explained why Asians should not be welcomed to come to this country (see table 5.2, where Asians score zero similarity based on our three similarity measures).

CONCLUSION

To explain the changed vote of white Protestants (WPs) in the 2012 presidential election, we ranked the candidates based on an internal similarity measure for WPs. Rick Perry was a true favorite WP candidate, but he also had to end his candidacy early in the primaries because of his own disastrous debate performance and other public relations miscues. Without Perry, Romney became a more favorable candidate than Obama based on our similarity measures. But the reasons why similarities are so important in politics require a sound theory which takes into account the importance of both in-group favoritism and out-group hostility. Our investigation into in-group favoritism and out-group hostility, both theoretical and empirical in consideration, led to an overall ordering of perceptions of external threats to the nation's long-time dominant group (WASPs). This ordering is presented in table 5.2.

Note that eight minority groups are listed in table 5.2. Four of these groups share the same racial identity with WASPs: Western European Protestants, Western European Catholics, Southern and Eastern Europeans (Catholics and Orthodox), and Latter-day Saints. The levels of similarities to WASPs for these four white groups were also based on their religious and geographic proximity in their European origin. Mexicans, on the contrary, because of "infusion of European blood," were partially similar in terms of race. Mexicans also were semi-similar to WASPs in terms of their Catholic religion when *the Treaty of Guadalupe Hidalgo* went into effect. Three other races (i.e., Native Americans, Asians, and Blacks) had no similarities with WASPs in terms of race, ethnicity, and religion. Though it is a well-known fact that Black Americans became one of the strongest and most coherent Protestant groups in U.S. history, in the early formation of racial order, WASPs had no intention of incorporating Black Americans into their religious establishment.

The count of similarities for these eight subordinate groups in table 5.2 provides an additional measure of the perception of an external threat. As discussed in Blumer's (1958) seminal work on abstract threat, WASPs as a dominant group defined and redefined these subordinate groups so that

WASPs could maintain their sense of superiority and continue to decide the allocation of power, resources, and privileges. In doing so, they were also concerned with the abstract group threats from these minorities on a collective basis. As shown in the last column of table 5.2, the ranking based on in-group favoritism provided WASPs with an additional mechanism to order these threats and govern them more effectively, a point to which we will turn to for more details in the following chapters.

Chapter 6

Hostility and Group Experiences

The ADVICE Principles (I)

The sudden surge of Michael Bloomberg in many national polls during February 2020 generated excitement and anxiety in the 2020 Democratic primaries. Would Bloomberg, the former popular mayor of New York City, become the acceptable alternative to former vice president Joe Biden and other candidates? Many Democratic voters were hesitating about their preferred candidate's real chances of beating President Trump in the general election. Bloomberg had not registered as a Democrat until shortly before the primary campaign, and many wondered if he would attempt to buy the nomination by spending nearly one-half billion dollars of his own money in television markets covering key primary states as well as social media platforms, such as YouTube. Another candidate, U.S. senator Elizabeth Warren from Massachusetts, talked about how to stop Bloomberg's run, during the televised live debate in Las Vegas on February 18, 2020. She said: "When Mayor Bloomberg was busy blaming African Americans and Latinos for the housing crash of 2008, I was right here in Las Vegas, just a few blocks down the street holding hearings . . . Banks . . . were taking away homes from millions of families" (Zaballos-Rolg, 2020).

Warren's attack proved effective. Bloomberg's poll numbers declined almost immediately, and media pundits widely praised Warren's debate performance. The morning after the debate, Warren's campaign announced that it had raised $2.8 million overnight. Warren's crisp attack linked Bloomberg to his controversial positions about the 2008 Great Recession, especially his remarks regarding the practice of redlining used by mortgage lenders. Neighborhoods that were redlined were stripped of mortgage opportunities that otherwise would have been favorable to residents in primarily Black and Hispanic communities. In 2008, when asked what caused the financial crisis, Bloomberg blamed the end of redlining, adding that "banks started making

69

more and more loans where the credit of the person buying the house wasn't as good as you would like."

It is a practical question to ask how the federal government can improve minority groups' access to housing and how to end notorious racial segregation practices still commonly seen in real estate markets across the country today. It is yet a more profound question to ask why redlining has had so much racial intent in the first place. To trace the origin of redlining, one has to return to 1933 when Roosevelt's New Deal initiatives led to establishing the Home Owners' Loan Corporation (HOLC), "primarily to refinance urban mortgages threatened with default. Unfortunately, HOLC gave the national government's imprimatur and a formal structure to practices of exclusionary 'redlining'" (King and Smith, 2011, 146). As "affirmative action" for whites, the New Deal programs played a historical role in their impact regarding the nation's long-lasting wealth gap between whites and Blacks (Katznelson, 2005). The Federal Housing Authority (FHA) was created in 1934. As Ira Katznelson (2005) pointed out, the FHA and the GI Bill for veterans "used redlining, local control, and overt discrimination to make it very difficult, often impossible, for blacks to qualify for mortgages" (p.163). FHA, for example, explicitly announced an official guidance in its 1938 *Underwriting Manual*: "If a neighborhood is to retain stability, it is necessary that proper ties shall continue to be occupied by the same social and racial class. A change in social or racial occupancy generally contributes to instability and a decline in values" (cited from King and Smith, 2011, 146–147).

More than eighty years after the publication of the 1938 FHA manual, the nation remains divided by the "racial class," which manifested itself not only through government programs but also through banks' loan practices and Americans' residential choices including the widespread white flight from the nation's urban centers to suburbs that gained momentum in the 1950s. To put into political context how to comprehend the enduring practices of racial segregation in the entire housing history, this book suggests studying the underlying forces of in-group favoritism and out-group hostility for context building, as discussed in the previous two chapters whites prefer to live close to the people sharing their own racial identity not only as a result of their attraction to their racial group but also due to their perceptions of external threats.

We already have introduced the foundations of in-group favoritism and out-group hostility. To recap our discussion of political groups in the last three chapters, we establish the following main propositions: the dominant group (DG) in a political system positions itself at the core to be superior to all other subordinate groups (SGs). Furthermore, the DG ranks and rank orders all of the SGs based on their similarities relative to the DG. This ordering is derived from the similarity-attraction principle. However, without considering out-group hostility, this ordering, at most, only applies to how the degree of favoritism DG prefers to allocate to a particular SG. The positional nature of inter-group relations holds that DG, in responding to the structure of group positions, perceives external and abstract threats from the SGs. Thus, the farther away a specific SG is positioned from the DG, the greater the perception of a threat. Hence, we write the first two axioms of group relations in a political system, as follows:

Axiom 1 (A1): In a political system, the DG ranks, orders, and positions SGs based on the attraction-similarity principle (which represents A in the ADVICE acronym)

Axiom 2 (A2): In a political system, the DG perceives external threats from all of the SGs. But, the extent of a threat from a particular SG also is based on the distance between the DG and this SG. The farther the distance, the higher the perception of threat. We label this as the distance principle.

These two axioms comprise a starting point for what may motivate groups, especially the DG, to act politically. Our discussion of group ordering will have no value in the study of politics, if group ordering does not correspond with political actions, especially institutional arrangements by the DG. As seen in the previous three chapters, the relationship between group ordering and perception of threat is pertinent to social psychology and sociology, but it also does not explain how that translates to political development, as long as a specific perception of threat does not lead to explainable political responses. Here, I define political development as progress at the system or group level in a political environment. Progress is a movement toward positive changes in terms of group status, rights, legal protection, political representation, and allocation of resources. Therefore, when one mentions progress for Blacks, it means that for this group there is a positive change for their group status, legal protection, rights, and political representation in the federal government.

To examine the implications of these first two axioms on political actions, we must define an additional crucial term. The term hostility refers to the level of intolerance, which a political group accepts as an affective response to another group. Because of the affective nature of hostility, a group relation concerning hostility is appropriately studied primarily on the emotional level. Thus, an increased level of hostility, for instance, simply means a stronger degree of emotional unfriendliness or even hatred toward another group. With respect to hostility, a natural corollary of the first two axioms (A1 and A2) is shown in figure 6.1.

Figure 6.1 orders four subordinate groups (SGs) from the WASP perspective. The vertical line shows the level of hostility toward these four groups. German Protestants should expect to receive the lowest hostility from

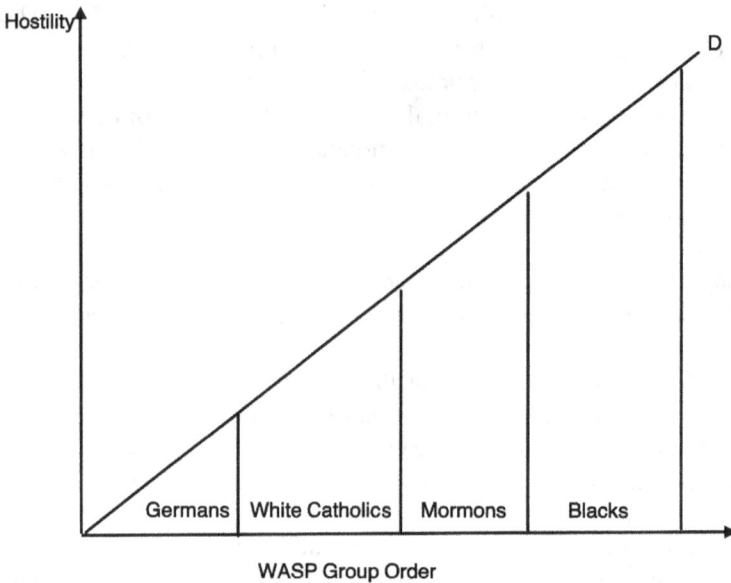

Figure 6.1   Group Ordering and Hostility. Created by the author.

WASPs, whereas Blacks would expect to be the highest. There is also a different level of WASP hostility generated toward white Catholics and Latter-day Saints. Based on the group order, Latter-day Saints, among all whites, receive the highest level of hostility from WASPs.

Logically, a higher level of hostility should translate to a higher level of aggression from the DG to a SG. This is based on the premise that human emotions, such as hostility, do drive these groups to act politically. In tandem, the concept of aggression is defined in more detail later in this chapter. However, it is worthwhile to examine in general some possible forms of aggression. For example, enslaving a SG outside political genocide should be regarded as the highest possible level of aggression exercised by the DG against a SG. On the other hand, assimilation would be the lowest possible level of aggression, because the goal of assimilation is converting a SG to be as similar to the DG as possible. If this logic is true, then we should see empirical evidence that Germans, indeed, were the group that WASPs were most likely to attempt to assimilate. Meanwhile, Blacks as a SG were most likely to be subjected to enslavement and later suppressed opportunities for social and economic mobility. In comparison, the aggression level against Latter-day Saints should then be higher than against white Catholics and Germans, but not higher than Blacks.

Now, we turn to evidence from American history about WASP political actions toward subordinate groups. We will then compare the subordinate group experiences to examine the validity of the first two axioms (A1 or attraction-similarity principle and A2 or distance principle) as discussed above.

GERMAN PROTESTANT EXPERIENCE

The growth of German Protestant immigrants in the original colonies, especially Pennsylvania, triggered concern from the Founding Fathers generation, which was expressed as a threat of "a colony of Aliens" that might "Germanize" WASPs. The strategy to respond to such a threat was labeled as "Anglo-conformity" rooted in the pre-Revolutionary era with the Society for Propagating Christian Knowledge among Germans. The group was founded in the mid-eighteenth century by Benjamin Franklin and Anglican minister William Smith with the goal of "the 'Anglicization' of Pennsylvania's large German population" (Kaufmann, 2004, 19–20). Franklin's Anglicization of Germans, based on his own description, was "to distribute them more equally, mix them with the English, establish English Schools where they are now to think settled" so that the Germans could "contribute greatly to the improvement of a Country" (Kaufmann, 2004, 41).

Franklin's vision of Anglo-conformity and his pragmatic approaches to German immigrants produced arguably the most successful assimilation model, to be followed later by all whites. But, the German immigrants' response, which sometimes resisted Anglo-conformity, required more time and greater effort than as expected in Franklin's original intentions. One example of this resistance occurred in Pennsylvania, when after the American Revolution, German immigrants attempted several times to have new federal laws printed in German and gain official recognition for the use of the German language in schools and courts. Of course, these attempts were quickly rebuffed and defeated. The new nation was not only able to assimilate the German population in Pennsylvania but also the Welsh and Scots "whose languages were all but dead in America by the early nineteenth century, as well as the Huguenots, who in the nineteenth century disappeared entirely" (Kaufmann, 2004, 20). Notably, President James Monroe was the first in history with Scottish origin.

Some German immigrants and their offspring spoke German in their homes and churches, while dual immersion language programs of some schools in the Lutheran-dominated Midwest states, such as Wisconsin, were popular among German Americans in more recent history. The experience of two world wars, nonetheless, eventually led to discontinuing the use of the German language as the primary one in schools and churches, though some churches ended it once and for all as late as the 1970s.

The success of German assimilation to WASPs was more evident in their acculturation and integration in communities. Cities, such as Milwaukee and Cincinnati and, to a lesser extent, Chicago and Cleveland, were dominated by German businesses. The political success of descendants of some German immigrants, as a result of assimilation, manifested itself, for example, through the election of Herbert Clark Hoover as the nation's thirty-first president. A better example of the long-term results of successful assimilation was the presidency of Dwight David "Ike" Eisenhower in the 1950s. He was a five-star general in the U.S. Army in World War II and served as Supreme Commander of the Allied Forces in Europe. As a descendant of a family with German and Pennsylvania Dutch ancestry, he had the ultimate responsibility to lead the American military to defeat Germany in World War II. The Eisenhower family name, in German, is Eisenhauer. The German name, Eisenhauer, was later Anglicized to Eisenhower. His ancestors immigrated from Karlsbrunn, Germany, to York, Pennsylvania in 1741.

BLACK EXPERIENCE

At the opposite end of successful German assimilation was the turbulent and harsh reality of enslavement and disfranchisement of Black Americans. Slavery epitomized the explicit intent to dominate completely a whole group. The dominance was not only political but also was extended to every aspect of life. American sociologist William Julius Wilson (1980) describes the daily experience of African American slaves as:

> The basic contacts between blacks and whites were essentially those involving the slaves and the small elite class of slave-owners—a relationship that was stabilized and reinforced by the vast discrepancy in racial power resources on the rural farms and plantations. Being symbiotic in nature, these contacts greatly decreased physical distance; however, social distance was enhanced by clearly defined patterns of dominance and subservience which included elaborate rituals of racial etiquette. (24)

The institutional dominance of WASPs over Blacks through enslavement would not have been ended without the nation's only Civil War. Ta-Nehisi Coates (2013), who has written extensively about the history of Blacks in America, added the postscript, summarizing the impact of the South's defeat: "In 1859 legally selling someone's five-year-old child was big business. In 1866, it was not." Considering the existential take of the war's outcome, the post-bellum era started unsteadily with the southern states' refusal to extend suffrage to Blacks, which led to the Civil Rights Act of 1866 and the 14th

Amendment being passed by the radical Republican-dominated Congress (Jarvis, 1992, 25; also see Kousser, 1999, 12–68). President Andrew Johnson, a Southern Democrat, assumed office after Lincoln's assassination, and he put the Republican racially egalitarian agenda in doubt (King and Smith, 2011). Racial discrimination in voting was not legally prohibited until the ratification of the 15th Amendment in 1870, which states, "the right of citizens of the United States to vote shall not be denied or abridged by the United States or by any state on account of race, color, or previous condition of servitude" (McClain and Stewart, 2002, 20).

Throughout the Reconstruction period when federal troops were dispatched to the former states of the defeated Confederacy to help enforce federal laws, white resistance in the South, often exercised through violence, was so widespread that three Enforcement Acts (1870, 1871, and 1875) were passed in an attempt to put judicial teeth into the 15th Amendment (Davidson, 1992, 10).

Meanwhile, many Southern state legislatures enacted "black codes" to disempower the affected groups economically. Adding to the problem was the U.S. Supreme Court decision on *United States v. Cruikshank (1876)*, in which the Court rejected applying the 14th and 15th Amendments to the prosecution of white defendants, who had killed about 100 Blacks in a mob attack. The Court simply reasoned that the white defendants were individuals, rather than states, and, as a result, they were not acting to represent the state, which, in essence, had rejected the Enforcement Act of 1870 without even reviewing its constitutionality.

The Reconstruction efforts ended with "the Compromise of 1877 in which Rutherford B. Hayes attempted to gain the support of the southern states in the contested presidential elections of 1876" (McClain and Steward, 2002, 21). The end of Reconstruction initiated a new round of disfranchisement and discrimination. "This disenfranchisement was achieved through a combination of structural discrimination (e.g., gerrymandering, annexations, at-large election systems, and appointive offices), violence, voting fraud, and eventually through disenfranchising conventions that rewrote state constitutions with clauses to prohibit Blacks from voting or participating in politics. By the 1890s, Blacks—primarily in the South but in some northern jurisdictions as well—had been legally and very effectively removed from the electoral process" (McClain and Steward, 2002, 21).

Moreover, the Supreme Court, with the 1896 *Plessy v. Ferguson* decision, upheld the practice of racial discrimination and the separation of the races in the South. The Ku Klux Klan flourished in the Jim Crow South, which practiced lynching and other extreme measures against Blacks' basic civil rights. The notorious "separate but equal doctrine" and the legacy of Jim Crow laws eventually led to the formation of civil-rights organizations such as NAACP to seek judicial protection of Black lives and liberty. Black political protests achieved the unprecedented success in the nation's Civil Rights Movement during the 1950s and the 1960s, leading to passage of the Civil Rights Act (1964) and the Voting Rights Act (1965) to protect the fundamental constitutional rights of African Americans throughout the country. The more recent history of Black political empowerment during the post-civil-rights era is discussed in chapter 11.

WHITE CATHOLIC EXPERIENCE

Discrimination against white Catholic immigrants started rapidly and spread widely in the first half of the nineteenth century. In addition to the accelerated expansion of immigration, one reason for WASP discrimination concerned the composition of the immigrant population, which, for the first time, changed from predominantly Protestant to mainly Catholic with primary origins in Ireland and German states. The City of Boston was already a quarter Irish as early as 1844, and it reached 40 percent Irish around 1840s (Kaufmann, 2004, 25). The Catholic churches were targeted in the first wave of anti-Catholic movement. WASP religious leaders in the nineteenth century, including Lyman Beecher, a Presbyterian minister who was cofounder of the American Temperance Society, warned that "the new immigrants were instruments of papal design who had to be converted immediately" (Kaufman, 2004, 24). Violent mobs, church burning, looting, and other forms of intimidation against Catholic churches became endemic in New England states, especially in urban areas, such as the Bible Riots of 1844 in Philadelphia.

Catholic immigrants often found themselves discriminated against in the workplace in the antebellum era. When the Mexican-American War began in 1846, the U.S. Congress authorized an additional 50,000 soldiers. The United States entered the war with an army that comprised in part 40 percent immigrants, especially Irish men who had just arrived after fleeing the devastating potato famine in their homeland. Another stark difference between them was religion, and their treatment fueled a sense of indignation. "The officer class was not immune to religious bias," Amy S. Greenberg, author of *A Wicked War: Polk, Clay, and the 1846 U.S. Invasion of Mexico*, explains. "Almost all officers were Protestants, and they not only refused to let Catholic soldiers attend mass in Mexican churches, they quite often forced them to attend Protestant service" (Uenuma, 2019).

The most important political response to the Catholic problem was the rapid growth of the Know-Nothing Party that dominated the elections of 1854. In urban areas where new immigrants tended to settle, the Know-Nothing Party was especially influential. For example, in the spring of 1854 election in Massachusetts, the Know-Nothing Party won 366 of the 377 state representative seats. The political agenda of the party included not only preventing Catholics from running for public office but also restricting the franchise to those who could read and write English, in addition to a twenty-one-year residency requirement for eligible voters and a twenty-one-year probationary period for new immigrants (Kaufmann, 2004, 25).

But, these radical measures against Catholic immigrants did not lead to a sustained national movement. The new Republican Party rose to become the leading force to shift the nation's attention to the slavery issue, but anti-Catholic mentality and discriminatory practices in social and economic spheres remained throughout the nineteenth century. Catholics were much more likely to take low pay and low social status jobs (if they could find one) than did WASPs.

The industrialization in the U.S. northeast and the western expansion, inspired by the lofty yet flawed doctrine of Manifest Destiny, signaled the demand for accepting Catholic immigrants as a necessity for the nation's growing economy. Toward the end of the nineteenth century, a new wave of anti-Catholic immigrant political antagonism emerged because of the influx of new immigrants mainly from countries in southern and eastern Europe. This time, it was the Populist Party and its later Progressive Party successor to engage in political campaigns against Catholics.

The Populists (also known as The People's Party) entered into national politics during a volatile political era (Fiorina, 2017). The ideal of cultural nationalism was championed as the new party was established in 1891 by James Baird Weaver and Leonidas L. Polk, and later joined by William Jennings Bryan. Meanwhile, patriotic organizations, with millions of members nationwide, sought answers to the nation's "Catholic problem," which threatened WASP cultural superiority and political domination. They worried not only because of the concentration of Catholic immigrants representing western Europeans but also more increasingly those located further south and east from the continent including Jews who tended to settle in major cities, such as Boston, New York, and Chicago. The anti-Catholic nationalist sentiments fueled by patriotic organizations such as the American Protective Association helped the People's Party (Populist Party) to rapidly expand at the national level. Bryan became the Democratic presidential candidate in 1896. Bryan failed to win the presidency, but the Progressives of the first years of the twentieth century found a coherent, yet short-lived supporting voice in preserving the national dominance of the WASP group and cleaning the "vice" of cities that were dominated by white Catholics and ethnically oriented political machines.

Another radical mass movement also took its own form of anti-Catholic, anti-immigrant, and white supremacist ideology. The Ku Klux Klan of the 1920s, in particular, who had called Bryan the "greatest Klansman of our time" for his plan to govern America, emerged as a national force that won numerous governorships and congressional seats. Though originally a Southern organization, the KKK promoted a national agenda to promote WASP purity, antifederal nationalism, and racist and violent attacks against minorities and immigrants. The KKK quickly became the major political force in states such as Indiana, Colorado, and Oregon.

In addition to mass movements, some of the nation's major academic institutions fueled anti-immigrant and WASP supremacy causes and legislations. For example, prominent eugenics scholars gathered by Yale University formed a collective "scientific" center, the Institute of Psychology, to prove the "disastrous" problem of mixing Slavs and Mediterranean Europeans with native Nordic blood (Dole, 2014). Sponsors of anti-immigration legislation secured major victories in the U.S. Congress. At first, the target was restricting the number of Asian immigrants (in the Acts of 1904 and 1907), but by 1921 the anti-Catholic fever had led to President Warren G. Harding's signing of America's first-ever law restricting European immigration that employed a 3 percent quota allocated to each nation, as based on their share of the 1910 immigrant population (Kaufmann, 2004, 32). "Since the immigrant population in 1910 was considerably less British and Protestant than the U.S. population stock," the 1924 National Origins Act was enacted to restrict immigration mainly from the southern and eastern European Catholic countries (Divine, 1957, 46). As a result of the restrictive national origin legislation, the representation of southern and eastern (Catholic) European immigrants dropped from almost 80 percent of the total immigrants in the 1920s to about 20 percent between 1930s and 1950s.

The ethnic concentration of urban Catholic voters, however, constituted a political force, especially inside the Democratic Party, which was too powerful to be ignored. Political bosses who organized and distributed economic and political goods along racial and ethnic lines in urban political machines increasingly served the role of national leaders, in spite of the Progressive Movement and Prohibition Era that attracted both Republican (e.g., Theodore Roosevelt) and Democratic (e.g., Woodrow Wilson) presidents to limit the ethnic and Catholic power in the name of political reform and progress. Alfred E. Smith, an Irish Catholic, became the presidential nominee of the Democratic Party in 1928 that "extended recognition, acceptance, and legitimacy" of white Catholics (Ladd and Hadley, 1975, 268–269). The New Deal Coalition assembled by President Franklin D. Roosevelt, with the white Catholic vote as a key component, would dominate national and local politics for two decades after the Great Depression.

The assimilation of white Catholics symbolically was ended when John F. Kennedy won the presidency in 1960. The anti-Catholic sentiment was still felt throughout his campaign. But, his success in convincing voters that he would govern as a president for the national interest rather than on order from the Holy See in Rome (a point many Kennedy opponents used to instill fear among undecided voters) was a major step for white Catholics to be recognized as joining the mainstream in U.S. politics. As a result of their success in economic and social status, the white Catholic vote quickly became "ripe for picking" for some Republican strategists, such as Kevin Philips (1969), who made the call in his influential *The Emerging Republican Majority.* Today Catholic politicians have represented both major parties in all branches and all levels of governments, such as U.S. speaker of the house, and numerous Supreme Court appointees. Their religious or ethnic backgrounds rarely matter as a political issue any longer—a clear manifestation of the successful assimilation for white Catholics in the end.

THE CHURCH OF JESUS CHRIST OF LATTER-DAY SAINTS

Compared to white Catholics, as figure 6.1 predicted, the Latter-day Saints endured a much harsher journey in their American experience. The persecution and oppression against the Church did not stop in the summer of 1844 when the founder of the new religion Joseph Smith and his brother were murdered by a mob attack. Before his death, Smith and the church leadership organization, then called the Council of Fifty, sent an investigative team, to seek safer environments outside the U.S. territorial boundaries of the time. Their negotiation with Sam Houston, the first and third president of the Republic of Texas, eventually failed to produce the settlement of the church community in the largely unsettled Nueces Strip, a contested area between the underdeveloped Texas Republic and Mexico (Foster, 2008, 61).

Smith's death led to the church's Quorum of the Twelve to rally behind the leadership of Brigham Young, the second president of the church. The leadership decided to migrate to the Rocky Mountains and Great Basin in 1846, where the vast areas of the Southwest and Pacific West were still under control of the Mexican government. A total of about 70,000 began the journey west, and the first group of Latter-day Saints arrived in the Salt Lake valley in 1847.

It would be the ensuing five decades after the settlement in Utah that differentiated the experience of Latter-day Saints from all other white ethnic or religious groups of that time. Finding themselves back again under federal control due to the 1848 *Treaty of Guadalupe Hidalgo* that declared the Rocky Mountains a part of new U.S. territory, the Mormons now had to renegotiate with the federal government for statehood recognition. Initially, the church "set up a government modeled on how they believed the millennial kingdom of God would be organized. The original government, which operated for fifteen months, was a theocracy, with the stake high council assuming both political and ecclesiastical functions" which had to be replaced by "a more permanent government, consisting of local probate judges, the first legislature, and a formal government entity named the State of Deseret" (Foster, 2008, 61–62).

Two problems triggered nearly five decades of disfranchisement for Latter-day Saints in the federal system. The first was the practice of polygamy. The second was the collective economy that was almost completely controlled by the church. "Brigham Young openly preached that non-Mormon merchants were a threat to Mormons' economic and social well-being; sometimes, Mormons who did not join the boycott were disfellowshipped by their local ecclesiastical officers . . . The policy of boycotting non-Mormon merchants endured well into the 1880s and became a point of suspicious inquiry during the U.S. Senate committee hearings" (Foster, 2008, 63–64). The Latter-day Saints even "printed their own currency and created their own coinage" in an attempt to create a self-sufficient nation-state (Foster, 2008, 64).

The U.S. Federal Government's responses to church ambitions were swift. The State of Deseret was ended, and before granting statehood, the Territory of Utah was established under tight federal oversight. Regarding controversial claims by federal officials that their lives were in danger in Utah, then president James Buchanan sent federal troops to Utah to put down the alleged Mormon Rebellion in 1857 and 1858. The so-called Utah War of 1857 and 1858 did not end with violent bloodshed but a series of standoffs. Young's orders to avoid direct conflict eventually led federal troops to retreat without entering the Salt Lake valley. On the surface, the church stood strong against the potential might of federal military control. The price was huge; however, statehood would not become a reality until 1896, which meant that the Latter-day Saints would not have representation in the U.S. Congress for forty-six years.

The Congress passed the Edmunds Act of 1882, which was followed by the Edmunds–Tucker Act in 1887 to disfranchise all polygamists and strip the rights of incorporation from the LDS Church. According to Foster (2008), "The Protestant majority in the United States responded with a series of laws, court tests, and political activities designed to break the back of the Mormon community and reshape it in the image of the remainder of the United States" (68). Many prominent leaders, including Romney's ancestors, fled and went into hiding as far away as in Mexico to avoid federal conviction and imprisonment as polygamists (Kranish and Helman, 2012).

Furthermore, the judges were replaced with federal appointees, and Utah's women who once were allowed to vote in elections lost their voting rights. The symbolic Salt Lake Temple was also under threat of federal confiscation.

The church president Wilford Woodruff in the end issued the Manifesto in September 1890 to end "official approval of new plural marriages" (Foster, 2008, 70). Following the official end of the polygamy practice, the church also ordered the disbanding of Utah's own People's Party in 1891 and encouraged church members to join the nation's two major political parties instead. Another church-affiliated party, Liberal Party, was also disbanded in 1893.

The federal granting of statehood to Utah in 1896, which became the nation's forty-fifth state, not only provided basic constitutional rights to the Mormons but also facilitated the assimilation into the nation's WASP establishment. Though still one of the most disliked religious organizations in the country (Putnam and Campbell, 2010), the members of the church made an astonishing turnaround in its social economic status throughout the twentieth century. In their study of successful minority groups, Amy Chua and Jed Rubenfeld (2014) list Latter-day Saints at the top. "In 1980, it was hard to find a Mormon on Wall Street. Today, Mormons are dominant players in America's corporate boardrooms, investment firms, and business schools," Chua and Rubenfeld note (2014, 5). In addition to Romney who was nominated by the Republican Party and ran for the presidency in 2012, prominent politicians also include Harry Reid, a former majority leader in the U.S. Senate; Jon Huntsman Jr., a former governor of Utah and U.S. ambassador to Russia and China in two administrations, former U.S. senator Orrin Hatch, and U.S. representative Morris Udall, among others.

The assimilation of church members has been impressive, but it has not been as complete as that for white Catholics. The Mormon problem, for example, emerged as an issue for Romney in his two presidential campaigns, but John Kerry, a white Catholic who was nominated by the Democratic Party and ran for the presidency only eight years prior in 2004, never encountered any religious problem in his campaign. Joe Biden in his 2020 presidential campaign, unlike Mitt Romney, did not encounter any serious problems related to his Catholic faith. In the next chapter, we introduce the third axiom, as represented in the ADVICE acronym: the volatility principle.

Chapter 7

Volatility

The ADVICE Principles (II)

One could claim that each subordinate group (SG) presents a unique case in terms of its experience in U.S. history. For example, the Latter-day Saints, as a religious minority, endured a long period of disfranchisement because of their polygamous practice which was ruled as unconstitutional. Not surprisingly, the U.S. Supreme Court upheld the federal law, such as the 1887 Edmunds-Tucker Act, prohibiting polygamy. The Supreme Court explained that polygamy "has always been odious among the northern and western nations of Europe, and, until the establishment of the Mormon Church, was almost exclusively a feature of the life of Asiatic and of African people" (Winkler, 2013). This explanation clearly had its reasoning based on what America ought to be, and the reasoning was a pure WASP racial antagonism against "Asiatic" and "African people." In response, the church argued that polygamy was sanctioned by God, as recorded in the Bible, or at least as it was practiced widely among Israelites, as described in the Old Testament.

The key was not whether WASP response to a minority threat should be unique or particular. The more important question is what defines the WASP norm with respect to how a minority group ought to be treated. It is in this sense that the study of group ordering can explain the similarities and differences between and among subordinate groups in terms of their experiences in the United States, especially during the nineteenth century when racial ordering was defined and redefined, as suggested by Blumer (1958). Thus, we see clearly that the minority groups we discussed above were treated differently. Also, their various paths reflected how WASPs perceived multiple threats from these groups and responses they finally chose, as based on their norm of group order, which was linked to how similar a particular SG was to the WASP dominant group (DG) in terms of traits in race, religion, and geographic proximity to Great Britain. Thus, German Protestants, when based on our approach for group comparison, undoubtedly received the most favorable treatment as they went through a gradual assimilation process, whereas white Catholics had to deal with episodes of discrimination that the German Protestants did not encounter. The Latter-day Saints, on the other hand, under the tight watch of the federal government, were disfranchised for most of the second half of the nineteenth century. None of these white groups, nonetheless, approached the circumstances enslaved African Americans encountered. The short-lived Reconstruction in the South succumbed to Jim Crow laws that disfranchised African Americans for almost another century and its effects continue to reverberate to varying degrees even today (Kousser, 1999).

Thus, our conclusion is clear: group order matters, and the political responses to multiple threats reflect generally how WASPs implicitly ordered the SGs in the first place. All the SGs, in this sense, had no choice of their own, as the group order was based entirely on how WASPs themselves felt whether or not a particular SG is close to them or is perceived as a stranger.

But, the investigation also takes us to another crucial aspect for understanding group relations: These minority groups also have experienced developments showing progress in the course of U.S. history. Again, I define progress for this theoretical discussion as positive changes in terms of group status, rights, legal protection, political representation, and allocation of resources. German Protestants were finally assimilated into WASPs, as did white Catholics at a later point. For Latter-day Saints, their accomplishments in many areas, especially in business and the economy, suggested that their assimilation has also been impressive, though not as complete as the white Catholics, because their religion remains a barrier to their penultimate political ambition. Even for Blacks, we saw that progress did occur in history as they gained their freedom, thanks to President Lincoln's Emancipation Proclamation, regardless of whatever Lincoln's original strategic intent might have been.

However, the progress observed certainly was not always linear nor upwardly trending in U.S. history. Measures of progress could be reversed easily by backlash, as shown in many national events and inconsistent public policies time and time again. The potential for African American gains in the political arena around 1870 which was written into the U.S. Constitution as the 14th and 15th Amendments, for example, quickly evaporated, as the post-Reconstruction *de facto* and *de jure* segregation and disfranchisement policies became the norm. The Mormon period of independence and peace in Nauvoo, Illinois, in 1844—even with evidence of political empowerment (Joseph Smith served as the mayor of Nauvoo, already a major city in the new Western frontier)—ended abruptly in political confrontation and death, a massive evacuation and Western migration through a bitter winter and the unbearable heat of the American desert.

White Catholics saw the growth of their political power in the urban centers at the turn of the twentieth century, and they gained political rule in several major cities. But, the rapidly spreading anti-Catholic movement and patriotic societies, as well as the prominence of academic eugenic studies pushed the U.S. Congress to enact in the 1920s discriminatory and restrictive laws mainly against white Catholic immigrants, who came from the southern and eastern regions of Europe.

In short, as far as a particular group status is concerned, there has been no guarantee for progress at a later point of time than the present, but the progress also has appeared to be inevitable in the long run. How can these twin and contradictory observations be possible for minority groups? To uncover the secret of these twin phenomena, I propose the third axiom of the book (A3). This axiom explains why, on the one hand, group order does have a clear effect on institutional treatment of subordinate groups. On the other hand, it is also important to note that group order does not predict how groups will be treated at a given time: Axiom 3 (A3): the volatility principle (which represents the V in the ADVICE acronym). The higher the perception of a SG threat, the greater the range of possible DG responses to such a threat, and thus the higher the political volatility a specific SG will experience.

RESPONSE RANGE AND MEASURES OF AGGRESSION

Figure 7.1 shows the effect of this third axiom (A3). To focus the discussion at this point, only four groups are listed from left to right as subordinate groups in figure 7.1. G1 is the group that is most similar to the dominant group, DG. Thus, following the first two axioms (the attraction-similarity and distance principles, respectively), the DG has the lowest perception of external threat from G1. As group order moves from left to right, the perception of external threat increases.

Based on the third axiom (the volatility principle), the possible range of responses (i.e., possible political actions taken by the DG) increases as the perception of external threat increases. Hence, G4 should experience a larger range of political response from DG than should G3; G3 should experience a greater range than G2; and so on. These ranges are depicted in figure 7.1 as r4, r3, r2, and r1. Obviously, the lengths of these vertical lines (i.e., the ranges of possible responses) increase from left to right.

Empirically, this translates into the WASP response ranges expanding as the group order shifts from German Protestants to white Catholics, to Latter-day Saints, and to African Americans, which represents precisely the discussion in this chapter.

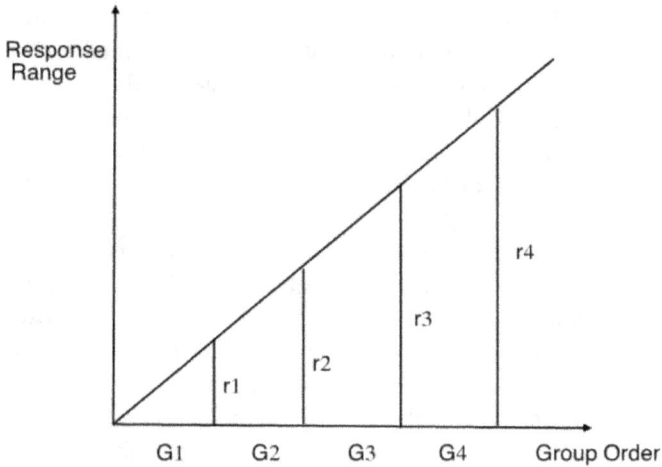

Figure 7.1   Group Order and Response Range. Created by the author with G1 through G4 denoting the subordinate groups.

African Americans have experienced political responses from WASPs, ranging from enslavement to emancipation and to disfranchisement and finally to empowerment. Latter-day Saints also experienced disenfranchisement and discrimination, but not enslavement. White Catholics endured discrimination, but not disfranchisement. German Protestants were assimilated into WASPs with comparable ease.

AGGRESSION: MEASURES ON SEVEN LEVELS

To test the validity and relevance of the hostility principle, one useful empirical measure can be constructed, as based on how aggressive the DG responds to a particular SG. Here, we will operationalize the measure of aggression of DG based on seven levels. These levels of aggression, from low to high, are assimilation, negotiation, discrimination, disfranchisement, exclusion, removal and, finally, enslavement. Let's take a look at each of these seven possible responses.

Assimilation

Assimilation represents the lowest level of aggression that a SG can experience from a political system controlled by the DG. It is a process of conversion, acculturation, and group-level conformity to the DG norm and its identities. This degree of conformity not only suggests the use of the dominant language but also cultural adaptation and political incorporation along with social and economic integration. The experience of German Protestants, as we reviewed above, certainly fits this process. But so did white Catholics whose assimilation encumbered more time and struggles, but eventually was achieved by the middle of the twentieth century.

In comparison, the Latter-day Saints also were assimilated into the economic system, as documented by Chua and Rubenfeld (2014), but their political assimilation also has not been completed, as shown by Romney's unsuccessful attempts to become president, a topic discussed in more detail in chapter 12. Other minorities have not been assimilated into WASP social identities and political system, compared to minority and religious groups who are white. As discussed in an earlier chapter, voting along racial identification is still the norm, rather than exception. African Americans and Hispanics, as well as American Indians are much more likely to have lower social, economic status than other groups. Here, one may raise the question about the successful run of Obama for president and his re-election. Does that success reflect the completion of assimilation for African Americans? Many media commentators, as well as academic observers, hastily claimed the United States had entered a so-called post-racial era as a result of the election of Obama as the nation's first Black president. But, this claim was premature and vigorously contested.

First, most white voters did not cast ballots for Obama in the 2008 and 2012 presidential elections, which means that race was still a big factor and certainly does not fit the definition of assimilation, as offered here. Second, the nation is still divided about what should be the way to "remedy" the legacy of enslavement and disfranchisement of African Americans. Affirmative Action programs have never been popular among the white majority (Liu, 2010). Third, discrimination and segregation still run deep based on many social and economic measures. Finally, the gain of African Americans in many areas including their election to high-profile office is better described as the process of negotiation rather than assimilation, a point to which we return in more details in chapter 11.

Negotiation

Negotiation is a political response by the DG to build a partnership with a specific SG for the purpose of mutual benefits, collective interests, or assuring stability of the political system. Negotiation normally occurs when a political coalition that includes minorities is established. Especially when such a political coalition wins elections, negotiation between the DG and the SG inside the coalition can become the norm for a relatively long time, through which a certain level of SG autonomy may be achieved with the DG's endorsement.

Negotiation as defined above provides a powerful perspective for us to understand why certainly minority groups can enjoy political success while not being assimilated into the WASP dominant group. For example, Black participation in the Civil War was based on the negotiation that Lincoln offered through his 1863 Emancipation Proclamation. In the modern era, Black loyalty to the Democratic Party in elections can be regarded as a negotiation tool for material improvement and social mobility through programs such as affirmative action and federal housing projects to assist the poor. Negotiation sometimes does allow the leadership of certain minority politicians to take on the major responsibility of a political coalition. An example is Alfred Smith's Democratic Party nomination in 1928 and Obama's nomination in 2008. Both candidates represented a major voting bloc (white Catholics and African Americans, respectively) inside their political coalition.

Discrimination

Discrimination is used to systematically manipulate the political system for the advantage of the DG at the expense of SGs. It is also a preemptive strike, through which SGs are limited in using legal means to seek expanded fair and equal treatments. Discrimination often is politically adopted at the time when the social norms allow intimidation, confrontation, and sometimes even violence against a minority group.

Almost all SGs, even white minority groups such as white Catholics and Latter-day Saints, have suffered from this form of WASP aggression. White Catholics, for example, were discriminated against as a result of Know-Nothings' policy on immigration, and southern and eastern Europeans were singled out as people not welcomed by the restrictive immigration laws in the 1920s. Discrimination against Latter-day Saints was common at the time of Joseph Smith, and even today they are discriminated against in workplaces and elections (Campbell et al., 2012).

Disfranchisement

Disfranchisement is a higher level of aggression than discrimination. This is because disfranchisement encompasses an intent of disempowerment, denial of basic citizen rights, and sometimes physical separation and isolation. Disfranchisement occurred in the second half of the nineteenth century for Latter-day Saints who had no political representation in the federal government.

Disfranchisement was the most effective method of aggression against all racial minorities. For example, the "free white persons" clause used in legislation and U.S. Supreme Court decisions consistently rejected the basic rights of all racial minorities including American Indians, African Americans, and Asians. More importantly, disfranchisement in the Jim Crow South completely denied African Americans' fundamental rights. Lynching and group violence against African Americans were the accepted social practice in the era of complete disfranchisement as African Americans had little to no power in even defending themselves in the court of law.

"Free White Persons" was among the most glaring examples of racist language used by the U.S. Supreme Court to deny all Asians from having basic citizen rights to protect themselves against WASP antagonism and aggressive policies. Asian immigrants, including the Chinese in their *Yick Wo v. Hopkins* (1886), Japanese in *Takao Ozawa v. United States* (1922) and Asian Indians in *United States v. Bhagat Singh Thind* (1923), were all victims of disfranchisement which disproportionally gave more power and protection to the dominant WASP group (Nakanishi and Lai, 2003, 47–88).

Disfranchisement has become a much more subtle practice by many state governments more recently. Political scientist Shauna Reilly (2020) was intrigued by the paradox that the nation elected its first Black president in 2008, which was supposed to lead to an era of post-racial politics, and she expected that older generation varieties of voting rights violations of the past history would be ended by a post-racial era. Yet, to her surprise [and many others], many states implemented more voting restrictions after 2008. Her initial thought was that these states were responding to unprecedented fiscal constraints, as the 2008 recession cut state budgets drastically across the country, which might lead to fewer resources for election administration and more restrictive laws. As a proponent of conservative fiscal policy, she initially did not believe that a voter identification requirement was a suppressive measure, as Democrats claimed in opposing it. She compiled a dataset containing all states that passed restrictive election laws between 2000 and 2016. The findings were surprising. For example, she examined the influence of race on the enactment of voter identification laws, and her findings showed that the race variable is statistically significant even after controlling for other variables, such as fiscal constraints, partisanship, and geographic location. "A proportionally greater black population would increase the odds of more restrictive voting laws" (100). Reilly's rigorous statistical analysis convinced her that the role of race in states' decisions to adopt more restrictive voting access rules "has been and continues to be a prominent one, and one that persists even in the face of countervailing political and economic pressures." And, as for why race is such a prominent factor, she explains that "it represents the threat response from elected officials as they attempt to engage the political process to their own advantage" (112).

Exclusion

Exclusion is used to eliminate any possible competition and challenge from a SG. While disfranchisement also minimizes political challenges from SGs, exclusion goes one step further to deny the entry of a SG into the political sphere. Disfranchisement does not reduce the numbers of the SG, but exclusion also can be used to extinguish the whole group in the long run.

Exclusion was used by U.S. Congress in 1882 to stop Chinese immigrants from coming to the Pacific shoreline. The Chinese population vanished quickly and disappeared from workplaces such as railroad construction and mining industry in the West. Those who did stay inside the United States endured dire circumstances in urban ghetto areas, the inability to bring relatives or start a family, and limited means that kept them in poverty (Takaki, 1998). A most recent example of exclusion involves Muslim Americans, and the disparagement many suffer even when they enter the political arena. The exclusionary language was frequently used not just by some radical groups in the social media. President Trump in July 2019 attacked his political opponents in Congress, especially those with Muslim backgrounds, adding that they should "go back and help fix the totally broken and crime infested places from which they came."

Removal

As an aggravated level of aggression against a SG, removal is used to force an SG from their home territory to a remote, undesirable site. The purpose of this violent and physically torturous process often is to occupy wholly the land previously owned by an SG. Through removal, the land becomes a property of the DG and the social and political control of SG is relocated to a distant area where no immediate threat can be initiated by the SG.

Following the *Indian Removal Act of 1830*, the forced relocation of Native American nations from southeastern parts of the country to present-day Oklahoma included many members of the Cherokee, Muscogee (Creek), Seminole, Chickasaw, and Choctaw nations. The Trail of Tears referred to the removal of the Choctaw Nation in the 1830s, which will be discussed in more detail in the next chapter. Another example of removal is the internment experience of Japanese Americans during World War II.

Enslavement

Enslavement is the highest level of aggression by the DG against a SG. It is the highest level of institutional dominance, coercion, and absolute control over an SG. (Note that we do not include genocide in our aggression measure, as genocide potentially is intended to accomplish the extinction of SGs, which erases any semblance of group relations in the political environment.) The members of an SG and their offspring work in extremely inhumane conditions without freedom and political rights. Slaves were considered legally the properties of their slave-owners, as indicated by the infamous *Dred Scott* decision (1857) of the U.S. Supreme Court. Within eight years, after a violent Civil War, the practice of slavery was abolished as unconstitutional and ended the Confederate States of America that was established to preserve it. Although slavery was abolished, the question of reparations always has remained in the political discourse, occasionally being amplified at particular points, despite concerted efforts by the WASP dominant group to control the extent to which it is being discussed.

In short, the legacy of slavery cannot be overstated. Acharya, Blackwell, and Sen (2018), based on their meticulous survey of the slavery and its impact on the current American politics, aptly put:

> [O]ur study has implications for how the United States is viewed compared with other Western democracies. Of these peers, the United States is not only alone in its historical prevalence of slavery, but it is also distinguished by taking the longest to abolish the institution . . . Around the time of the Civil War, approximately twelve percent of the entire population was enslaved . . . Ten percent of Americans were completely disenfranchised before 1965, and the United States federal and state prisons currently incarcerate 1.4 percent of its population and 4.3 percent of its black population. Again, opposition to more progressive approaches on these issues has come from conservative Southern delegations . . . (212)

CONCLUSION

Based on the levels of aggression illustrated above, the WASP responses to multiple threats from SGs are shown in table 7.1. The perception of threat increases from the left to the right in table 7.1, while the level of aggression against SGs increases from the bottom to the top. As table 7.1 indicates, a higher level of perception of threat can lead to a higher level of aggression from the DG. More importantly, we can also see that the third axiom (the volatility principle) is empirically supported by the outcomes affecting SGs. The response range is enlarged as the group order shows enhanced perception of external threat from an SG. Furthermore, the pattern of the increase of response range shows a clear triangulated distribution, as depicted in figure 7.1.

Note that the + sign denotes that the presence of the particular experience is not as far reaching as those for other groups with X signs. The implication

Table 7.1   WASP Responses to Multiple Threats from Subordinate Groups (SGs)

	Germans	White Catholics	Latter-day Saints	Latinos	Asians	Native Americans	Blacks
Enslavement							X
Removal						X	
Exclusion					X		
Disfranchisement			X	X	X	X	X
Discrimination		X	X	X	X	X	X
Negotiation		X	X	X	X	X	X
Assimilation	X	X	+				

Source: Created by the author with + sign denoting that the presence of the particular experience which is not as complete as those for other groups with X signs.

represented in table 7.1 is that while WASPs have the option to deploy a high level of aggression against a group they perceive with a corresponding high level of threat, such as African Americans, the WASP response to a perceived Black threat at a given time does not have to be a high level of aggression. In contrast, WASPs have limited options to react to low threatening groups, especially German Protestants. This is because German Protestants are regarded as being the closest to the in-group of WASPs, based on their similarities. Meanwhile, African Americans constitute the most distinct out-group. WASPs have the options to react to SGs based on the group order they defined in the first place.

But the large range of response options and political volatility for high threatening groups, such as African Americans, invite other questions: Under what conditions would WASPs react more positively to African Americans? What causes the positive changes in terms of the group status for African Americans? What causes a backlash against them? Most importantly, what have been the sources of political volatility these "high threatening" groups have experienced in U.S history? To answer these questions, we need to expand beyond the three axioms we have introduced to this point: attraction-similarity, distance, and volatility. No theoretical construction can be complete by focusing on only the relationships between the DG and SGs. One must probe deeper into the inner structure of the DG itself, which is the task set forth in the next chapter.

Chapter 8

Internal Threat, Competition, and the Atomic Structure

The ADVICE Principles (III)

As we have seen from the previous three chapters, a key enduring political reality is that the presence of multiple subordinate groups (SGs) means multiple threats to the dominant group (DG), often occurring simultaneously. This puts pressure on the DG to respond politically to these simultaneous multiple threats. Chapter 4 examined how the DG manipulates the racial, ethnic, and religious ordering to develop a spectrum of political responses to perceived multiple political threats from SGs.

Remember that a more distant SG usually receives much harsher treatment from the DG than an SG closer to the DG. But, the greater range of possible responses to a distant SG's threat also motivates the DG sometimes to raise the political status of this distant SG as well. For example, the politics of Reconstruction in the immediate aftermath of the Civil War led to governmental efforts that enhanced African Americans' group status. In contemporary politics, affirmative action programs have also been facilitated African Americans gaining access to a broader range of economic opportunities. It is important to understand the conditions upon which an SG's political status may change.

The underlying reasons for a change in SG group statuses comprise the focus of this chapter. We have used the term of political volatility to refer to unexpected, unpredictable characteristics of changes in group status for various SGs. To say that the changes are unexpected or unpredictable, one emphasizes that the changes often have resulted from the DG's internal political struggles rather than being driven by the political success of specific SGs. To understand this feature of volatility, we begin with an infamous historical event—the Trail of Tears. Here, the political fate of a subordinate group is not simply a result of how this SG challenges the political rule of the dominant

group—more often than not—it also is a result of the internal threat that DG
members have perceived from within.

TRAIL OF TEARS

In their passionate recounting of the Trail of Tears, historians Perdue and
Green (1995) wrote:

> When United States soldiers arrived in the spring of 1838, few Cherokees had
> made preparation to go west. The troops began rounding up people and plac-
> ing them in stockades. The summer heat, poor water supplies, disease, and
> inadequate provisions quickly took their toll on those awaiting deportation to
> the West. Seeing his people's suffering, [chief John] Ross finally accepted the
> inevitability of removal and secured permission for the Cherokees to conduct
> their own emigration that fall. Except for scattered families and a small group
> of Cherokees whose 1819 treaty rights permitted them to stay in North Carolina,
> the remaining [16,000] Cherokees moved west in the winter of 1938-39 on what
> has come to be known as the 'Trail of Tears'. (20-21)

An estimated 2,000 to 6,000 Cherokees died during their forced journey to
destinations in Oklahoma. The removal of Native Americans no doubt had
its roots in the perception of their threat. As discussed in previous chapters,
racial minorities are ordered by the dominant group to deal with the problem
of multiple threats. Immediately before the Indian Removal Act of 1830,
for example, a U.S. Senator from Georgia described Indians as "a race not
admitted to be equal to the rest of the community; not governed as completely
dependent; treated somewhat like human beings; but not admitted to be free-
men; not yet entitled, and probably never will be entitled, to equal civil and
political rights" (Perdue and Green, 1995, 15).

Native Americans, however, were never treated uniformly throughout
U.S. history. Their group status was subject to the volatility principle, as
discussed in the last chapter. The relations between WASPs and Native
Americans in the first fifty years after the nation gained its independence,
in fact, did not arrive at a level of crisis that would threaten the internal
unity of WASPs, despite the fact that some Indian nations joined British
forces against the WASPs in wars during that time. The Cherokee Nation,
in particular, fought against the United States until 1794. But, peace and a
period of autonomy followed. John Collier, U.S. Commissioner of Indian
Affairs from 1933 to 1945, commented that before the Trail of Tears, "The
Cherokees met every test of peacefulness, of practicality, of Christian
profession and conduct, of industry and productiveness, of out-going

friendliness to the whites, of 'progress' in domestic order and in education" (Steinfield, 1970, 49).

In the 1820s, tensions quickly grew to crisis levels between American Indians and states where their territories were located. One chief reason for the tension was the drastically increased demand for American Indian land as a result of the economic boom and population growth moving westward from the Appalachian Mountains to the Mississippi River region. The U.S. government tried to negotiate with American Indian tribes to buy the lands, but tribes adamantly refused to sell their lands and leave their territories. The removal of Indians from the southeastern areas of the United States to west of the Mississippi River finally became the dominant view shared by many politicians, including Presidents James Monroe and John Quincy Adams. The key engineer of the American Indian removal project was Andrew Jackson, who was commander of the U.S. army's southern district and the government negotiator for American Indian treaties. For Jackson, the issue could be solved only through Congressional action that treated the American Indians as subjects of the Republic rather than as sovereign entities. Therefore, the U.S. Congress should "legislate their boundaries" so that American WASP citizens could develop the land and prosper.

The compliance of American Indians would be guaranteed by "the arm of government" (Perdue and Green, 1995, 16). Jackson won the 1828 presidential election largely because of this policy position, which won him nearly unanimous support from the southern states. His American Indian removal plan was used to measure loyalty to the Democratic Party (Perdue and Green, 1995, 17), and the U.S. Congress finally passed the Indian Removal Act, which was signed by President Jackson on May 28, 1830. According to the Act, "the Indians could choose to remove west of the Mississippi River or submit to state law" (Hobson, 1996, 171).

In Georgia, the American Indian crisis went all the way to the U.S. Supreme Court. The state government of Georgia had hoped that the federal government would purchase all Cherokee lands in Georgia on behalf of the state. To do so, the federal government would pay back the land between Georgia's current western boundary and the Mississippi River that once had belonged to Georgia but had been ceded to the United States in 1802. But Georgia's wish didn't happen, and "by the 1820s little progress had been made in extinguishing Indian titles. The Cherokees had taken up agriculture and refused to sell any more of their lands. In 1827 they adopted a constitution and declared themselves an independent state. In response Georgia enacted a series of laws seizing Cherokee territory, extending state law over this territory, and annulling all Indian customs and laws" (Hobson, 1996, 171).

The Cherokees, represented by Chief John Ross, appealed to the Jackson administration initially to seek federal protection, which President Jackson rejected based on a states-rights claim. The Cherokees then brought their case, *Cherokee Nation v. Georgia* (1831), to the Supreme Court, in an attempt to restrain the state of Georgia from executing its laws in Cherokee territory. The Court refused to take jurisdiction and ruled that the tribe "was not a foreign nation" (Steinfield, 1970, 50).

Within two years, in a stunning Supreme Court decision concerning *Worcester v. Georgia* (1832), Chief Justice Marshall, writing for the majority, changed his heart and ruled against the government of Georgia. Marshall forcefully articulated the rights of Cherokees in his opinion (Perdue and Green, 1995, 73–74):

> The Indian nations had always been considered as distinct, independent, political communities, retaining their original natural rights . . . and the settled doctrine of the law of nations is, that a weaker power does not surrender its independence—its right to self-government—by associating with a stronger, and taking its protection. The Cherokee Nation, then, is a distinct community, occupying its own territory, with boundaries accurately described in which the laws of Georgia can have no force, and which the citizens of Georgia have no right to enter, but with the assent of the Cherokees themselves, or in conformity with treaties, and with the acts of Congress.

The dramatic shift of Marshall's American Indian position poses an important, and yet intriguing, question about the main reasons for such a change. Arguably one of the greatest U.S. chief justices, for establishing Supreme Court precedents, Marshall stood tall in his influence in the formation of the American legal system, particularly for the birth of, and continuing power of, judicial review. He was a major political figure in the generation of leaders who led the United States to its establishment as an independent nation. Therefore, his views about American Indians and minorities help us understand not only the early group status of minorities but also the trajectory of group relations in American history.

The change in the nature of Marshall's rulings from *Cherokee Nation v. Georgia* (1831) to *Worcester v. Georgia* (1832) indicates that there were different opinions about how American Indians should be treated in the Republic's formative years and how differences of opinions could develop within such a short time for a single WASP public figure. One popular explanation for this change was based on moral terms. It was said that Marshall was unhappy about his decision on *Cherokee Nation v. Georgia* because it was against his moral conscience that the American Indians should be treated equally. "The conscience of the Court was troubled by this Pilate-like decision [in *Cherokee Nation v. Georgia*]," said John Collier. Serving in the same court, U.S. Justice Joseph Story was also reported saying that by using the *Worcester* decision, the U.S. Supreme Court could "wash their hands clean of the iniquity of oppressing the Indians, and disregarding their rights" (Steinfield, 1970, 51).

More recently, scholars have noticed the inadequacy of using moral factors alone to explain Marshall's changed position on American Indian affairs (e.g., Hobson, 1996). Indeed, if *moral* factors were the real cause for making the moral decision in the *Worcester* decision, why would the same moral reason have not applied in the *Cherokee Nation* decision? Was it because Marshall did not notice the dire consequence of white oppression of American Indians during his consideration of the *Cherokee Nation* case? But, Marshall already wrote privately, as early as in 1828, that it would be the right cause "to give full indulgence to those principles of humanity and justice which ought always to govern our conduct toward the aborigines when this course can be pursued without exposing ourselves to the most afflicting calamities" (Hobson, 1996, 175). For the *Cherokee Nation* case itself, Marshall expressed his sympathy to Indians so vividly:

A people once numerous, powerful, and truly independent, found by our ances- tors in the quiet and uncontrolled possession of an ample domain, gradually sinking beneath our superior policy, our arts, and our arms, have yielded their lands by successive treaties, each of which contains a solemn guarantee of the residue, until they retain no more of their formerly extensive territory than is deemed necessary to their comfortable subsistence. (Hobson, 1996, 175)

Given so much sympathy expressed not only in private but also in the Court decision itself, why did Marshall still choose the way against his "moral conscience" concerning the Indian suffering in *Cherokee Nation v. Georgia*? Legal scholar and Marshall biographer Charles Hobson (1996) pointed out that "As a pragmatic jurist, not a moralist, the chief justice was concerned only with finding the 'legal' answer'" (173). Clearly, for Marshall, the legal answers were different between the *Cherokee Nation* case and the *Worcester* case, though his expression of sympathy toward American Indian suffering might have been the same in both cases. As already noted, the *Cherokee Nation* case was an original case brought by the Cherokee Nation in order to stop the state of Georgia from potentially confiscating the Indian lands. However, the *Worcester* case brought a new legal dimension to the Court for consideration.

The *Worcester* case involved the plaintiff, Samuel A. Worcester, a white American who left his home state of Vermont and went on a Christian mis- sion with other two white persons in the town of New Echota, a territory of Cherokee Nation located inside the state of Georgia. The three white mis- sionaries were accused of practicing religion without a license and refusing to swear an oath of allegiance to Georgia. "They were arrested, chained together, and forced to walk twenty-one miles behind a wagon to jail. Two Methodist preachers intervened against the brutality; they were chained with the others and thrown into jail with them. The missionaries were tried and sentenced to four years' hard labor in the state penitentiary" (Steinfield, 1970, 51).

The Marshall court, in its opinion delivered by the U.S. Chief Justice, emphasized the fact of the Christian missionaries as "being white persons" and their imprisonment as a result of Georgia's "assertion of jurisdiction over the Cherokee nation" (cited from Perdue and Green, 1995, 72). The U.S. Supreme Court, however, declared that "the whole intercourse between the United States and this [Cherokee] nation, is, by our Constitution and laws, vested in the government of the United States" (cited from Perdue and Green, 1995, 74). Thus, Georgia's state statute was seen "as being repugnant to the Constitution, treaties, and laws of the United States, and ought, therefore, to be reversed and annulled" (cited from Perdue and Green, 1995, 75).

It is clear then that for Marshall his legal concern was not whether the Indians should be removed West. Not only did he decline to take the *Cherokee Nation v. Georgia* case, which would otherwise have allowed him to express clearly his view on the removal, but he also remained silent on the Indian Removal Act, which had been passed recently by the U.S. Congress. His sympathy toward American Indian suffering apparently was not strong enough for him to publicly issue his opposition to American Indian removal. Even after the *Worcester* case was decided and the state of Georgia was forced to free the white missionaries, the Marshall decision effectively did not halt the Trail of Tears, particularly during the winter of 1838–1839.

But, Marshall's forceful opposition to the state-sovereignty doctrine was effectively rendered in the *Worcester* case. As a steadfast federalist, the Chief Justice set his eyes firmly on protecting the U.S. Constitution and the supremacy of federal over state laws. As Hobson (1996) suggested, "Sympathetic as he was to the dire predicament of the Cherokees, Marshall had other reasons for seizing the opportunity to pronounce the law in their case" (180). Put differently, protecting Indians' rights and equality did not describe Marshall's fundamental goal. As a federalist, Marshall had every intention to use American Indian autonomy to make treaties with the federal government as a legal instrument to defeat the states-rights advocates' doctrine of nullification of federal laws. The federal government, of course, did not make any further peaceful treaties with the American Indians to keep their lands intact after the Indian Removal Act. But, through the *Worcester* decision, the state of Georgia was forced to acknowledge the power of federal government including judicial review and free the three white missionaries. It was a legal victory for the federalists, indeed, though the Cherokees eventually would not escape from the fate of forced removal.

ABSTRACT THREAT AND
CONCRETE THREAT REVISITED

The difference between the federalists and states-rights proponents on the American Indian issue in the early nineteenth century deserves greater scrutiny, as it reflected a trend within the dominant group that has continued to today. The dominant WASP group from the beginning of the Republic already diverged on how subordinate groups should be treated. To understand the divergence within the dominant group, we should revisit the coexistence of abstract and concrete threats. As discussed in chapter 5, the DG perceives multiple threats from SGs, but the threats also can be classified as abstract and/or concrete. All members of the DG can perceive the abstract threat from a minority group, such as the American Indians. This is simply a result of the first two axioms in our theoretical proposition: the attraction and the distance principles, respectively. American Indians can be perceived as a threat to all WASPs, because they do not resemble them and they are located further away from the positional system initiated and defined by WASPs themselves.

Historians Perdue and Green (1995) found that WASPs formed a consensus quickly after the formation of the Republic that American Indians, after all, could not be "civilized" because they were "racialized" as different from whites (14-15). Even Cherokees, who were often regarded as the most advanced among the American Indians, were regarded as "a race not admitted to be equal to the rest of the community" (15). As a result of these racist thoughts, as noted by Perdue and Green (1995), WASPs "rejected the idea that American Indians could ever be fully 'civilized' [or, more accurately, assimilated] and insisted that one cannot change through educational characteristics determined by race alone. Therefore, the reasoning continued, there could be no place in American society for Native American people and, furthermore, it made no sense to pursue an Indian policy that aimed to achieve an impossible goal" (14).

This shared view of Indians as otherness explains well why even Marshall, as sympathetic as he was to American Indian suffering, refused to take the *Cherokee Nation v. Georgia* case under consideration, and thereby avoid the question about halting their fate and whether or not removal was constitutional. It also explains why the Marshall court did not pursue forcefully after the *Worcester* case the constitutional legal grounds arguing for real American Indian autonomy to reverse their increasingly inevitable fate of removal.

But, not all WASPs faced the same concrete threat from American Indians. If the Cherokees in the state of Georgia were not separated or removed from their tribes, they formed a concrete and direct threat to those WASPs (including white slave owners) who demanded more land for economic opportunity and population growth. It is for this reason the states-rights proponents were mainly from southern states where American Indians posed a concrete threat. Elected officials (e.g., President Jackson), hence, focused on exercising all of their political power to strengthen their domination over American Indians. Furthermore, this domination was theorized as being for the good of American Indians, a point illustrated by Perdue and Green (1995):

> Jackson built his defense of removal on the twin themes of the sovereign rights of Georgia over the Cherokees and the normal imperative to protect Indians from the deleterious effects of exposure to American frontier settlers. Such contact, he explained, had always resulted in the degradation and ultimate demise of the Indians and only their isolation in a safe and distant haven could save them. (18)

The WASPs from the northeast did not see the Indians as a concrete threat. On the contrary, they saw the domination of American Indians only as increasing the power of southern states that had already gained disproportional influence through provisions such as the three-fifths compromise. During the Congressional debate about the Indian Removal Act, representatives from the northeast argued against American Indian removal by using moral accounts mainly derived from Christian missionary works inside the tribes (Perdue and Green, 1995, 18).

For the federalists who had been losing national elections to Jeffersonian Republicans for several decades, the internal WASP concrete threat from the states-rights proponents was perceived as much greater than the external abstract threat from American Indians who politically were powerless. Because of the power struggle between the federalists and Jeffersonian Republicans, the question of removal became a heated political issue. The two coalitions, though both situated within the dominant WASP group, diverged more widely on how American Indians should be treated. This leads to the fourth axiom of the book's theoretical proposition:

> Axiom 4 (A4): The internal-threat principle (which is represented by I in the ADVICE acronym). The divergent positions on a SG's group status are the effect of and reinforcement of the internal threat between the two coalitions inside the DG and the concrete SG threat relative to only one of the coalitions.

Having seen how this axiom applies to the divergent views of federalists and Jeffersonian Republicans on the American Indian removal issue, we can also expand the discussions of this freshly introduced axiom to other minority groups. Table 8.1 lists how the two WASP coalitions were built around concrete minority threats throughout U.S. history. The first WASP coalition was built because of the shared perception of concrete minority threats. For

Table 8.1   Concrete Minority Threats and the Dualism in the U.S. Politics

	Black Threat	*Indian Threat*	*White Catholic Threat*
WASP Coalition #1: the Threatened	White Southerners, Democrats	States-Rights Supporters, Jeffersonian Republican, Southerners	WASP working class, Know-Nothing Party, Populists
WASP Coalition #2: No Concrete Minority Threat Perceived	Republicans, Abolitionists	Federalists, WASP Clergy, Northeasterners	Expansionists, Pro-growth politicians, Republicans, Big Business, Settlement Movement Participants

Source: Created by the author

example, for the American Indian threat, the affected WASPs were states-rights proponents, Jeffersonian Republicans, and group members from southeastern states such as Georgia. The second WASP coalition included those federalists, WASP clergy who had missionary experiences in the American Indian territories and northeastern residents who experienced no concrete threat from the American Indians.

If access to land was the main reason for the concrete threat of American Indians to states-rights proponents, the use of slaves placed WASP slave-owners on continuous alert to any concrete threat to such an institution. As Wilson, the American sociologist, explains, "In early Virginia and Maryland, and later in other colonies, as slavery gradually received legal sanction, the laws not only granted masters overwhelming power over their slaves but also codified white supremacy by restricting slave status to nonwhites and prohibiting interracial marriage" (Wilson, 1980, 25). Strict racial order was established under slavery. Moreover "the most advanced fraction of the slaveholders—those who most clearly perceived the interests and needs of the class as a whole steadily worked to make their class more conscious of its nature, spirit, and destiny. In the process, it created a world-view appropriate to a slaveholder's regime" (Genovese, 1974, 27).

The domination over African American slaves brought not only economic benefits to slaveholders but also enormous political power to southern plantation owners. The three-fifths clause gave them disproportional power in the U.S. Congress, which facilitated a succession of favorable congressional decisions in the antebellum era. In the deep South of Florida and Louisiana, slavery was the norm. The Missouri Compromise further extended slavery across the Mississippi River, and, thanks to the annexation of Texas, slavery was consolidated in the southwest. The 1854 Kansas-Nebraska Act dramatically opened the Western expansion to slavery. Three years later, the Dred

Scott decision of 1857 provided federal government protection of slavery in the aforementioned territories, magnifying southern influence in the federal government, which was determined to sustain slavery into the future.

Despite the widespread deeply misplaced belief that African Americans were inferior to WASPs and the abstract threat that they might foster to all WASPs, the institution of slavery did not bring equal benefits to all WASPs. The disproportionate power of slaveholders and southern states did breed resentment and political opposition from WASPs in northeastern states. This was notable among members of the newly formed Republican Party, for whom southern politicians, as indicated by *The New York Times* in 1856, were "held together like the feudal barons of the middle ages by a community of interests and of sentiment; and [act] together always for the promotion of their common ends" (cited from Wilson, 1980, 26).

Historians have debated and questioned the reason for WASP politicians, such as President Lincoln, to use political means to raise the political status of a minority group. One particular puzzle was why there was historical evidence about Lincoln's racist attitude toward Blacks but yet he also was hailed as the "great emancipator" of African American slaves (Bennett, 2000). This seemingly contradictory trait can be explained by the coexistence of abstract and concrete threats. As a member of the dominant WASP group, one may perceive the abstract threat from an SG such as African Americans, which explains why Lincoln expressed willingness to consider sending African Americans to another nation (notably, Liberia, which became a destination for freed slaves and free-born African Americans). This "racist" position is again based on the attraction principle (A1) and distance principle (A2), as discussed in earlier chapters. Racist views reflect upon the relative group positions, as suggested by Blumer (1958). However, abolitionists such as Lincoln saw southern slave owners as a greater political threat (again an internal threat). On the contrary, Lincoln and the Republican Party did not see Black slaves as the concrete threat. Lincoln was accused of hating white Southerners in his time as well because of his abolitionist point of view and his opposition to the South. For him, equality was the best moral principle that he could use to fight against his WASP opponents. He wrote passionately and persuasively in 1855 to his friend Joshua Speed, a slave owner in Kentucky (Abraham Lincoln Speeches, online): "How can anyone who abhors the oppression of negroes, be in favor of degrading classes of white people?" He then emphasized the moral value of equality not yet applied to all: "As a nation, we began by declaring that "all men are created equal." We now practically read it "all men are created equal, except negroes." When the Know-Nothings get control, it will read "all men are created equal, except negroes, and foreigners, and Catholics." Liberating slaves could pay more political dividend to the Republican Party, especially when the political cause was seen as moral as well.

Another potential opposition to southern slave-owners' political power came from southern working-class WASPs. As Wilson (1980) pointed out,

> Throughout the period of legal servitude, the ownership of slaves was a privilege enjoyed by only a small percentage of free families in the South. Of the 1,156,000 free southern families in 1860, only 385,000 (roughly one-fourth) owned slaves. However, the majority of slaves were owned by families that possessed at least twenty slaves each. (24)

It turned out that working-class white southerners, in fact, did not oppose slavery on any significant measure.

Two potential explanations could be made for remaining silent. One was the successful southern racial ideology that gave working-class white southerners a sense of superiority over Black slaves, as suggested by the attraction principle. The second was that they might have feared labor competition from Blacks for relatively higher-paid jobs if slavery came to an end. Wilson (1980) also noted that poor white working-class in the South did not have the political organizational power and unified class consciousness to challenge the well-organized slave-owner class (27).

We do see, however, the well-organized working-class WASP political opposition, not directed toward Black slavery, but instead toward white Catholic immigrant workers in the first half of the nineteenth century and later toward Chinese labor in the second half of the century. The Know-Nothing Party was stitched together from disparate small political parties and patriotic organizations (Kaufmann, 2004, 25). But, the issue of slavery turned out to be the major national event that dragged the whole nation, including the Know-Nothing Party, into the crisis. As the Republican Party established itself as a major new force, the Know-Nothing party faded and dissolved, while new anti-immigrant sentiments again were ignited by a populist movement after the Civil War. Populism was organized by two major forces—the Protestant clergymen and the rural masses, with the target at Catholic immigrant-dominant urban centers. Rather than from the South, populism had its origin in New York State back in 1868, and quickly spread to many other states. With anxiety over vanishing rural self-sufficiency because of the nation's reliance on urban-based banks, industrial powerhouses, and railroads which all demanded Catholic migrant laborers, the Populists grew 300 branches in New York State alone before 1874 (Kaufmann, 2004, 27). Elite WASP clergymen, such as the "Social Gospel preacher" Josiah Strong, used mass publications, especially Strong's *Our Country* to warn Americans that "they would be overwhelmed by foreign immigrants as the Romans were by the Goths and Vandals" (Kaufmann, 2004, 28). Before the beginning of the twentieth century the Populists dominated the Democratic Party, supporting Bryan as the presidential candidate in 1896.

While Bryan lost the presidential election, his WASP nationalistic vision continued to influence subsequent progressive movements, as well as the radical Ku Klux Klan. The anti-Catholic immigrant agenda was expanded to wholesale attacks on anybody non-WASP, and the Klan had grown into not only a southern regional power but also a national force that set the congressional agenda for southerners, as well as WASPs in other parts of the country. With massive power at the grassroots level—for example, one out of every four white men in Indiana in the 1920s was a Klansman—the movement "engendered a sense of community . . . drew together disparate social groups through a powerful appeal to white Protestant ethnic Identity" (Moore, 1985, 296).

Not all WASPs saw Catholics as a concrete threat nor shared the view of anti-immigrant Know Nothing Party, Populists, and Ku Klux Klan. In particular, Western expansionists, pro-growth politicians, and laissez-faire capitalists voiced their opposition to the anti-Catholic movements. William Lloyd Garrison, a major figure in the anti-slavery movement, pointed out:

> I cannot feel any heartrending emotions . . . in contemplating the condition of a people who are not under despotic or dynastic sway . . . who are free to make their own contracts and sell or employ labor according to the law of supply and demand . . . You express the conviction that the present relation of capital to labor is "hastening the nation to its ruin" . . . I entertain no such fears. Our danger lies in sensual indulgence, in a licentious perversion of liberty, in the prevalence of intemperance, and in whatever tend to the demoralization of the people. Abhorring all injustice, class legislation and usurpation of power. (Garrison [1868–1879] 1981, 388–389)

Moreover, state governments, thanks to state enforcement power in immigration issues prior to the mid-1880s, competed with each other to lure immigrants from Europe and Asia due to rapid advances in mass manufacturing, railroad construction, and gold mining. The Sewardite, expansionist wing of the Republican Party was an important channel for the immigrant-friendly policymaking. In 1864, for example, in reaction to labor shortages, the Republican Party enacted a statute that encouraged the importation of contract labor, while its 1864 convention "reaffirmed the historic role of the United States as an asylum for the oppressed of all nations, and endorsed a 'liberal and just immigration policy, which would encourage foreign immigration'" (Foner, 1970, 236–237).

Even within Protestant religious circles, universalism, which emphasizes the value of humanitarianism toward Catholics, also launched its own
movement in the late nineteenth century and early twentieth century. The
American Settlement Movement, for example, "grew rapidly after 1891, from
6 Settlements to 74 in 1894, 100 by 1900 and over 400 by 1910" (Kaufmann,
2004, 96). Especially in Chicago, led by social reformer Jane Addams, the
Settlement Movement emphasized the dignity of every individual. "Catholic
and Jewish immigrants in inner-city New York and Chicago were thus considered just as worthy of respect as Protestants in rural or suburban districts
. . . Americanization along Anglo-conformist lines . . . was considered humili-
ating to their sense of dignity" (Kaufmann, 2004, 97).

The intellectual community also split on the treatment toward Catholics,
especially those from southern and eastern European countries. John Dewey,
widely known as America's quintessential public philosopher, passionately
argued that all ethnic groups contributed to what America is. Along with
Jane Addams, Dewey led the Ethnic Culture movement that valued cultural
mixing. He remarked that "neither Englandism nor New Englandism, neither
Puritan nor Cavalier, any more than Teuton or Slav, can do anything but fur-
nish one note in a vast symphony" (Lissak, 1989, 156). Dewey's intellectual
leadership at The University of Chicago along with Franz Boas of Columbia
University cultivated the New Social Science movement as a major source
to combat and discredit claims and theories related to biological racism and
eugenics, the center of which was headquartered at Yale University in the
1920s (Gleason, 1992, 156–157; Doyle, 2014, 52–54).

DUALISM IN U.S. POLITICS

Building upon the discussion in the previous sections, one can observe how
divergent views on how SGs should be treated by the WASPs led directly to
the two political coalitions that have appeared consistently throughout U.S.
political history. As discussed above, Republican Party emerged from the
debate over slavery. Democrats meanwhile held anti-minority and anti-Catholic positions throughout the nineteenth century. Curiously, these two parties
transformed their positions regarding the group status of various SGs in the
twentieth century, a topic to be discussed in the next two chapters.

As Beck and Sorauf (1992) indicate, "a underlying duality of interest in the
American society has sustained the American two-party system" (43). Our
fourth axiom (the internal threat principle) suggests that the duality of interest
in American WASP society originated in the concrete threats perceived by
one coalition of the WASPs, but not the other. Whether or not it was "the initial sectional tension between the eastern financial and commercial interests

and the western frontiersmen" or the later "the North-South conflict over the issue of slavery and the Civil War, and then to urban-rural and socioeconomic status divisions" (Beck and Sorauf, 1992, 43), one can comprehend more fully the formation and durability of the American two-party system by tracing it to the roles played by divergent views regarding SGs.

Beck and Sorauf (1992) also described the so-called "natural dualism" within the American democratic system—"party in power versus party out of power, government versus opposition, pro and anti the status quo, and even the ideological dualism of liberal and conservative. Thus, social and economic interests or the very processes of a democratic politics—or both— reduce the political contestants to two great camps, and that dualism gives rise to two political parties" (43).

With respect to minority groups in the U.S. political system, this natural dualism has a vital implication—the political fate of minority groups at a given time depends upon which political coalition wins major elections at the federal level. Therefore, the fifth axiom of the book's theoretical proposition emerges to extend the discussion:

> Axiom 5 (A5): The competitive-election principle (which is represented by the C and E in the ADVICE acronym). Through a competitive election, the winning coalition inside the DG gains more power temporarily to determine the political status of SGs within the respective response ranges.

Winning elections does not guarantee change in group relations, but it provides the opportunities for substantive changes in the status of SGs. Dualism also suggests that neither of the two major political parties can dominate the federal elections cycles for too long. Otherwise, there would have been no substantial changes in the status of various SGs. This new axiom makes the political fate of a SG volatile over time, as the two coalitions both are capable of winning elections and governing.

One of the reasons for why the two parties "take turns" to govern is provided by the minimum winning coalition theory proposed by William Riker (1962). Riker's minimum winning coalition thesis is the counterpoint to Downs' (1957) maximum coalition and median voter theory as discussed previously. Winning is the fundamental goal of political parties, according to Downs' rational choice theory. As a result, political candidates, especially at the federal level, always have the incentives to build a coalition as large as possible. Moreover, the best way to build such a grand coalition is to support campaign agendas that reflect the median voters' policy positions.

But, many scholars of racial relations point out that Downs' assumption about median voters does not apply to the United States because of inevitable voting dilemmas faced, especially by minority voters who have been caught between two major parties and can only choose a major party regardless of their own preferences (e.g., see Kim, 2007; Frymer, 1999). Riker offered yet another compelling alternative to Downs' thesis. For him, winning is, of course, vital to coalition building process, but governing is important as well because it is through that process where political parties finally exercise their political power to reward their electoral coalition members. Moreover, a smaller number of winners lead to a higher yield of power and prestige.

Despite their fundamental differences, it is beneficial to combine the insights from both Riker and Downs. Governing is important, but political parties also must win in the first place to gain that privilege. Furthermore, in order to win, parties do not have to build an overwhelming majority coalition; the minimum winning coalition is the only precondition to govern.

Politicians may eventually build a dominant coalition to govern more effectively, but establishing a minimum winning coalition is the primary objective. Sometimes, when a political party grows to the extent where it represents an overwhelming majority or grand coalition, there is a strong incentive for the respective party leaders to minimize it. This is because "every coalition has internal conflicts over the division of spoils" (Riker, 1962, 66). Riker (1962) elaborates,

> When pressure from an opposing coalition is great, so great in fact that the opposition may win and thereby deprive the coalition of any spoils to distribute, these internal conflicts are minimized. But when pressure from the outside diminishes, there is less urgency to settle the internal conflicts amicably simply because they are not so dangerous to the oversized winner as to the minimal winner. (66)

Riker's minimum winning coalition thesis forces researchers to focus on the sizes of electoral coalitions. Clearly, the minimum winning coalition notion is useful when election outcomes are close rather than as a landslide. It offers a plausible explanation for why the two American major parties are competitive over time. Riker's notion of a minimum winning coalition is especially valuable for studies of racial relations, though Riker himself never built any model around race or religion. In the following section, I propose taking the five principles outlined in the first part of the book to a theoretical framework about the atomic structure of group relations that can explain the effect of the two political coalitions on the ebbs and flows regarding the political status of subordinate groups throughout U.S. history.

THE ATOMIC STRUCTURE IN AMERICAN POLITICS

Before we explain the application of our atomic structure of group relations in American politics in part II, let us review the five axioms (or principles) discussed so far. They comprise the ADVICE acronym:

Axiom 1 (A1): In a political system, the DG ranks, orders, and positions SGs based on the attraction-similarity principle (which represents A in the ADVICE acronym).

Axiom 2 (A2): In a political system, the DG perceives external threats from all of the SGs. But, the extent of a threat from a particular SG also is based on the distance between the DG and this SG. The farther the distance, the higher the perception of threat. We label this as the distance principle (which represents the D in the ADVICE acronym).

Axiom 3 (A3): The volatility principle (which represents the V in the ADVICE acronym). The higher the perception of a SG threat, the greater the range of possible DG responses to such a threat, and thus the higher the political volatility a specific SG will experience.

Axiom 4 (A4): The internal-threat principle (which is represented by I in the ADVICE acronym). The divergent positions on a SG's group status are the effect of and reinforcement of the internal threat between the two coalitions inside the DG and the concrete SG threat relative to only one of the coalitions.

Axiom 5 (A5): The competitive-election principle (which is represented by the C and E in the advice acronym). Through a competitive election, the winning coalition inside the DG gains more power temporarily to determine the political status of SGs within the respective response ranges.

The five principles—*a*ttraction, *d*istance, *v*olatility, *i*nternal-threat, *c*ompetitive *e*lection—collectively represent the *ADVICE* principles. In chapters 6 and 7, we discussed the first three axioms, which are mainly concerned with the effects of abstract threats on the political responses of the dominant group (DG) to the subordinate groups (SGs). We see how SGs are positioned because of the abstract threat perceived by DG. Moreover, an SG's political status is volatile, though it is within the specific response range determined by how distant a SG is from the DG.

To further analyze the political volatility experienced by SGs, in this chapter we examined an internal threat within the DG itself and the concrete threat perceived by a subset of the DG rather than by all members of the DG. We discovered that the divergence due to the internal threat perceived by the two opposing coalitions inside the DG is connected to A4 (the internal threat principle) and A5 (the competitive election principle) as based on how one of the two existing coalitions forms a successful minimum winning coalition.

Note that all five axioms work simultaneously, and they collectively function as a political structure that leads to the (in)stability of a political system. We now are ready to examine how the atomic structure works. We use the term atomic structure for two reasons. First, the structure reduces a political system to the fundamental elements and configures them in a specific structure so that the elements interact with each other to form a system, which is capable of adapting continuously to external environmental changes. Second, there are some resemblances in our political system to the atomic structure as studied broadly in the world of chemistry. But, caution must be exercised, as the two worlds are certainly not exactly the same. We proceed with figure 8.1.

In the political system, there is the core, which is composed of the members of the dominant group, denoted as D, in figure 8.1. The role of the core is to determine the relative position of each group in the system based on how the perception of abstract threat takes a certain form due to the first three axioms of the ADVICE principles concerning attraction, distance, and volatility. The core is further split between two coalitions (C1 and C2) that are antagonistic on issue positions relating to how to treat peripheral groups, and therefore see each other as an internal threat, according to the fourth axiom. It is important to remember that C1 and C2 are located inside the core, which is like the nucleus contained in an atom.

The two coalitions are differentiated because of their own attributes, just like protons and neutrons in a nucleus. In chemical atoms, protons are positively charged, and we use the plus signs in our figure 8.1 to represent the feature of C2. In our case, the positive signs represent the characteristics of members of C2 who desire increased levels of power for specific subordinate groups (SGs) which they identify as partners of their electoral coalition. These are egalitarians, as based on King and Smith's classification (2011). For example, we discussed how Lincoln Republicans wanted to liberate African Americans from slavery and enacted constitutional amendments and federal laws to protect their civil and voting rights.

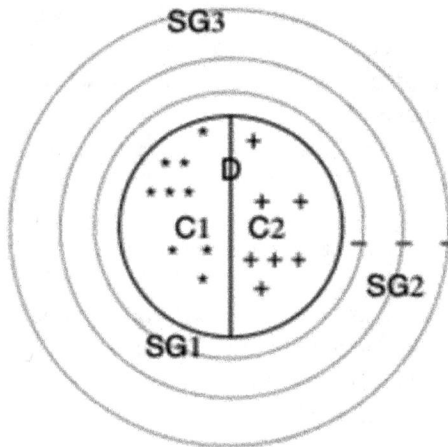

Figure 8.1   The Political Atomic Structure. Created by the author with SG1 through SG3 denoting subordinate groups, and C1 and C2 denoting the two internal competing coalitions inside the dominant core of atomic structure.

On the other hand, the members of C1 do not see the necessity of increasing the power and political status of the specific SGs because they are more likely to perceive the concrete threat by the SGs. They are more likely to be traditionalists. Thus, we use star signs to denote the desire to maintain the status quo, or perhaps achieve more domination over the SGs.

In the political atom, the SGs are located in positions along the periphery because SGs have no direct control over the relative positions of all groups in the system. More simply, the SGs do not govern. Just like electrons negatively charged in chemical atoms, SGs in the political system have the natural motivation to reduce the domination of the core over the peripheries. Therefore, we use negative signs to designate the political tendency of SGs. The SGs are represented by the three circles around the core in figure 8.1. They are positioned in their particular orbits. The inner circles around the core are more similar to the core based on our attraction principle (A1). Some SGs are closer to the core, while other SGs are more distant from the core, D (i.e., the distance principle, A2). The circles have different diameters—a measurement of not only distance (A2) but also the response ranges (A3 or the volatility principle).

In a chemical atom, neutrons are the collective force to balance or cancel out the attraction between protons and electrons and keep electrons outside the nucleus. In this way, the atomic structure can be stabilized. In the political system discussed in this book, C1, through its domination over the SGs, enjoys disproportional power and attempts to counter act against the coalition between C2 and the peripheries.

Take, for example, the three-fifths compromise, as a result of the 1787 constitutional convention, which gave more political power to southern WASP slave owners at the expense of northeastern WASPs, because Black slaves were counted, though disproportionally, for establishing Congressional representation. But, these slaves were not given voting rights which empowered the southern whites even further. Let's call these southern whites, especially the slave owners, C1, and WASPs in the northeast, C2. Of course, in our political atomic structure, C2 has an internal need to challenge the power of C1, and often it starts with C2's political campaign to raise the status of SGs and eliminate the special privilege that C1 members had enjoyed over the SGs.

We saw the abolitionists' call for civil rights, though white racial discrimination also was widespread in the Northeast as well, as vividly captured by Tocqueville in 1831 (Tocqueville, 2000, 343). Again it is important to emphasize that the members of C2 are more likely threatened by C1 than SGs, which we call an internal threat (fourth axiom). The successes of the Lincoln Republicans in 1860 and 1864 were the key to the enhanced political status of Blacks, though white racism itself was still deeply rooted in the nation's social fabrics (fifth axiom or the competitive-election principle).

To reiterate, it is essential to examine the atomic structure based on all five axioms (i.e., ADVICE principles) simultaneously. Especially, the last two axioms concerning internal threat inside the dominant core and competitive elections make the American atomic structure a constitutional democracy rather than a static, caste-like hierarchical system. Many other non-American societies (some of which formed a pyramid-like racial or ethnic hierarchy) are also subject to the first two axioms (the attraction and distance principles) of this book. This is because the attraction-similarity and distance-threat principles apply to all humans, as represented in the micro-level, social-psychological, and biological needs of all individuals in all societies. But to understand the volatility of the American atomic structure (as indicated in the third axiom or principle), one has to go beyond the first two principles, and pay attention to internal threats within the dominant core, and competitive elections which lead to the possible changes of SG's group status.

The American political system reaches its most volatile tipping point when the two electoral coalitions are evenly matched in federal elections (a typical phenomenon occurring in the most recent two decades). Neither of the two coalitions can enjoy a clear advantage over the other, which puts more pressure on them to maintain their respective policy positions on group relations in order to keep voters' loyalty to win elections.

But, this tipping point may not exist forever, if at all possible, as society does evolve. This occurs because of major demographic shifts, economic development, and changes in cultural and social mores, and the members of dominant group do change over time and political issues concerning the concrete SG threat evolve as well. The key to understanding how these changes, or volatility, may transform the political system from one particular configuration of the atomic structure to another is to analyze the memberships of the two coalitions, and how the two opposing sides inside the core differ on the SGs' political status, and which side wins competitive elections (especially in presidential years), and for how long. These questions will be discussed in the chapters of part II in this book.

Part II

APPLYING THE ATOMIC STRUCTURE THEORY TO AMERICAN POLITICAL DEVELOPMENTS

Chapter 9

The Shift Away from
WASP Domination

The aim of this chapter is to set the stage for applying the atomic structure and its ADVICE principles to explain the implications for the group status of the nation's dominant ethnic and religious group, White Anglo-Saxon Protestants (WASPs), a term coined by Lawrence Fuchs in 1952 (Wright, 2004, 33). An important note before we proceed: Some key players in the founding of the U.S. were Catholic. For example, Daniel Carroll, a signatory of both the Articles of Confederation and the U.S. Constitution, was an influential Catholic figure among the founding fathers.

As introduced in part I, WASPs have been the most dominant group since the founding of the Republic, and its domination continued throughout the nineteenth century and at least through the 1920s, when it enjoyed its peak dominant status. But, since then, that dominant status has ebbed and continued to diminish. The same level of domination that the WASPs group enjoyed for nearly three-fourths of the country's history is no longer applicable.

This chapter takes us through four sections. The first briefly discusses the key roles of the dominant group in the atomic structure, and it points to the most recent peak of the WASP power in the 1920s. The second section introduces two competing views in the research literature on why the WASP decline has occurred—namely, the cultural explanation and the assimilation theses. The third section challenges propositions from these two competing views and subsequently links the WASP decline in dominant status to the atomic structure presented in this book. The atomic structure opens the door to synthesizing cultural and assimilating dynamics without needing to prefer or exclude prior assumptions associated with these two competing views. The fourth section brings the chapter's entire discussion into a cohesive summary to set up the book's remaining chapters.

DOMINANT CORE IN A POLITICAL SYSTEM

Before discussing how WASP domination approached its end in U.S. history, it is imperative to examine the role of the dominant group in a political system. A starting point of agreement references Anthony D. Smith, a prominent scholar of comparative ethnic studies, who argues the dominant ethnic core is the main reason for how modern nation-states were formed (Smith, 2004). Three factors contribute to why the ethnic core took on such a prominent role, according to Smith. First, there is a "relative ethnic homogeneity of the core" that unites the nation, but also expands it. Second, religion often serves as a "unifying factor." Third, the common lineage based on "shared historical memories and an 'ethno-history' . . . provided a repertoire of ethnic myths and symbols of heroes and saints, exploits, battles and sacrifices, on which later generations of the dominant ethnie [ethnic group] have been able to draw when they and their state have been under threat" (Smith, 2004, 20).

Clearly, one could comprehend why WASPs constituted for so long the dominant ethnic and religious core in the United States by incorporating Smith's discussion of the formation of nation-states. English as a language has had that uniting power throughout the nation's history. As noted elsewhere in the book, WASPs became the super-majority of the population at the founding of the Republic. If we use the atomic structure to describe the political establishment when the U.S. Constitution was ratified, WASPs undoubtedly were situated at its core while American Indians, African Americans, and some very small white ethnic and religious groups (e.g., Catholics) were located at the peripheries. Hispanics were not a significant part of the American experience until Florida became a part of the U.S. territory in 1819 (as well as Texas in 1845, along with California and other western states in 1848). The Chinese entered the Pacific West as demand for cheap labor soared as early as in the 1840s, but they also did not gain a significant population presence in the western states until the 1860s. Later, the major influx of eastern and southern Europeans took place between 1880s and 1920s.

Throughout the period of territorial expansion, WASPs strengthened their dominant status. Within the atomic structure core, as discussed already in the last five chapters, WASPs defined and redefined the positions of all groups in the American political system on their own terms. The most recent peak of WASP domination could be seen from the Volstead Act of 1919, prohibiting the consumption of alcohol along with the Johnson-Reed Act of 1924, restricting immigration as based on a quota system for European nations and the complete exclusion of Asians. Both Acts were designed to keep the nation emblematic of the image of WASPs. The Volstead Act was signed by President Woodrow Wilson, a progressive Democrat whose father was a Presbyterian minister. Wilson's Progressivism would "prove remarkably congenial to southern prejudices—as president, he would resegregate the District of Columbia and drive from office many black federal employees" (Kesler, 2012, 35). Defending southern resistance to Reconstruction, Wilson (1902) wrote in his *A History of the American People*, considered then an influential text of the nation's history: "[T]he white men of the South were aroused by the mere instinct of self- preservation to rid themselves, by fair means or foul, of the intolerable burden of governments sustained by the votes of ignorant negroes and conducted in the interest of adventurers" (58).

President Calvin Coolidge, who signed the 1924 immigration quotas law, embraced the idea of the Republican Party as a "lily white" party. He alienated African Americans by declaring that the federal government should not interfere with southern states' local issues (i.e., segregation policy).

As suggested by Smith (2004), the ethnic core's domination also can be demonstrated by its ability to deal with any potential challenge to its governing strengths and squashing any and all external threats. In 1928, Al Smith, who was nominated by the Democratic Party to run for the presidency, was a Catholic anti-prohibition candidate who won numerous supporters in many of the country's urban centers. However, southern white votes and Protestant rural votes formed a united WASP front against the first Catholic nominee from a major political party. Smith was defeated by Herbert Hoover, the Republican candidate, in a landslide.

COMPETING VIEWS ON THE
END OF WASP DOMINATION

If the presidency is used as the only yardstick, surely the two presidential elections after World War II marked the beginning of the end of WASP domination. Dwight D. Eisenhower, a German American, won the election in 1952, and John F. Kennedy, a Catholic, won in 1960. Many scholars have suggested that WASPs lost its domination in the 1960s (Kaufmann, 2004a). Peter Schrag, in noticing the historical change, published his book *The Decline of the WASP* in 1971.

There are three points indicating the loss of WASP domination in the 1960s. First, the Democratic Party was transformed into a multiethnic organization that was dramatically different from the party of Woodrow Wilson, in that Irish, Catholics, and labor unions now played more visible leadership roles.

Second, the U.S. Congress enacted a stream of legislation, which significantly weakened the power of WASPs. The ground for transformative legislation was set by a landmark ruling in the U.S. Supreme Court: *Baker v. Carr* (1962), which confirmed that redistricting was a legitimate constitutional question for federal courts to consider. The practical effects of this ruling reduced the disproportionate power of WASP-dominated rural America. It also handed strong representation geared toward equal redistricting in the country's growing urban centers, thanks to landmark legislation passed by the U.S. Congress and signed by President Lyndon Baines Johnson (e.g., Civil Rights Act, 1964; Voting Rights Act, 1965). Also, the immigration laws were radically changed by replacing the 1924 quota law with the 1965 McCarran Act, which opened the door to Asian and Hispanic immigrants, in particular. In the twenty-first century, attempts to overhaul and modernize the system established by the McCarran Act, because of major demographic shifts representing new immigrants, have been adamantly resisted by many WASPs group members, who would prefer to see immigration law and enforcement return to standards not seen since the peak of WASP-dominant group status in the 1920s.

Radical changes in the political landscape in the 1960s, while providing convincing evidence that WASPs were not as dominant as they were in the 1920s, seemed so strange that one has to raise the questions about why such sudden changes occurred. Also, why WASPs were ceding their status powers to emergent racial and religious minorities? One intuitive answer comes from the political struggle and demands of minorities themselves. Surely, the Civil Rights Movement in the 1950s and 1960s shocked the nation's moral conscience, and racial and ethnic equality issues constituted a driving force for the country's desire for political change.

However, the minority explanation for the loss of WASP domination is certainly not sufficient, to say the least. Consider the timeline: the election of Eisenhower, a Republican, had little if anything to do with the internal changes occurring within the Democratic Party. Kennedy was elected in 1960 before *Baker v. Carr* was decided in 1962, also occurring prior to the most significant and tangible influences of the Civil Rights Movement. Furthermore, the Civil Rights Movement, which was oriented toward protecting minorities already in the country, seemed to be a "stretch" for the cause of immigration liberalization to open the door to potential foreigners of different racial and ethnic backgrounds.

Acknowledging the scale of changes that occurred in the 1960s and the landmark legislation being passed by a still WASP-dominant Congress, some scholars have concluded that the cause for changes could not have been external. Kaufmann (2004b), for example, claimed that "the minorities' struggle against oppression is more of a universal phenomenon and cannot account for key policy and identity shifts" (28) and "it is vital, however, to focus upon the divisions that were emerging within the WASP" (65).

Kaufmann's focus was on WASP elites, and he insisted that "the elite were more strongly pro-immigrant than the rural majority or urban working class" (65). It was one subgroup of elites in particular, which Kaufmann called the "WASP cultural elite," which "abandoned the organic Protestant reform crusades of the early Social Gospel Movement in favor of Liberal Progressivism" (2004b, 78). The birth of Liberal Progressivism, according to Kaufmann, occurred between 1905 and 1917. The WASP cultural elite, furthermore, became the leading voice for policy changes in universities such as University of Chicago and Columbia University, which caused "a pattern of pre-1939 dominant ethnic hegemony slowly giving away to greater openness in the 1940s and 1950s, followed by collapse in the 1960s" (Kaufmann, 2004b, 78). In sum, for Kaufmann, the decline of WASPs in the United States was due to cultural changes primarily of the WASPs' own doing.

Kaufmann's approach of analyzing WASP internal ideological makeup resonates in a more recent study by two Yale University law professors. Chua and Rubenfeld (2014) argue that "modern principles of equality tend to undercut [WASP] group superiority complexes" (20). Moreover, WASPs' previous success as a dominant ethnic group "softens" the urge to be more competitive, and a sense of insecurity has already been eroded among WASPs. More importantly, WASPs' "freedom-loving, get-it-now culture" also "undercuts impulse control" (20).

The cultural analyses surrounding the cause of the WASP decline by Kaufmann, Chua, and Rubenfeld and others with similar conclusions, however, are more speculative than scientific. First, the egalitarian ideology ran much deeper than the political thoughts of the Progressive Era. As demonstrated by Desmond King and Rogers Smith (2005), the egalitarian order, along with the white supremacist group, has always defined the nature of political development in the entire U.S. history. It is not clear why Liberal Progressivism at the beginning of the twentieth century would have become the watershed moment that eroded the unity sustaining WASP homogeneity.

Second, individualism, along with the ideals of work ethic and the "pursuit of happiness," formed the fundamental characteristics of the nation's founding WASPs. "Freedom-loving" and "get-it-now" were as true in the belief system of Thomas Jefferson as it is now for ordinary Americans. Third, survey data, time and time again, have shown that modern whites still hold strong negative opinions against minorities because minorities, especially African Americans, are regarded as those who they perceived to violate the traditional WASP/American values of hard work and self-reliance (Kinder and Sanders, 1996). There is no empirical evidence to make a convincing conclusion that the white electorate in the United States has embraced the equality principle, as advocated by Liberal Progressivism, at the expense of deep-rooted WASP individualism (see chapter 11 for more discussion on racial divide on public opinions).

Indeed, using cultural variables to explain group behaviors has always been an elusive assignment in social science history. Sociologist Steve Bruce blames the decline of Protestants on individualism rather than the egalitarian principle. "Protestantism has at its heart a principle that undermines all group identities: individualism," said Bruce (2004, 129). He elaborates, "If Protestants are true to their stated principles, then they must accept the right of others to disagree with them. If such others become a majority, then, with the appropriate safeguard for the rights of individuals, the Protestants must accept defeat" (129).

No matter whether it is individualism or the egalitarian principle (or both), which has contributed to the decline of the WASP-dominant group status, it is worth noting that individualism (or individual liberty) and equality often appear as contradictory to each other, especially when the issue is how members of social groups should be treated by political institutions (Satori, 1987). It is exactly for this reason why the cultural explanation for the decline in WASP-dominant group status often is controversial. Political scientists have tried to go beyond the limit of cultural explanations. Obviously, the decline has been such a profound event, as evidenced in the politics of the first two decades of the twenty-first century. As a result, it has commanded attention from explanations of more than just one ideological point of emphasis within the WASP community since the beginning of the twentieth century.

Theodore P. Wright, for example, has treated the decline of WASP group dominant status as a much longer, gradual process, which asks for a structural explanation. Wright sees a difference in the United States unlike other areas of the world where ethnic groups lost their political dominance, such as in India, where Muslims in the northern part of the country saw their position eroded between 1757 and 1857. Therefore, it "is possible for this 'ethnic succession' in power to take place more gradually and peacefully with a minimum of violence as the final confirmation of a long trend such as differential migration or birth rates as in the United States" (Wright, 2004, 36). Immigration is essential to comprehending Wright's perspective on WASP decline, as it is a simple fact that WASPs were eventually outnumbered. As he put it, "By 1970 White Protestants comprised a bare majority (55 percent) and 1980 only 20 percent in the census identified themselves as of English descent" (33).

The pace has accelerated recently: "In 2018, there were 151 U.S. counties where Hispanics, Blacks or two much smaller racial and ethnic groups—American Indians and Alaska Natives—made up a majority of the population, according to a Pew Research Center analysis of U.S. Census Bureau data. That was an increase from 110 such counties in 2000" (Schaeffer, 2019). And, notably, "The South and Southwest of the U.S. hold most of the counties where Hispanic, black or indigenous people make up a majority of residents" (Schaeffer, 2019). Wright's point is amplified by changes in how the U.S. Census measures race. There were only three categories in 1790: free white males; free white females; all other free persons and slaves. Up until 1960, it was enumerators who determined an individual's race. In 2000, the census provided options for individuals to select more than one race and, in 2020, the census allowed all Americans (regardless of race) to give more information about their origins.

However, the loss of WASP dominance certainly could not be realized with only the rapid growth of the non-WASP population. Human history has shown that a minority can rule a much larger majority, as was the case in the Yuan Dynasty of China where a very small circle of Mongolian rulers dominated all aspects of political life in fourteenth-century China. Returning to the United States, the question becomes how were non-WASPs able to eventually reach a level of political power that ultimately challenged and ended the WASP-dominant group status?

Wright listed factors that contributed to the demographic and political changes in the country: separation of church and state, democratic franchise, free public education, and cheap land. Most importantly for Wright (2004), assimilation, through the American immigration experience, especially "genetic melting pot" (34), was the penultimate reason for the end of the WASP-dominant group status. Because of the genetic melting pot, "paradoxically, the survival of ethnic group dominance may be dependent, as in the WASP case in America, on failure of 'boundary maintenance', which eventually undermines or completely redefines group identity which is no longer from ancestral origins" (35).

What, then, has become the eventual dominant ethnicity (or ethnies) in the United States, if the original members of the WASP-dominant group lost because of the collapse of their boundaries? Interestingly, Wright concludes with the following:

Thus one must ask: have the WASPs really lost their ethnic dominance in the United States? . . . What strikes me as more accurate is to posit the approaching assimilation, both culturally and linguistically, of all European-origin ethnies plus some Asian into an amorphous amalgam of Euro-Americans (Alba, 1990), distinct from a huge underclass of African-Americans, Native Americans and the darker of Hispanics. So the dominant WASP ethnie has survived, if at all, by so weakening its boundaries in the past two generations and incorporating other groups that it is no longer the same group. (34)

Therefore, for Wright, assimilation led not only to the loss of WASP domination but also a new transformed core in America with a mixture of original members of the WASP-dominant core, all European Americans and some Asians. But, this core also excludes the "huge underclass of African-Americans, Native Americans and the darker of Hispanics," as Wright continues.

This new America is visibly different from the old WASP-dominant America, but it also does not suggest in any way that the old political structure has changed completely. For Wright, the WASPs are still in the core, but that same core now also contains other groups that had been marginalized in the past. It is at this point Wright and other structural analysts (e.g., Anthony Smith, 2004) differ fundamentally from cultural analysts, such as Kaufmann. For cultural analysts, the loss of WASP-dominant status also means that a new American national identity has been born. It is worthy to examine more closely Kaufmann's thesis.

The importance of liberal progressivism for Kaufmann's cultural argument is not only that it led to the decline of dominant ethnicity (i.e., WASPs) in the United States but also that it marked the beginning of a new era of "multiculturalism" in which "dominant ethnicity clearly has no place" (Kaufmann, 2004a, 284). This is because, according to Kaufmann (2004a), "the idea of *dominant* ethnicity represents a violation of both liberal and egalitarian thinking" (284, emphasis in the original) and "the discriminatory legacy of the past provides liberal-egalitarians with a compelling narrative with which to underpin their normative sanctions of 'political correctness'" (288). Praising the following as "surely sound and has been ratified," Kaufmann cites the words from Yael Tamir who stated that "liberals often align themselves with national demands raised by 'underdogs,' be they indigenous peoples, discriminated minorities, or occupied nations, whose plight can easily evoke sympathy."

To what extent is the "liberal and egalitarian thinking" exercising its influence on current political realities? What has been the actual effect of multiculturalism on the WASP's political status? Kaufmann (2004a) claims that "the repression of national ethnicity [e.g., the WASP] is a pan-Western phenomenon" (287). He cites the "white" "British" majority in not only the United States but also Canada and Australia "whose numerical, cultural, socio-economic and political dominance" has disqualified them from multicultural activities or funding. Kaufmann (2004a) argues that "minority ethnic communities were now replacing the old Anglo-Protestant ethnie (or ethnic group) as the recipient of collective privilege" (3).

The disagreements between cultural analysts such as Kaufmann and assimilation scholars such as Wright are about how the American political system has endured various forms of threats while sustaining its structure, which originally was put into place by WASP elites. Their disagreements have led scholars to focusing on different facts. Kaufman emphasizes the scale of changes and the extent to which minorities now can gain group benefits which are not accessible to the white majority. As he puts it, "one might better conceive of what is happening as a continuation of the narrative of dominant ethnic decline as whites and Protestants lose ground to others year after year" (Kaufmann, 2004b, 70).

Wright, on the other hand, stresses the fact that the decline of the WASP-dominant group status was a result of a necessary, successful strategy to embrace demographic changes in American society and its communities. For Wright, "declining dominant majority groups like the North American WASPs may preserve some of their status by extending their boundaries to include kindred populations, but thereby jeopardize the survival of their distinctive identity" (Wright, 2004, 38). To illustrate his point, Wright, provided one example as follows: "My Yankee [WASP] ancestors surrendered Boston politically to the Irish long ago and retreated to business, banking and law from which they could exert indirect influence. This shrewd strategy allowed them to co-opt the Kennedys when that clan reached to the top of Samuel Lubell's 'ethnic ladder' of offices" (Wright, 2004, 38).

The atomic structure approach presented in this book attempts to bridge the differences between the cultural arguments preferred by Kaufman and the assimilation thesis as proposed by Wright. As mutually exclusive as they may sound, there is a way to incorporate the strengths of both scholarly viewpoints. What is missing in both Kaufmann and Wright's accounts of WASP-dominant group status decline is a general theory to explain both the increasing power of liberalism (by no means the only influential ideology today) and why the new white majority group, which has evolved from the old-stock WASPs to all white European descendants, can preserve some of its dominant status in the current political system. Both schools of thought have brought something important to light regarding group relations, such as the increased power of minority groups (who sometimes even enjoy certain policy benefits not available to the white majority), and the central role of whites as a group instead of the originally described WASPs. Nonetheless, what is lacking in both schools is a general theory that can explain coherently for both the end of WASP domination and the political volatility experienced by peripheral groups. This is exactly what the atomic structure and its ADVICE principles are designed to do, as seen in the next chapter.

Chapter 10

Atomic Structure and the WASP Decline

Our examination of the decline of WASP-dominant group status continues from the insights of Kaufmann and Wright, as discussed in the previous chapter. The rising power of minorities has occurred in U.S. politics (according to Kaufmann), but that also does not suggest that the original WASP group has lost its position at the core of the political system (according to Wright). The core now has been enlarged to include all whites of European origin. But, this observation does not automatically lead to the conclusion that there has been no progress in terms of the rights and political power of other minorities.

The coexistence of the increasing influence of liberalism (as reflected by the enhanced group status of minorities) and the preservation of the old WASP status as a part of the core combine to explain the WASP decline. Often the debate between the views of culturalists and assimilationists on WASP decline has treated the enhanced power of minorities and WASP assimilation of certain original peripheral groups as somehow mutually exclusive in a political zero-sum game. The theory introduced in this book, however, allows one to see how both statements are natural consequences of the ADVICE principles that govern the atomic structure. Whites are still much more influential in the atomic structure today than other racial minorities, but also the minorities at the peripheries have made unprecedented advancement toward equality in the political system (see chapter 12 for more details). The conditions for both to occur are related to the political volatility, which naturally occurs within the atomic structure.

To understand the causes for the end of WASP-dominant group status, we need to place the historical role of WASPs back into the original atomic structure. Originally, WASPs were located at the core of the structure because of the group's dominant position. As Harold Lasswell (1936) explained, politics is about "who gets what, when and how." This stresses the importance of politics as an allocation of resources, which is basically a reward-driving defi-nition. Politicians reward those who voted for them. In our atomic structure, the WASPs had the original power to determine the allocation of resources. But due to the existence of multiple groups, WASPs needed to deal with potential threats by way of how WASPs allocated resources.

Threat is especially politically salient because during a voter's information search threat represents negative information, which requires an immediate response. Politics is not just about allocating public resources but also manag-ing threats during volatile periods.

THE RELATIONSHIP BETWEEN
THE CORE AND PERIPHERIES

To prioritize external threats, the dominant group ranks and orders minor-ity groups. Following the attraction and distance axioms (A1 and A2), one can visualize how the minority groups are structurally positioned along the peripheries of the atomic structure. The WASPs initially manage threats through institutional decisions and laws because of their dominant position at the atomic structure core.

In our atomic structure, minorities work to mitigate WASP dominance, which makes their political struggle an external threat to the WASPs. But, such a threat remains at the abstract level because it also represents a chal-lenge to the WASP's overall position at the atomic structure core. The power of abstract threat is, as demonstrated in chapter 5, that it determines the response range a particular minority group will receive from WASPs. The more distant a group appears to be from WASPs, the more threatening it is to the WASP core (the distance principle), thus the response range is enlarged to include some potentially harsh political treatment (the volatility principle). It is, however, the existence of concrete minority threat that divides WASPs about how a minority should be treated at a given time. We dig deeper here.

The existence of a concrete threat suggests that some WASPs feel "con-cretely" threatened by a minority, and therefore they have a natural political tendency to demand more political domination over the threatening minority group. This applies to southern WASPs during slavery who saw Blacks as a concrete threat, and their political choices had been based on how they could maintain their dominance over Black slaves for their own benefits. But not all WASPs subscribed to this during the antebellum period. WASPs in the north-east U.S. along with members of the newly established Republican Party did not see Blacks the same way. On the contrary, they saw southern WASPs as a greater threat on the issue of slavery, because the political advantage of south-ern WASPs came at the expense of northeastern and Republican WASPs.

In sum, the coexistence of abstract and concrete threats naturally led to two competing political coalitions inside the WASP core (the internal threat principle). Furthermore, the winning political coalition temporarily plays a greater role in determining the political status of the minority group under discussion (the competitive-election principle).

THE RELATIONSHIP BETWEEN THE
TWO POLITICAL COALITIONS

Obviously, from the perspective of WASPs as the dominant core, the atomic structure based on the ADVICE principles is a collectively beneficial political structure if they can maintain it. It is exactly for this reason the political coalition, which is concretely threatened by a minority group (as such, in this book, members of this coalition are referred to as traditionalists), always campaigns based on the theme that WASP collective group interest should be more important than the dispute between the two WASP political coalitions. For example, Stephen Douglas, then the Democratic Party leader, said during one of the Lincoln-Douglas debates in 1858:

> It must be borne in mind that when that Declaration was put forth every one of the thirteen colonies were slave-holding colonies, and every man who signed that instrument represented a slaveholding constituency. Recollect, also, that no one of them emancipated his slaves, much less put them on an equality with himself, after he signed the Declaration . . . this government was made by our fathers on the white basis. It was made by white men for the benefit of white men and their posterity forever, and was intended to be administered by white men in all time to come. (Steinfield, 1970, 28–29)

Douglas's appeal would have sounded persuasive if WASPs only looked at their group interest as the sole element of the decision-making process. Jumping forward, racist policies such as the 1924 immigration-quota law were based entirely on a discredited ideology backing eugenics and manipulated elements of social Darwinism that glorified the WASP position. But, in the long run, these racist views have been difficult to sustain and prevail, especially as political control of the U.S. Congress has changed and taken on new leaders. This is not just because, as culturalists would argue, this view requires a deep-seated, never-changing racist ideology. More importantly, from a structural perspective, if the peripheral groups of the political system are disenfranchised, then the internal threat within the dominant group naturally becomes the largest threat to each other.

One good example of this greater internal threat when there were minimum external threats from other racial and religious minorities is the women's suffrage movement occurring when the WASPs themselves were reaching the peak of their political power in the 1910s. The demand for suffrage of [white] women also reached the peak, culminating in a victory in 1920, which threatened the status quo inside the WASP-dominant group. Note, coincidentally, that many early feminists were hostile to African Americans in the South, and they believed in WASP superiority (see Elizabeth G. McRae 2018's *Mothers of Massive Resistance* on southern white women's role in protecting racial segregation during the 1920s and 1940s).

It must be emphasized that the internal threat, due to the two political coalitions, is also a threat to the allocation of resources that benefits one coalition at the expense of the other (Axiom 4). As discussed in chapter 8, there is always competition between the two alliances that conceivably can win elections through minimum winning coalitions. Moreover, the two coalitions represent the institutional power of the U.S. government, because they have amassed a long track record of governance. The two coalitions must compete for partisan loyalty, and the two coalitions find their enemies in any groups who threaten their probabilities of winning. The threat can be internal coming from members of the same dominant group or external from members of out-groups. The fact that not all members of the dominant group are in the winning and governing coalition determines the main evolutionary process of U.S. politics.

Of course, our atomic structure could allow the permanent domination of WASPs over the minority groups based on one condition: the political coalition inside the WASPs core becomes an overwhelming majority entity which dictates the federal institution to implement racist policies. In other words, "one of the major parties substantially disappeared" when an overwhelming majority coalition is formed (Riker, 1962, 56). This overwhelming majority coalition, or labeled as a grand coalition by Riker, did exist in U.S. history. Riker (1962) examined three "grand coalitions" in the nineteenth century: the "era of good feeling" when the Jeffersonian Republican dominated (ca. 1820); the period after 1852 when the Whig party dissolved; and the period around 1872 "when the Democratic party substantially disappeared from Presidential politics" (56). The first two of these three grand coalitions led to some of the most racist policies enacted and slavery was protected.

But no grand coalitions can sustain forever or even for long periods in the experience of American constitutional democracy. The internal divisions that emerge inside grand coalitions in addition to the disproportional benefits of dominating the minority group, such as Black slaves, jointly have led to the disintegration of grand coalitions. The fixed racist super-majority, even within the WASP-dominant group, could not have been sustainable over time, due to the nature of our proposed atomic structure and its ADVICE principles.

More importantly, the electorate itself changed over time, as eloquently described by Wright (see the last chapter). The most important consequence of the change in the national electorate refers to the probabilities of winning for political parties in competitive elections, and thus the cyclical rise and fall of political group status (the competitive election principle). In the next chapter, we will return to this important point in the context of the more recent eras. The changing racial composition of the electorate could be seen, on the one hand, as a function of immigration. For example, immigration was triggered by the labor demand of major industrialization projects, such as railroad construction and gold mining in the West, and economic competition that forced big business to seek cheap labor (Wright, 2004).

On the other hand, the change in the electorate's racial composition, it should be pointed out, can also be political. Political parties may intentionally plan to change the electorate so that they can be in an advantageous location in the coalition space. According to Riker (1962), for example, the first major defeat of a former majority party (the Federalists) in 1816 occurred because of the strategy of Jeffersonian Republicans to enlarge the electorate by admitting new trans-Appalachian states (56–57). Similarly, the postbellum Reconstruction Era created opportunity for the Republican Party to attempt incorporating southern Black voters into the Republican Party. FDR's New Deal Coalition was expanded because of the incorporation of loyal white Catholic voters and the working class.

Sometimes, when a political party grows to the extent where it represents an "overwhelming majority" or "grand coalition," there is strong incentive for the party leaders to "minimize" it. This is because "every coalition has internal conflicts over the division of spoils" (Riker, 1962, 66). The New Deal Coalition was "restructured" because LBJ (President Johnson) realized southern whites were not a loyal sector in the Democratic Party, and he "threw them out of the coalition" in exchange for Black voter loyalty and potentially new minority immigrant converts. In this way, he helped reduce the previous overwhelming New Deal coalition to a size close to a minimum winning coalition. In doing so, the original minority groups may be integrated into the governing political coalition, and the dominance of WASPs as a whole is naturally weakened. Overall, the atomic structure, especially with its internal threat and competitive election principles (Axioms 4 and 5), produces a continuing political dynamic which leads to conditions of stability, as well as volatility affecting all groups.

THE RELATIONSHIP BETWEEN THE PERIPHERIES

As briefly discussed above, all minority groups located at the peripheries in the atomic structure seek to reduce the domination of the core group (e.g., the WASPs in the United States) for enhanced group status of their own. This creates a possibility for coalitions among minority groups for a common purpose. They can be united to fight for the equality of all groups. But, throughout American history, this united front of all minority groups against the dominant majority has not occurred as often as one might have perceived. The Civil Rights Movement during the 1960s and 1970s and the Obama electoral coalition were arguably the most exemplary of such a united front.

Throughout history, however, more often we see examples of conflicts between and among peripheral groups. "Although black, Latino, and Asian American elites were building coalitions, the masses of these three groups were increasingly in competition for scarce resources" according to a study of multiple minority groups (McClain et al., 2008, 162). A graphic example of race riots involving minority groups fighting against each other occurred in 1992 in Los Angeles, after a jury acquitted the police officer who used excessive force and a deadly weapon against Rodney King. The riot continued for more than six days and killed fifty-three people and was ended only when the military was called.

Let us look at the reasons for potential conflicts, rather than cooperation, between minority groups. First, the reduction of core group dominance will not lead to an equal distribution of benefits to the groups located at the peripheries. This is because, based on our attraction axiom (A1) and distance axiom (A2), peripheries do not rise to the same level of external threat to the core, and historically the peripheries have been treated differently by the core because of these volatile threats (A3). Thus, the relationships between the peripheries are structured by the ranking order of the groups from the perspective of the dominant group.

For example, reiterating a point brought up in part I, German Americans are much closer to southern Europeans (who are mostly Catholic), than, to say, African Americans. In this sense, it is important to remember that the peripheral groups as minority entities are "ordered" in terms of their potential threat to the core group in the first place. Recent studies, for example, have shown that African American resentment toward the American Jews, despite their political alliance during the Civil Rights Movement, was related to their perception that Jews had gained more benefits from the political system, which favored white Jews more than African Americans (King and Weiner, 2014; also see Marc Dollinger 2018's *Black Power, Jewish Politics* for an analysis of the complexity of relationships between Blacks and Jews, and the unique Jewish perspective on racial alliance).

Second, from the perspective of minority groups themselves, all other minority groups are also ordered, based on how they perceive threats from other minority groups. The minorities' perception of external group threats also follows the attraction principle. For example, white Catholics may perceive a racial minority as a major threat to themselves, and this minority threat is greater than the threat from the dominant core group because white Catholics have shared more similarities with WASPs. In the 1860–1880s, white Catholics regarded the Chinese immigrants as their major political threat, even though white Catholics in general preferred more friendly immigration policy toward other Europeans.

The anti-Chinese labor movement was led by Denis Kearney's Workingmen's Party. Kearney was a white Catholic, and he "accused the Chinese of working hand-in-hand with monopolies, of accepting slave wages, and of robbing the white man of his job . . . Kearney's speeches always ended with the slogan, 'the Chinese must go!'" (Steinfield, 1970, 125). Major violent acts were conducted by white Catholic laborers against their Chinese counterparts in various industrial sites where Chinese laborers worked side-by-side with members of the white working class.

> During this period, the Chinese were stoned and robbed, assaulted and murdered. Hoodlums would organize attacks against the Chinese camps as sport, for they knew the Chinese could not obtain redress. In the spring of 1876, the Chinese were driven from small towns and camps, their quarters burned. Some Chinese were killed or injured. In June of 1876, a violent attack was made upon them at Truckee . . . In 1885, the infamous massacre of twenty-eight Chinese in Rock Spring, Wyoming, occurred. (Steinfield, 1970, 125–126)

Third, different minority groups are perceived differently by the WASPs not only because of abstract threats from these minority groups but also due to various concrete threats perceived by particular WASP subgroups. As a result, different political coalitions may be formed, and minority groups may find themselves on opposing sides. We again use the Chinese exclusion legislation of 1882 as an example. It is tempting to assume that the exclusion law was a product of WASP discrimination against the Chinese. But, in reality, WASP discrimination against the Chinese was not a significant factor at all. Many WASP subgroups actually favored the Chinese immigrants. These subgroups included elite Protestant Republicans, Protestant clergymen, big business, and "mainstream press (out of the West)" (Kaufmann, 2004a, 59).

The New York Herald, for instance, published an editorial in 1870 to welcome Chinese labor. The editorial, however, deployed racist language against African Americans:

They [Chinese] are intelligent, industrious, frugal . . . Shall a race of these qualities be ruled out of a constitution that has taken in the depraved, slothful, stupid and brutal African? . . . If it falls to our lot to give to the human family that unity which it has lost—to make it one in language, one in religion, one in nationality—we shall not as a people, have lived in vain . . . I say Welcome to John Chinaman. (Harper, 1980, 219)

Because of the concrete threat from newly freed African Americans, even southern WASP elites welcomed the Chinese laborers. Politicians, even southern KKK founder Nathan Bedford Forrest, supported welcoming more Chinese immigrants to contain Black labor demands after the Civil War (Kaufmann, 2004a, 63–64). At the end of the political confrontations concerning the Chinese labor issue, the coalition between WASP working class and the white Catholics prevailed. The unionized workers of this political coalition, such as the Knights of Labor, won major legislative battles at the federal and state levels. In addition to the *1882 Chinese Exclusion Act*, federal and state laws also enacted strict bans on contract labor and the restriction of foreign-born workers from some specific types of employment (Higham, 1988, 46–49).

On the surface, the exclusion of the Chinese, stretching from 1882 to the end of World War II, seemed to suggest that the dominant WASP group would become even more dominant, as the Chinese (as well as other major Asian groups in the following decades) were excluded from the political system. In actuality, there was a price to be exacted, as far as the dominant WASP group status is concerned. The Chinese exclusion facilitated the integration of white Catholics, especially those with northern and western European ancestry, into the dominant core of the atomic structure.

ASSIMILATION OF WHITE CATHOLICS TO THE CORE

Within the atomic structure, the peripheral groups form three kinds of threats. First, they may be a threat to the whole dominant group. Second, they may be a concrete threat to a subset of the dominant group. Third, they may also be a threat to other minority groups.

For the first type of threat (i.e., when a peripheral [or subordinate] group is perceived as threatening the dominant group as a whole), the dominant group will respond hostilely to the subordinate group. For example, before the 1848 Guadalupe Hidalgo Treaty, Mexicans did not constitute a threat to the WASP core. Despite opposition from southern elites, Western expansionists successfully secured the treaty, which granted citizen and property rights to Mexicans. But, the expansionists quickly turned hostile toward Mexicans and used all means possible to occupy Mexican lands. Mexican Americans, who had no support from inside the WASP core, were seen as a threat.

However, it is the second and/or third type of threats—that is, threats to a subset of the dominant group and/or threats to other minority groups that most likely have the potential to change the atomic structure. In such cases, one or more subordinate groups will become useful (at least, temporarily so) for winning federal elections. Let us examine a few possible scenarios.

When a subordinate (or peripheral) group can be used to achieve political gain for a key subset of the core group, especially the winning coalition, this subordinate group could face heightened hostility, especially if it is used as a scapegoat. For example, the Republican Party used the issue of polygamy as a weapon against the Democratic Party in the 1850s. "The Democratic-supported Kansas–Nebraska Act of 1854 had given the people the right to choose whether their states would be slave or free. The Republicans asserted that if this kind of choice were lawful, then the people of Utah would be able to vote in polygamy as lawful in their area" (Wald and Calhoun- Brown, 2011, 300). In this scenario, the LDS Church became the political scapegoat and Utah would not be able to gain statehood until more than forty years later.

In a scenario where the subordinate group is treated with minimum hostility by WASPs, it becomes useful for neutralizing the risks of economic loss such as those posed by strikebreakers. Both African Americans and Asians (especially the Chinese) were used as strikebreakers to deal with potential threat from WASPs and members of the white Catholic working class. Sometimes, a minority group is given the political privilege to which even some WASPs are denied access. For example, affirmative action policies have been used to offer Blacks, Hispanics, American Indians, and other historically marginalized groups previously unavailable opportunities to gain education and/or find jobs or career promotional paths. This mandated privilege is normally supported by one electoral coalition and opposed by the other, because the minority group support is vital to the electoral success of one of the two coalitions inside the core. Again, it is important to remember that peripheral (or subordinate) groups often will be taken advantage of by the dominant group. But, the benefits and/or payments are usually not the same for the two coalitions inside the dominant groups. This often is the driving force for the internal competition inside the dominant core.

A lasting impact of the second and/or third sort of threats on the atomic structure, however, occurs when a minority group is completely integrated into the political core. This integration certainly has happened to whites of European origins, as Wright (2004) has explained regarding the broken boundary of the original WASP. As discussed above, white Catholics achieved a major political victory by joining the WASP working class in unionized organizations to legislate immigration policies in their favor.

The final political integration of white Catholics into the core of the atomic structure, nevertheless, took five more decades after the 1882 Chinese Exclusion Act. A crucial development, in addition to the growth of immigrant population from eastern and southern Europe in those decades, was the rise of political machines in major cities, such as Chicago and New York. The machines not only trained white ethnic groups politically at the local level but also made them a formidable force inside the Democratic Party at the national level. FDR's New Deal coalition finally consolidated the role of white Catholics in the core of the atomic structure. Before the end of the 1980s, the integration of white Catholics into the nation's core economic and social systems was also completed based on all major social-economic indicators (Wright, 2004; Kaufmann, 2004a).

The integration of white Catholics into the core signaled a monumental change in the atomic structure of the U.S. political system. The core was enlarged to the extent that today it basically contained whites of all European origins, though the Latter-day Saints as a religious minority group still struggled to gain full acceptance into the core, as we have seen from Romney's two presidential campaigns. The original WASPs, in the meantime, have lost the monopoly in making nation's institutional decisions to their group's preferences. This change, however, does not mean that WASPs nowadays have become secondary in the atomic structure. Unlike the argument of minority advantage made not only by scholars such as Kaufmann (2004) but also by white politicians today (see the next three chapters), the white electorate remains the core of the atomic structure. Also, it is white voters still playing a primary role in shaping the nation's public policies in spite of the fact the label of WASPs is becoming irrelevant at an accelerating pace. We will empirically examine this claim in the next chapter.

The nature of the atomic structure compels all minority groups hoping to be integrated into the dominant core. But, to date, the integration of minorities, other than non-WASP European Americans, has been unsuccessful. Wright (2004) argues that lighter-skin Asians already have been assimilated into the WASP-dominant coalition status, but not African Americans, Native Americans, and Hispanics. However, Wright does not provide an operational definition of assimilation. Scholars such as Yinger (1985) and Hero (1992) emphasize that assimilation as a process should be multidimensional. A peripheral group that has been assimilated is a "group of persons with similar foreign [or ethnic] origins, knowledge of which in no way gives a better prediction or estimation of their relevant social characteristics than does knowledge of the behavior of the total population of the community or nation involved" (Yinger, 1985, 30–31). For Hero (1992), "a group may be defined as a group, but as it becomes more assimilated it becomes less noticeably different—socially, politically, economically—from the rest of society"

(45). At least, politically the assimilated groups should have similar rates of registration, voting and officeholding as the dominant core, and economically "full integration would mean that occupational and income distribution of an ethnic group matched those of the whole society" (Yinger, 1985, 32).

The above measures of assimilation certainly would not indicate that assimilation has been fully achieved for Asians, African Americans, Native Americans and Hispanics, with the only exception of Asian Americans' economic status. The next chapter will examine the political, especially electoral, power of these minority groups in greater detail, and show why given the rising electoral power of minority groups, the newly expanded core (i.e., all whites of European origin) still constitute the dominant power in the atomic structure of the American political system.

CONCLUSION

Since the founding of the Republic, WASPs had dominated the nation's political system for more than 150 years. The prohibition and immigration laws passed in the 1920s marked the last peak of WASP power, when the United States was utterly against anything non-WASP in its public policymaking. This overwhelming power of the WASP-dominant group, however, hid an internal mechanism that has worked against its intentions of total domination. The WASP decline seemed to occur overnight, relatively speaking. In the 1960s, the WASP monopoly of political power was clearly gone. What happened before the 1960s? And, what happened next?

The scholarship on the WASP-dominant group status decline is divided into two competing views. The first suggests that the internal ideological division within the WASPs themselves, especially arising from cultural and ideological differences, was the main reason for the loss of WASP domination. In particular, this view holds that liberal progressivism took over not only the academic world but also the political arena. A new political system was born to represent the ideas grounded in egalitarian principles. Furthermore, the once dominant WASP power was replaced by a new political structure that emphasized the minority powers in the name of multiculturalism.

The second view offers a different perspective. Indeed, the WASPs lost complete control of the system. But the loss was due to the broken boundary of what defined WASPs in the first place. Assimilation, especially the "genetic melting pot" by using Wright's phrase, made the original WASPs a new dominant group, enlarged by mixing with other white ethnic and religious groups. Assimilation may even include some racial minorities, such as light-skin Asians, but other traditionally marginalized groups, such as African Americans, Native Americans, and Hispanics, are still at the peripheries.

In this chapter as well as the previous one, I argued that both camps of scholarly analysis brought some important insights into the factors that contributed to the decline of the WASPs. But they also missed the fundamental structure that has caused some of the phenomena, as discussed in these two views. Certainly there was always division among the WASPs, but it was not for ideological reasons only that the division contributed to the decline. We must consider the two electoral coalitions that formed different relationships with the minority groups, which fundamentally changed how politics evolved throughout history. In the meantime, assimilation did occur for whites of European origins, but not for the "genetic" reason primarily advanced. The assimilation was actually a result of WASPs' internal struggles and their responses to a political environment filled with multiple threats.

In the United States, there has been a constant need for groups to deal with multiple threats simultaneously. The atomic structure, as introduced in this book, could elucidate how to sort out clearly the complex relationships between voters and political figures, including the relationships between and among minority groups. To go beyond the existing research literature, I illustrate in this chapter how groups, including the dominant WASPs, reacted to each other when various threats were perceived. By using particular historical events, such as the 1992 racial riots in Los Angeles and the 1882 Chinese Exclusion Act, I have placed all of the groups back into the atomic structure and have analyzed how such groups may act differently. White Catholics, for example, were the main force behind the *Chinese Exclusion Act*, and they were assimilated for the WASP electoral coalition to defeat its main political threat—the other WASP electoral coalition.

The complete integration of white Catholics, including political, economic, and social assimilation, was finalized in the 1960s, which made the WASP as a concept politically less irrelevant. The current structure, however, unlike the view of culturalists such as Kaufmann, maintains the original characteristics of the atomic structure, though the core now is much larger as it contains European Americans. Minorities have enjoyed unprecedented electoral success, but it also does not mean that whites, the new core of the atomic structure, are not politically powerful. On the contrary, their domination (certainly much less than that of historical WASPs) is still the primary factor shaping national politics. We turn to this topic in more detail in the next chapter.

Chapter 11

The Core of the New Atomic Structure

The previous two chapters explain how the external multiple threats and the internal competition within the WASP-dominant group had led to the most significant political development in the atomic structure—the end of WASP domination at its core. The redefined core of this atomic structure now includes all whites of European origins. The ethnicity of their European origins has become irrelevant in their political status, and they have been incorporated into the core of the atomic structure, which, in turn, has expanded and diversified the core.

The implications of the increasing amplitude of heterogeneity among whites at the core of the new atomic structure, as WASP domination has ended, cannot be overstated. Chief among these implications are the fragmentations of the white electorate, which has enhanced the level of internal threats inside the atomic core, and the multiplicities of issue politics which allow more feasible ways to build electoral coalitions (e.g., climate crisis, reproductive rights, safety nets for economically disadvantaged, immigration reform). In short, the updated core of atomic structure since the Civil Rights Movement Era has led to an era of political volatility, a topic to be discussed at greater length in the next two chapters. For now, the focus is on the relationship between the core and the peripheries. Put differently, we examine the relative influences of the white electorate *vis-a-vis* racial minorities.

Along with this change of the atomic core is a body of laws intended to secure unprecedented constitutional and legal protections for minority rights of enfranchisement. The landmark *Voting Rights Act* of 1965, for example, effectively enfranchised minority voters at the federal, state, and local levels, which eventually led to elections of non-white politicians at all levels of local, state, and federal government. There is no dispute that the political influence of minorities reached a new level with Obama's election in 2008 as the nation's first Black president, especially if we consider the significance of descriptive representation of minorities in the federal government. For example, "more than one-in-five voting members (22%) of the U.S. House of Representatives and Senate are racial or ethnic minorities, making the 116th Congress the most racially and ethnically diverse in history" (Bialik, 2019). As a comparison, the 107th Congress (2001–03) had sixty-three minority members so the makeup represented a gain of 84% in sixteen years. As the 2020 general election was decided, the 117th Congress included fifty-nine African Americans, forty-five Latinos, eighteen Asians, and five Native Americans (a total of 127 minorities, or a gain of more than 100% in 20 years).

But, whether or not the rise of minority political status has occurred at the expense of white voters at the core of the atomic structure remains a divisive and unresolved issue. Mo Brooks, U.S. Representative for Alabama's 5th congressional district, claimed in 2014 that "if you look at current federal law, there is only one skin color that you can lawfully discriminate against. That's Caucasians—whites." According to a survey conducted by the Public Religious Research Institute, Brook's view was shared by many whites, and two-thirds of the Republicans, in particular, agreed with Brooks from Alabama (Ingraham, 2014).

There have been political changes that appear to support the view expressed by Brooks. The perception of many white voters (especially in the electoral base of President Trump's support) of the rising power of minorities at the expense of the white racial group is not just a reaction to unprecedented minority electoral success at the federal, state, and local levels across the country in the past four decades. More importantly, there have been laws, which also have been affirmed by federal courts, as well as the U.S. Supreme Court, that were aimed at protecting minorities. These new laws addressed historic inequalities, many of which were designed to remedy past racial discriminations against Blacks and other minorities (Smith and King, 2011). The creation of "majority-minority districts" (MMDs) perhaps has led to the most widespread white resentment against the "special favor" given to the minorities. Furthermore, "such districts," as King and Smith indicated, "had long been under attack by proponents of color-blind decision makings and by many proponents of race-conscious approaches who regarded majority-minority districts as often operating to weaken, not to enhance, the political influence of nonwhites" (168). In the minds of many white citizens as well as political writers, the creation of MMDs and the use of voting rights litigations, just like affirmative action programs, simply revealed the fact that whites had been subjected to reverse discrimination (Thernstrom and Thernstrom, 1999). Even President Obama "did not explicitly advocate majority-minority districts" (King and Smith, 2011, 168). During the Trump administration, the emphasis on protecting minority voting rights came mainly from private plaintiffs rather than the U.S. Department of Justice (DOJ) as in previous Republican and Democratic administrations. Between 2018 and 2020, there was not a single voting rights case brought up by the Trump administration, according to DOJ's own online publication.

Politicians on the left, described as "the racial-conscious alliance" by King and Smith (2011), emphasize that despite the legislative and judiciary decisions aimed to protect racial minorities, measures of income disparity between whites and minorities, among many other important socio-political factors, continue to show that minorities disproportionally suffer from unequal material conditions and the effects arising from past or current racial discriminatory practices in the workplace, education, and other areas. But, it also should be emphasized the conditions of economic inequality existing in the United States do not alone change the perception of white voters that minorities are protected by certain federal laws, programs, and regulations (including, for example, affirmative action) not available to white voters.

Furthermore, whites as a racial group are no longer the clear winner in the measure of median family income for more than a decade (see table 11.1). Asian Americans, as a racial group, have been on top in terms of median family income. Conservative thinkers have long been attacking the use of economic indicators as the basis of political changes. As early as in the 1970s, Harvey Mansfield, a prominent white conservative philosopher from Harvard University, summarized the Democratic left as the party preoccupied by an unrealistic agenda based on material "sameness" (1978). Black conservative thinkers, such as Shelby Steele, even accuse minority politicians and their white Democratic colleagues of using the political tactic of "white guilt" in an attempt to morally "highjack" white voters for the liberal agenda. For Steele (2008), Obama was simply the political beneficiary of this unfair Black advantage.

The political confrontational style and racially charged rhetoric by both the left and right led to partisan gridlock and polarization during the Obama Administration, dynamics which were cemented in the subsequent Trump Administration. *Still a House Divided* (Smith and King, 2011) documents the historical rivalry between the race-conscious and color-blind alliances. The two racial alliances attack each other by selectively using empirical evidence for the benefit of their own arguments, and no compromise seems likely given the contentious nature of the rivalry between the two alliances. I submit in this chapter that there is another way to determine whether or not white voters have become the victims of the reconfiguration of the atomic structure since the end of WASP domination.

More importantly, I argue that the atomic structure presented in the previous chapters explains why it is possible that the rise of minority political

Table 11.1   Median Household Income in 2019, by Race

Race	In U.S.$	Rank
Asian	$98,174	1
White	$76,075	2
Hispanic	$56,113	3
Black	$46,073	4

Source: Created by the author with the source from https://www.epi.org/blog/racial-disparities-in-income
-and-poverty-remain-largely-unchanged-amid-strong-income-growth-in-2019/

influence occurred simultaneously with the integration of all white Europeans into the core of the atomic structure, starting in the 1960s. And, to be direct, there is a continuing and, relatively speaking, greater influence on the federal government from white voters over their non-white peers. The feature of white voters at the core of the atomic structure regarding their ability to exercise the central role in the decision-making process of governance, especially at the federal level, has endured to date. The point will be made more precise if we consider Harris and Liberman's (2013) call: "What remains relatively unexplored and unexplained, however, is how to account for variation in the state's capacity and inclination to protect civil rights and promote racial equality—over time, across policy domains, and across geography, among other sources of variability" (20). I suggest that the atomic structure, especially the one that has evolved since the end of WASP-dominant group status, potentially offers an ideally comprehensive, coherent explanation for the variability (or volatility, as applied in this text) that Harris and Liberman asked scholars to consider.

Though it is possible that sometimes one group's gain arrives at the loss of another, this zero-sum type of policy output is not always true in the atomic structure. The tendency to regard the racial competition as a zero-sum game itself, either by whites or minority groups, indicates that most Americans still perceive the political world along the racial lines—which is a manifestation of how our attraction principle (A1) still holds true today. But, it also is the positive, productive feature of the atomic structure (i.e., making progress for multiple groups in the long run—a point I will return in the concluding chapter) which often is lost in the debates between the race-conscious and color-blind electoral coalitions. Thanks to the atomic structure, the race-conscious alliance succeeded in electing Obama, but the color-blind alliance also was able to come out of the Obama era to elect the candidate of their own: President Trump. These elections, as this book demonstrates, are the results of the built-in competitive and volatile nature of the political struggles occurring in the atomic structure.

Let's focus initially on why whites as a group still enjoy relatively greater influence on the federal government, a key feature of the atomic structure in the period following the Civil Rights Movement Era. This chapter will examine the position of whites at the core of the modern-day atomic structure, as based on their central roles in the two-party system, the presidential and congressional elections, and their representation in the legislative policy-making processes. In order to establish the claim that whites still reside at the core of the contemporary atomic structure, one should acknowledge that white voters remain the dominant force in the Republican Party and a key voting bloc in the Democratic Party. Thus, they remain the center of attention for candidates from both parties.

Second, the white turnout in presidential elections remains a formidable majority, although the size of that majority has been decreasing steadily since 1984 from roughly 85 percent in 1988 to just below 74 percent in 2016, according to political scientist Michael McDonald's longitudinal turnout measure (United States Elections Study Project, 2020). The early data from the 2020 exit polls (not as reliable as in the past due to COVID-19 effect on election-day voting) showed that at least 67 percent of the 2020 electorate were white voters. Finally, I will demonstrate that the federal government has indeed responded to white political demand at a disproportionally greater rate than to those of racial minority groups.

WHITES AS A GROUP

To establish our claim that white voters remain at the core of the new atomic structure after the end of WASP domination, let us revisit the first axiom introduced in this book—the attraction principle (A1). Are white voters in general still subject to this principle in the contemporary era and, by and large, are they attracted to each other at least based on measures of affect? We will focus on affect presently and leave the consideration of white cognitive component of political attitude to the next chapter. This is because the validity of the atomic structure is grounded on the fundamental principle of human psychology, which indicates that voters are more likely to be affectively attracted to people who are similar to them. This was a major claim of intuitionists starting from the day of David Hume (as referenced in the introduction to the book). To claim that there is still an atomic structure after the end of WASP-dominant group status, it is critical to prove that the attraction principle (A1) is still operational. The new atomic core is still a political group, though it is no longer WASPs only. The grouping of whites (not WASPs but more commonly referred to as non-Hispanic whites) as a whole has become much more politically robust today than ever, a theme that Trump highlighted repeatedly in his 2016 campaign (see chapter 13).

We use the thermometer ratings on racial groups to examine empirically the validity of the attraction principle. Scholars of ethnocentrism recently have relied on this measure of group ranking based on affect (e.g., Kinder and Kam, 2010). In the American National Election Studies (NES) data, the respondents were asked to rate their own racial group, as well as other racial groups between 0 and 100. The higher the score, the warmer the feeling toward a group. A 50° mark suggests that the respondent does not feel "particularly warm or cold" toward a racial group. Figure 11.1 shows the long-term trend of racial attraction gaps for non-Hispanic whites, as based on NES data from 1976 to 2016.

It is clear that non-Hispanic whites have consistently shown the warmest feeling about themselves in the last four decades. The mean of non-Hispanic whites' thermometer scores of themselves has been within the range of 70 and 80, while none of the other racial minority groups has scored more than 70 throughout the comparable period. This finding supports the central claim of the proposed atomic structure. That is, white voters are attracted more

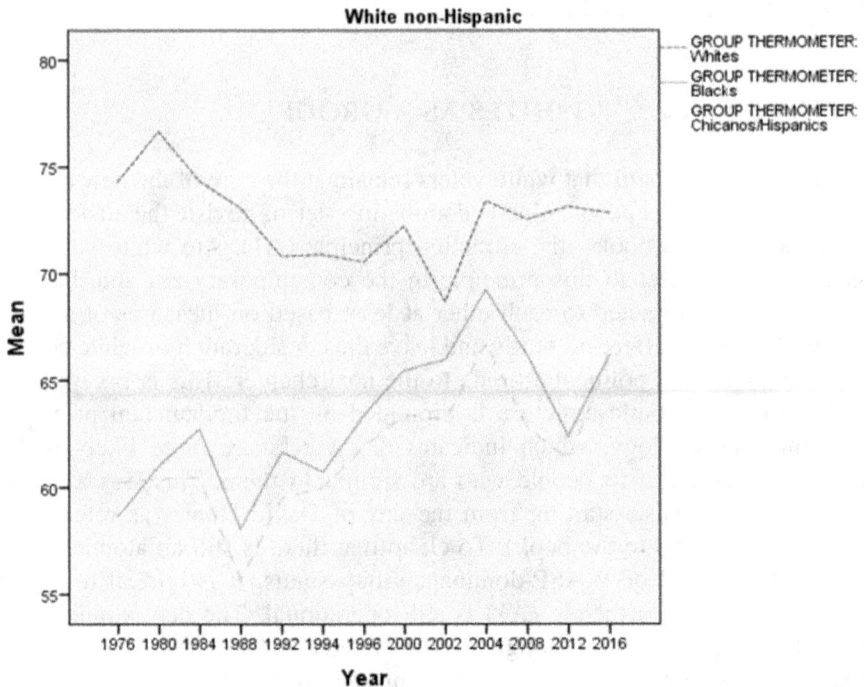

Figure 11.1   Non-Hispanic Whites' Racial Group Thermometer Ratings, NES 1976–2016. Created by the author with the data source from American National Election Study (ANES), 1976–2016.

likely to those who are similar to themselves. The white racial category still matters to them, at least emotionally.

Figure 11.1 also shows that the racial attraction gap between non-Hispanic whites and racial minorities has narrowed during the last three decades of the twentieth century. In fact, non-Hispanic whites were "closest" to Black and Hispanic voters during both terms of President George W. Bush. That "warm" thermometer reading of whites toward these two minority groups, however, turned out to be short lived. The emotional racial gap, as far as non-Hispanic whites were concerned, widened significantly during the Obama Administration, especially in the 2012 presidential election.

To examine non-Hispanic whites' religious thermometer ratings, we use figure 11.2, as based on the ANES survey data. Two important observations deserve attention. Protestants, as the dominant religious group, have lost their most favored group rating since the end of the 1960s. Meanwhile, Catholic and Jewish religious affiliations have been received as warmly as Protestants in more recent decades. The end of WASP domination in the atomic structure, thus, was not only reflected by the fact that WASPs lost their dominant political status but also, more importantly, was revealed through the affect dynamics of the white electorate. Incidentally, the NES did not ask respondents to

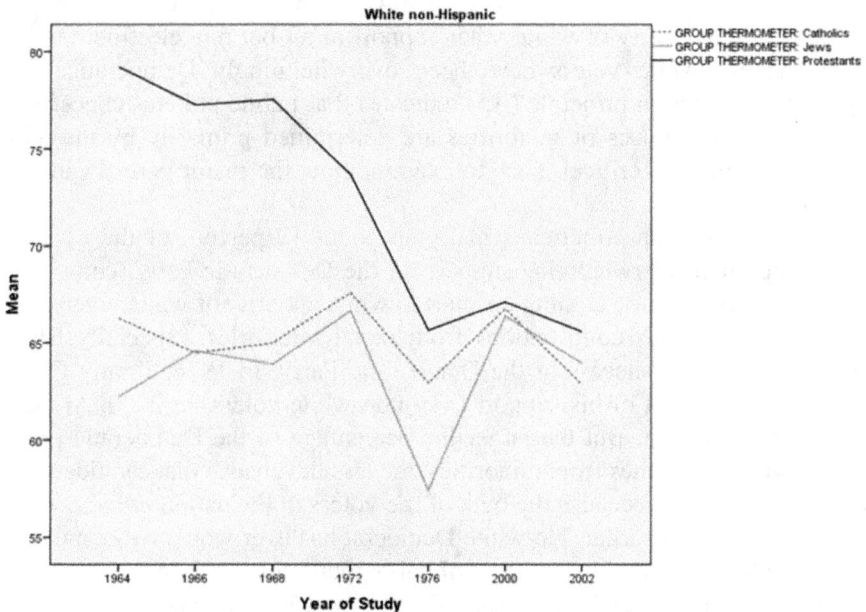

Figure 11.2   Non-Hispanic Whites' Religious Group Thermometer Ratings, NES 1964–2002. Created by the author with the data source from American National Election Study (ANES), 1964–2002.

rate Latter-day Saints as a religious group in all of their surveys. We will evaluate white voters' reaction to the candidates from that religious minority group in the next chapter.

RACE AND POLITICAL PARTIES
IN CONTEMPORARY ELECTIONS

After we examine the amplitude of cohesiveness among whites, as based on the measure of their affect, we can turn toward their political influence in American democracy. The best starting point to examine relative group influences on U.S. politics is through the analysis of presidential elections. The internal-threat principle (the fourth axiom or A4) suggests that despite the warm thermometer reading toward their own racial group, white voters belonging to the two major parties differ greatly about the nature of concrete minority threats, as well as the differences of perception in how minorities should be treated, which allowed them to build two electoral coalitions to win competitive elections (as explained by the fifth axiom or A5).

Table 11.2 displays the different levels of racial support for the two major parties in the presidential elections, spanning from 1952 to 2016. Democrats have lost the majority of white voter support in all but one election. On the contrary, non-white voters have been overwhelmingly Democratic. The competitive-election principle (A5) indicates that public policies concerning the temporary statuses of minorities are determined primarily by the winning coalition. It is critical, thus, to examine how the major parties can win elections.

Although African Americans make up about 12 percent of the nation's electorate, their overwhelming support for the Democratic Party (coinciding with the party's efforts coming up short to win a majority of white voters) has generated enormous contributions from racial minorities, especially Black Americans, to the success of the Democratic Party. In 1976, Jimmy Carter received 18 percent of his support from non-white voters. In 2000, Al Gore received 20 percent. But the larger the percentage of the Democratic presidential vote that comes from minorities, the less the chance that candidate has of winning. This is because the bulk of the voters in the nation remain white, a point referenced earlier. No white Democrat has ever won a two-candidate race with less than about 60 percent of ballot totals coming from white voters. Even for the historical 2008 presidential election, which elected the nation's first Black president, 61 percent of Obama's total came from white voters (see Liu, 2010). Thus, both Republicans and Democrats remain primarily dependent on white votes. A Democrat can lose a majority of whites and still

Table 11.2 White and Minority Vote in Presidential Elections: 1952–2020

Election	Republican		Democrat		Other		Total		Winner
	White	Non-White	White	Non-White	White	Non-White	White	Non-White	
1952	57	21	43	79			100	100	R
1956	59	39	41	61			100	100	R
1960	51	32	49	68			100	100	D
1964	41	6	59	94			100	100	D
1968	47	12	38	85	15	3	100	100	R
1972	68	13	32	87			100	100	R
1976	52	15	46	85	1		99	100	D
1980	56	10	36	86	7	2	99	98	R
1984	66	13	34	87			100	100	R
1988	59	18	41	82			100	100	R
1992	41	11	39	77	20	12	100	100	D
1996	45	12	46	82	9	6	100	100	D
2000	52	12	39	78	9	10	100	100	R
2004	57	17	43	83			100	100	R
2008	56	10	44	90			100	100	D
2012	57	19	39	78			96	97	D
2016	57	21	37	74	6	5	100	100	R
2020	58	26	41	71	1	3	100	100	D

Source: Created by the author with the source from Gallup Poll (1952–2004), CNN.com (2008–2020).

prevail, but to win, Democrats still have to narrow the gap as much as possible, when it comes to white voters.

In 2016, Trump won with many states in the south, the Intermountain West and the Midwest. In the south, Alabama, Arkansas, Florida, Georgia, Louisiana, Mississippi, South Carolina, North Carolina, Tennessee, Texas, and Virginia (that once were 11 states of the former Confederate States of America) have a combined population of more than 84 million, constituting the largest geographic section in the country. As of 2020, its 160 Electoral College votes represent 59 percent of the 270 needed to elect the president; its 138 representatives represent 63 percent of the 218 votes needed to control and pass legislation in the U.S. House of Representatives; its 22 senators represent 43 percent of the 51 votes needed to control and pass legislation in the U.S. Senate. Today, the south is solidly Republican in presidential elections.

In the early nineteenth century, the south's great regional rival was New England, with its six states. In 2020, New England had only thirty-one electoral votes, twenty-two representatives in the House, and twelve members in the Senate. In the late nineteenth century, the south's great rival was the block of eleven states which comprised the Midwest. In 2020, those states had only 118 electoral votes and 94 representatives. The five Pacific Coast states, largely liberal and Democrat, had only eighty-two electoral votes and seventy-two representatives. The three Mid-Atlantic states—New York, New, Jersey and Pennsylvania—are also mainly liberal and Democratic but, in 2020, totaled only sixty-three electoral votes and fifty-seven representatives. The remainder—six border states and eight mountain states—in 2020 were politically similar to the south in general, although together they had only eighty-one electoral votes and sixty-nine representatives. All these statistics point to an inherent Electoral College advantage for the Republican Party which, as explained above, has relied on mostly white support for their presidential votes.

Between 1840 and 1960, the south was the region most loyal to Democratic candidates. For much of that period, the "Solid South" meant solid Democrat. After the Civil War, the Republican Party in the South, with certain exceptions, was confined to Blacks who, with limited voting rights and limited numbers, could not outvote white Democrats. The 1964 presidential election changed the nation drastically and it represented the official end of the WASP-dominant group status.

Table 11.3 shows the racial breakdown of the Presidential vote, spanning 1952 to 2016. While Black Americans began leaving the Republican Party during the New Deal period of the 1930s, their desertion to Democrats was not completed until 1964. Before 1964, Republicans did not get less than 20 percent of the non-white vote. After 1964, however, Republicans never again received 20 percent of those voters.

Table 11.3 Presidential Support by Four Racial Groups, 1992–2020

Year	Vote	White	Black	Asian	Hispanic	Total
		Non-Hispanic				
1992	Democrat*	39	83	31	61	43
	Republican	40	10	55	25	38
	Other	20	7	15	14	19
	Total	99	100	101	100	100
1996	Democrat*	43	84	43	72	49
	Republican	46	12	48	21	41
	Other	9	4	8	6	8
	Total	98	100	99	99	98
2000	Democrat	42	90	54	67	48
	Republican*	54	8	41	31	48
	Other	3	1	4	2	2
	Total	99	99	99	100	98
2004	Democrat	41	88	58	56	48
	Republican*	58	11	41	43	51
	Total	99	99	99	99	99
2008	Democrat*	43	95	62	67	52
	Republican	57	5	38	33	48
	Total	100	100	100	100	100
2012	Democrat*	39	93	73	71	51
	Republican	59	6	26	27	47
	Total	98	99	99	98	98
2016	Democrat	37	89	65	66	49
	Republican*	57	8	27	28	46
	Other	6	3	8	6	5
	Total	100	100	100	100	100
2020	Democrat*	41	87	61	65	51
	Republican	58	12	34	32	47
	Other	1	1	5	3	2
	Total	100	100	100	100	100

Source: Created by the author with sources: CNN.com (2008–2020); Marjorie Connelly. "Election 2004 How Americans Voted: A Political Portrait." *New York Times* Sunday November 7, 2004 page 4.

The reason for the change was complex, but it certainly had a racial connection. In 1964, President Johnson pushed Democrats to racial liberalism. His party would be the home for civil rights legislation. Johnson knew that he was making a strategic decision to win the presidential election, and yet he might have paid a big price for the future. On the evening he signed the

1964 *Civil Rights Act*, President Johnson told Bill Moyers: "I think we just delivered the South to the Republican Party for a long time to come" (Clymer, 2002). Senator Barry Goldwater, the 1964 Republican candidate, who was wedded to the principles of conservatism and small government, voted against the *Civil Rights Act*. Goldwater won only his home state of Arizona, and more importantly, all five deep south states. Goldwater's vision changed the political future of the Republican Party and laid a foundation for today's configuration of red-and-blue states.

Southern whites witnessed the collapse of the New Deal coalition of southern race-based politics with northern liberal politics. The result was a swing of southern whites to the Republicans and Black Americans to the Democrats. Republicans were able to campaign in the increasingly conservative south as conservatives without the race baggage of the old southern Democrats, while southern whites continued to view northern liberal Democrats with suspicion.

Since 1964, the only white Democratic presidents have been mainly southerners—Johnson from Texas, Carter from Georgia, and Clinton from Arkansas. Obama, however, was from Illinois, and Joe Biden was from Delaware. Republicans have taken a majority of the white vote thirteen times since 1964. Democrats never have won a majority of the white vote after 1964. While racial issues may not always be vocalized in campaigns, America is racially polarized in elections. There is no evidence that racial polarization is diminishing, even with the election of Obama (see below).

Table 11.3 shows the major racial vote breakdowns between 1992 and 2016. In four of these seven elections—2000, 2004, 2008, and 2012—the two major parties gained 95 percent or more of the vote. In three (1992, 1996, and 2016), minor parties gained between 5 and 10 percent of the vote. Bill Clinton clearly benefited from the third-party candidate from the right (Ross Perot) in 1992 and 1996, but Hillary Clinton was hurt by pro-Sanders progressives from the left in 2016. Furthermore, the apportionment structure of the Electoral College evidently favors the Republican Party, as they lost the popular vote but still won the White House in two presidential elections (2000 and 2016).

Because Black voters have been extremely loyal Democrats, Republican presidential and Congressional candidates in areas with substantial Black populations (the south, for example), need a landslide, representing at least 60 percent of the non-Hispanic white electorate. Republicans have cultivated issues oriented toward religious whites (especially the evangelical Christian voting bloc) along with middle-class social and economic concerns. Before Trump, Republican candidates, for the most part, attempted to downplay race and issues directly connected to race. They constitute what King and Smith (2011) labeled as the color-blind alliance.

Democrats also could not stress race as part of their campaign strategy. To win elections, Democrats needed to build a coalition of moderate and liberal white non-Hispanics while energizing minority voters. Since the 1970s race has not worked well as a campaign theme for Democrats. The reason is simple. Democrats could already count on a disproportionate share of the minority vote. They also needed issues directed at whites. Thus, this has contributed to racially polarized politics while race, itself, had been depoliticized, up until to the 2016 presidential election.

Blacks are clearly the most loyal Democrats, which operates as a strength and weakness for the party. There are other minorities as well who value different policy proposals. Hispanics and Asians are growing as a result of immigration concerns. Hispanics are not categorized as a single race and can be classified as white, Black, Asian, or American Indian. Many Hispanics after migrating to America for multiple generations do not call themselves as Hispanic. Rather, they either identify themselves as white or define themselves in terms of heritage and place of origin, such as Puerto Rico, Mexico, Cuba, and Central America (an option made more accessible, for example, on the 2020 U.S. Census form). Republican presidential candidates have not won a majority of Hispanic voters in the last three decades, but George W. Bush did win between 30 and 43 percent of the Hispanic vote and won the White House twice. In 2016, Trump received only 28 percent of the Hispanic vote.

Contemporary Asian Americans are another diverse minority, having origins in the Philippines, China, Japan, India, Pakistan, Korea, and many other regions. In 1992 and 1996, they supported Republican presidential candidates but more recently they have supported Democratic presidential candidates. Generally, Asians are a small minority, although they are located throughout the country. Asian Americans are elected to public offices in the greatest number in Hawaii where they have become the majority of the population. In 2018, 72.3 percent of 137 Asian American candidates for state legislative races throughout the country won election (the highest percentage to date). As of 2016, three Democratic U.S. Senators, all women, were elected to represent Hawaii, Illinois, and California. Furthermore, four Asian U.S. House Representatives were elected to represent Washington, California, Illinois, and Florida, respectively. Compared to other minority candidates, Asian American candidates usually run based on mainstream messages that appeal to diverse groups of voters because of their small population representation.

Oklahoma is the state with the largest number of Native Americans while Alaska has the largest Native-American population in proportion. Native Americans live in all fifty states and typically have tribal organizations recognized by states and the federal government as sovereign within a specific state. Oklahoma tribes, for example, have their own tribal governments and exercise their sovereignty by issuing motor vehicle license plates and collecting their own fuel and tobacco taxes on Indian-owned land, but not state taxes.

Tribes can enter into compacts with states by which the tribe can operate gambling facilities. In California, more than sixty tribes have had compacts which typically permit the tribe to operate gambling establishments in exchange for the state getting a share of the proceeds. Tribes have clashed frequently with state governments on issues such as regulation of hunting and fishing, taxes, and regulation of gambling. In 1837, Minnesota Chippewa agreed to a treaty by which they ceded land but retained the right to hunt and fish on it. In the 1980s, when Minnesota attempted to regulate hunting and fishing for conservation reasons without exempting American Indians, the Chippewas sued, and, in 1999 won their case in the U.S. Supreme Court. As a result, Minnesota was obligated to negotiate with the Chippewas. Similar disputes have occurred in Wisconsin and other states. In a recent Supreme Court decision, *Tribe v. State* (2019), the Crow Tribe won a major victory to protect its hunting rights in the state of Wyoming.

The political representation of American Indians in the federal government, however, has been rare. In 2016, two Oklahoma Republican House Representatives—Tom Cole, a Chickasaw, and Markwayne Mullin, a Cherokee—were elected as the only tribal members in Congress. But, in 2021, President Joe Biden nominated and won Congressional approval for Deb Haaland, an enrolled member of the Laguna Pueblo who had just completed a term as a House representative for the New Mexico Congressional delegation, as the nation's first Native American cabinet member (U.S. Department of the Interior).

The small numbers of Native Americans combined with tribal-based interests have motivated them to exert their political influence through lobbying and campaign support as opposed to depending solely on their voting numbers. They act politically more like corporations and business associations as opposed to a conventional minority politics model. In the 2003 California gubernatorial recall election, American Indian tribes contributed $6.7 million, about 20 percent of the total spent, making the tribes "the state's newest and biggest special interest" (Simon, 2003).

Yet, Native Americans also can organize protests and demonstrations. It makes a politically effective combination. One example was the campaign for designating Bears Ears—an area encompassing nearly 2 million acres in southern Utah—as a national monument under the *U.S. Antiquities Act* of 1906. It was an unprecedented effort, as a coalition of five tribal governments—Navajo, Hopi, Ute Indian Tribe, Ute Mountain Ute, and Zuni—were involved. Tribes have been consistently excluded or relegated when it comes to discussing public lands. Near the end of his second term, President Obama designated the Bears Ears monument, as the tribes had desired, an act that immediately was set upon to be reversed after President Trump took office in 2017. The Trump Administration proposed reducing the designation significantly while making plans for mining, drilling, and grazing. The tribes have sued with the support of the Natural Resource Defense Council to stop the Trump Administration's actions. The court battle continues at time of publication. Meanwhile, the Biden administration, with the notable inclusion of a Native American cabinet secretary at the U.S. Department of Interior, is considering reversing his predecessor's decision and restoring the monument designation.

The growing political power of the aforementioned minorities, compared to the long history of racial suppression, is hard to dispute. But, none of these minorities has any electoral power to challenge the core of the atomic structure—the white electorate. Both major parties have yet to find effective balanced, comprehensive messages that do not alienate white voters. One more important factor that may shape the reconfiguration of the atomic structure is the changing demographic makeup of the country. Will the growth of minorities completely end the majority status of whites, thus redefining the atomic structure within the near term?

MIGRATION, DEMOGRAPHIC CHANGE, AND MINORITY POLITICAL POWER

The U.S. population has diversified at a steadily gaining pace since the 1960s. However, with respect to the residential patterns, one still sees a segregated society. Immigrant minorities have tended to move to urban centers, while the waves of white flight from urban centers to suburbs continued during recent decades. Though the urban revival has also provided an economic boom in certain cities largely due to the high-tech revolution, the Electoral College system still favors those states with less dense population concentrations. Many scholars believe that the migration pattern overall may benefit the Republican Party, because the growth of population in the sunbelt states (i.e., the south and the west) is occurring within the current stronghold of the GOP, while the northeast and Midwest, which have been critical areas of support for the Democratic Party, have seen out-migration. The white working-class voters, who lacked sufficient high-tech skills to move to the south and west for jobs, have expressed their frustration about globalization, the loss of manufacturing and Trump's victory in 2016 was not possible without the surprising margin of success in three Midwest states—Wisconsin, Pennsylvania, and Michigan. In comparison, well-to-do whites have moved to the south and contributed to the growth of the Republican Party in those areas (Gimple,

1999). The 2020 census results further strengthened the Republican Party at the Electoral College, as Texas gained two more electoral college votes, and Florida, Montana, and North Carolina each gained one more. Only two Republican strongholds, West Virginia and Ohio, lost one electoral college vote each. In comparison, the Democratic Party gained only two more electoral college votes in its strongholds (Colorado and Oregon) while losing five (California, New York, Illinois, Michigan, and Pennsylvania).

On the other hand, the growth of the racial minorities in the country has also led to changes in the political calculus. According to the 2020 census, the African American population share was 13.4 percent of the total population. The Asian American population grew because of the 1965 immigration system overhaul, which ended a long history of discrimination against Asians. But, their population share, less than 5.9 percent, is still small. Hispanics have quickly become the largest minority in the country, and the 2020 census data show that they constitute more than 18.5 percent of the total. Their size will continue to grow because of higher birth rates compared to other demographic sectors of the U.S. population. Correspondingly, the white population share has declined. The 2020 census data show that non-Hispanic whites represent about 60.1 percent of the total population.

The demographic changes already have impacts in political representation. In the 2020 election, forty-two Hispanics (six more than in 2016) were elected to the U.S. House of Representatives, and a fifth and sixth Hispanic were elected to the U.S. Senate (both Democrats) representing New Mexico, and California, joining Hispanic senators (two Democrats and two Republicans) from Florida, New Jersey, Texas, and Nevada. In the 2020 election, fifty-seven Blacks (all but two Democrats) were elected to the U.S. House of Representatives (12 more than in 2016), one Blacks (a Democrat) was elected to the U.S. Senate, representing, Georgia, who joins two others representing, respectively, South Carolina (Republican) and New Jersey (Democrat). This is significant progress but there is still plenty of room for growth: Blacks make up 11 percent of the total 535 members of the U.S. Congress in 2020, still below their share of the U.S. population.

With the growing sizes of minorities and their increasing political representation at the federal government, the question remains whether or not minorities can determine who will win major elections. Are minorities actually today's political battleground? It is certainly not correct to suggest that politicians do not pay attention to race when they design their campaign strategies. In 2001, for example, President Bush ended military-training exercises on Vieques, a Puerto Rican island. Many believed that this step and Bush's proposal to introduce a new immigration policy for undocumented immigrants that would enable them to obtain temporary visas for stays of limited duration were designed to attract Hispanic votes. But, after Bush introduced his immigration reform proposal, members from his own political party attacked its details. Eventually, the issue of immigration was omitted from the GOP platform in 2004 and at the Republican national convention, Bush did not mention any policy proposals related to immigration or racial issues.

At the same time, the Democratic Party did not want to draw too much attention to racial inequality. In the 2004 Democratic national convention, it was John Kerry as the candidate, a war hero whom some believed would appeal to white male voters. Meanwhile, during the primary season when Kerry already had secured the nomination, there were concerns that his campaign had done little outreach toward Hispanic voters in Arizona, Nevada, New Mexico, and Florida. In 2000, Bush lost New Mexico by 366 votes and his re-election campaign wanted to ensure that another narrow defeat would not occur. In May, 2004, for example, "in each of the three other battleground states where the Latino vote is pivotal—Arizona, Nevada and Florida—the same is true: Bush has staff and headquarters; Kerry does not. Bush also has run television ads in Spanish in each of those states; Kerry has not" (Finnegan, 2004).

To focus on minority issues in presidential campaigns, however, can be a self-defeating move. Between 2008 and 2016, President Obama repeatedly emphasized to the American people that he is the president for all Americans and should not be judged solely as a president for Black Americans (Haines et al., 2019). His signature domestic achievements—the *Affordable Care Act* and legislation raising the federal minimum wage—were carefully promoted as assistance for all working Americans. Throughout the 2008 campaign, Obama cautiously executed a "deracialized" strategy to woo voters, which was moving forward without controversy with white voters until his connection with Reverend Jeremiah Wright from Obama's church in Chicago became a national political story. The highly publicized video of Wright's Sunday sermon criticizing white America jeopardized the efforts to promote Obama's image as a bridge builder for reconciliation. Obama responded by making the most important speech of his campaign in Philadelphia on March 18, 2008, which called for understanding the painful history of racial conflict from the perspectives of both whites and minorities. In his speech, Obama invoked his biracial background repeatedly, using the story of racial fear told by his own white grandmother as a reminder of America's uneasy past on the issue of race.

WHITE GROUP INFLUENCE IN AMERICAN ELECTORAL POLITICS

Obama's carefully designed campaign messages, especially the one delivered in Philadelphia, helped him undercut a potential political crisis in his primary momentum. After the speech, many of his white supporters gained confidence in his ability to win not only the primaries but also the general election. His Philadelphia speech, however, was seen differently by political scientists such as King and Smith (2011), who indicated that the message "contained few insights into the policy challenges racial inequalities pose in modern America" (8).

But King and Smith also missed an important electoral connection. The strategy used by politicians such as Obama to minimize the effect of racial confrontation and to focus on other non-racial issues in their campaigns is called "deracialization" in the political science literature (Wright and Middleton, 2001; Clayton, 2010). More specifically, deracialization is used when, for example, candidates try to defuse the polarizing effects of race by avoiding explicit reference to race-specific issues while using symbolic Black and Latino faces in their campaign literature or advertisements (McCormick and Jones, 1993). Why do politicians want to adopt a strategy of deracialization? From their perspectives, it is imperative to analyze the strengths and weakness of all voting groups (see Daniel Gillion 2016's recent work on the effect of deracialization on governing, especially during Obama's first term). To win an election, there are at least four elements candidates need to evaluate in relation to any given minority group: its size, its homogeneity, its distribution, and its turnout level.

In terms of size, Hispanics and Blacks are more powerful than Asian Americans, but none of these groups is big enough alone to guarantee a major party's success at the national, or even state, level. Blacks are the most homogeneous group, and thus the most powerful one. But, their strongest regional location is in the south where Republicans hold a strong base of white voters.

Hispanics are much less homogenous than Blacks. There are mainly three groups comprising residents from the southwest, Florida, and northeast. Cuban Americans most likely live in Florida and have supported Republican candidates. Mexican Americans are more loyal to the Democrats in the southwest states such as New Mexico, but they also may vote for GOP candidates, as in Texas where they supported President Bush. The Latino support for Trump in Texas increased to an impressive 41 percent level in 2020. Puerto Ricans, concentrated in New York, are more likely to support Democrats. It should also be noted that Blacks and Hispanics have supported the Democratic Party in those states with the nation's largest urban centers in California and New York.

Asian Americans are not homogeneous. There are many ethnic groups, such as Chinese, Japanese, Koreans, Indians, Pakistanis, and Filipinos, and they differ culturally and politically. Another limitation is that they are spread out among the states, and thus cannot constitute a strong enough unified force in any state, except Hawaii and California.

No matter how large a group is represented in the population, its political power can only be realized when its members vote. Table 11.4 shows the reported turnout data in presidential elections from 1964 to 2016. Non-Hispanic whites participated at the highest rate in all but one presidential election in the past five decades. They also have had the largest number of voters. In 2000, white non-Hispanics cast 83.8 percent of the votes and 84.2 percent in the 2002 election. In 2016, whites still cast 71 percent of the total votes. In comparison, in a typical national election, only 12 percent of the votes come from Blacks, 11 percent, Hispanic, and about 4 percent, Asian.

Given the limitations on the political power of minorities in competitive elections, it is rational for politicians to focus on the white majority and to employ a deracialization strategy. Indeed, politicians at both national and state levels emphasize issues like jobs, the economy, and foreign policy, not racial inequality issues. Increasingly, race-based public policies have met challenges in the administrative and legislative branches of the federal government, as well as in the public discourse. More minorities, in fact, have been elected as Republicans than ever before. One was Mia Love, a Haitian American, elected in the white-dominant 4th Congressional District in Utah in 2014, who lost narrowly a bid for a third term in 2018 to a moderate white Democrat (Ben McAdams). That district was returned to the Republicans in 2020, with the election of Burgess Owens, a Black newcomer to politics. Other prominent elected minority Republicans include U.S. Senators Tim Scott of South Carolina, Ted Cruz of Texas, Marco Rubio of Florida. Asian

Table 11.4 Voting and Registration in Presidential Elections by Race and Ethnicity 1964–2016, Percent of Voting Age Citizens Who Reported Voting

Year	White	White Non-Hispanic	Black	Asian	Hispanic
1964	70.7		58.5		
1968	69.1		57.6		
1972	64.5		52.1		37.5
1976	60.9		48.7		31.8
1980	60.9	62.8	50.5		29.9
1984	61.4	63.3	55.8		32.6
1988	59.1	61.8	51.5		28.8
1992	63.6	66.9	54.0	27.3	28.9
1996	56.0	59.6	50.6	25.7	26.7
2000	56.4	60.4	53.5	25.4	27.5
2004	60.3	65.8	56.3	29.8	28.0
2008	64.4	66.1	64.7	47.6	49.9
2012	62.2	64.1	66.6	47.3	48.0
2016	62.9	65.3	59.6	49.0	47.6

Source: Created by the author with the source, "Voting and Registration in the Election of November" 1964–2016, U.S. Census.

American Nikki Haley was also a Republican elected as the governor of South Carolina, and later served as the Ambassador to the United Nations in the Trump administration.

The judiciary also has been a major focus in cases involving political interests vital to liberal minority groups. For example, in 2016, a major test of affirmative action policies in college admissions ended with a 4-3 split decision from the U.S. Supreme Court which upheld the race-conscious admission policies of The University of Texas, an outcome welcomed by affirmative-action advocacy groups. The use of race in redistricting has, on the other hand, caused major controversies between civil-rights groups such as the NAACP and state legislatures controlled by white representatives. In 2016, the U.S. Supreme Court ruled unanimously that three Virginia Republican House members challenging the district boundaries drawn by a federal court lacked standing to bring the case—a major win for minority groups and the Democratic Party. Nonetheless, as pointed out by King and Smith (2011), the voting rights litigations and a series of Supreme Court decisions such as *Shelby County v. Holder* (2013) and others in the past two decades have in general favored the color-blind racial alliance, thereby diluting the effectiveness of the 1965 Voting Rights Act and its subsequent amendments (most notably, adopted in 1982) in protecting the opportunities of minorities to elect the candidates of their choice. In her new book, *The Trifecta in Voting Barrier Causation*, Shauna Reilly (2020) concludes that recent systematic changes in voting procedural laws at the state level across America have had a clear racial purpose of weakening, sometimes disenfranchising, minority voters.

In sum, minority groups' aspirations to enter the core of the nation's atomic structure must be met with strategic thinking about the nature of racial threats. On the one hand, minority politicians must maximize the electoral opportunity to win. This maximization means the ability to convince white voters that they are not a threat to their corresponding interests. On the other hand, the minority politicians also need to present themselves to their respective groups, and more importantly, they must be able to build cross-racial coalitions as Obama accomplished in 2008 (and to a somewhat lesser degree in 2012, See Crotty, 2012 for the pragmatic side of Obama in his governing approach as a centrist and moderate). With the perceived conservative advantage in the U.S. Supreme Court, the judiciary as a path to enhance racial minority influence becomes increasingly difficult. Next, we turn to another measure of relative group influences based on how groups are represented by elected politicians at the federal level and to what extent that whites as the core of the atomic structure maintain relatively a greater influence in U.S. Congress than do racial minorities.

GROUP INFLUENCES IN THE LEGISLATIVE ARENA

What we have discussed above in this chapter can be mostly summarized as the potentials of white group influence versus all other minority groups in the atomic structure post–WASP dominant group status. But, just because a group has a disproportionally larger size and a higher level of turnout doesn't automatically lead to the conclusion that this group's influence will materialize in the legislative and executive arenas of federal government. To argue that the white racial group is at the core of the atomic structure in the new era, one has to examine how legislators make laws in reaction to group demands, and how the executive branch represents a racial group. We will turn to the presidential elections in the next two chapters. Here, we focus on the legislative branch of the federal government. In this regard, political scientists John Griffin and Brian Newman (2008)'s *Minority Report: Evaluating Political Equality in America* provides the most systematic and vigorous empirical analyses.

Griffin and Newman's first step of analyses looks at political opinions and representation of minorities in relation to those of whites. By focusing on the differences in their opinions, Griffin and Newman were able to examine whether or not variation in racial attitudes eventually led to corresponding shifts in Congressional lawmaking. Griffin and Newman also compare the general ideology of each racial group, finding that Black Americans are the most liberal leaning while Hispanics can be found somewhere in the middle, and whites are the most conservative. When comparing political opinions by Blacks and whites, it is easy to see their differences on civil rights issues, such as affirmative action and job discrimination, among other indicators. Black Americans generally believe that there should be more government spending toward education, health care, and welfare. White voters have deep disagreements on these issues. Based on their opinion data, they show that, for example, while 69 percent of Black Americans say that the government should do more to reduce income disparities, only 47 percent of whites agree with that sentiment.

According to Griffin and Newman (2008), most minority groups are on "the losing side," as far as representation in Congress is concerned, and there is a clear racial "policy gap." The members of Congress who are elected under plurality electoral rules are usually from districts that are home to far more whites than minorities. Griffin and Newman's data show the "proximity gap", in that minorities are farther on average from their representatives than most whites in terms of political representation in Congress. Unfortunately, for minority voters, Griffin and Newman also show that those voters who are closer to their representatives in terms of their political views do find a higher response rate to their political desires (which is a clear advantage for white voters, in general). Even Hispanics and African Americans with a co-partisan connection with their respective representatives are still significantly further away from their representatives than whites. Racial minorities do have a chance being represented in Congress if they coalesce their resolve in their attitude (a strategy promoted by pluralist scholars such as Robert Dahl), and "be loud", or if they elect members from their own racial groups. Congress, nonetheless, has enacted overwhelmingly more laws based on the policy wishes of whites, rather than those of racial minorities.

In short, through public opinion and roll-call vote analysis, Griffin and Newman use empirical data and vigorous statistical analyses to show that the white electorate enjoys a greater advantage in U.S. Congress. Their advantage is reflected by the disproportionally larger number of white legislators who have taken into consideration the values of whites.

CONCLUSION

Griffin and Newman (2008) demonstrate that elected officials respond to white opinions and ideology at a much greater rate than they do to racial minorities, which is consistent with our proposition of an atomic structure. To establish the claim that the integrated white group (including those of European origin) is located at the core while racial minorities stay at the peripheries, we use longitudinal National Election Studies (NES) data to show that whites are affectively much warmer toward their own racial group members than any other minorities. Whites comprise more than 70 percent of the population and a moderately higher proportional rate of participation in national elections. The aspect of racial identity matters to this super-majority.

Is it possible that the greater influence of white voters on elected officials can be simply an artifact of the disproportionately larger size of the white group, which aligns with the majority rule of a democratic political system? The empirical analysis in this chapter finds no evidence to conclude that whites have become victims in the aftermath of the end of the WASP-dominant group status in the atomic structure. On the contrary, they continue to enjoy a clear group advantage in the electoral system and in terms of representation in Congress. And, this white advantage is even greater than what the size of white electorate would suggest, as Griffin and Newman contend.

The central role of whites as a group in the atomic structure, however, does not diminish the assessment of the progress in minority group efforts for equity and parity. For one, minority representation in the federal government has grown to an unprecedented level (though still below their population proportions). Most importantly, the two-party competition has allowed racial minorities to find their political support from the Democratic Party. Minorities alone, however, cannot determine their political fate, which is conditioned upon whether they can find enough white voters to support their cause. This fact, again, continues to show that key features of the atomic structure still works today. Whether or not white support for minorities' struggle for equality is sufficient from an electability perspective is the source of volatility we have experienced throughout history. More recently, the level of volatility is at historical highs, as demonstrated in recent presidential elections, the topic taken up in the next chapter.

Chapter 12

Racial Minority versus Religious Minority

The 2012 Presidential Election

On February 5, 2020, the U.S. Senate voted to acquit President Trump on two articles of impeachment. The first article of impeachment was abuse of power, for which forty-eight senators voted yes and forty-two voted no. On the second article of impeachment, obstruction of justice, forty-seven senators voted yes and fifty-three senators voted no. The U.S. Constitution requires two-thirds of the U.S. Senate to convict, thus Trump was acquitted on both accounts, and would remain in office. The votes were cast almost completely along party lines, but the sole vote for impeachment on the first article by a Republican was from Mitt Romney, a first-term U.S. Senator from Utah. It also was the first-ever vote in an impeachment trial from a senator who is a member of the same political party as the impeached president. On that day, Romney, in a moving and emotional floor speech, said his faith played an important role in his decision to vote against Trump's acquittal. (Romney would repeat this act in 2021 when Trump was again impeached, post-presidency.)

After the vote was announced, Trump expressed his anger in a public statement: "I don't like people who use their faith as justification for doing what they know is wrong." At the National Prayer Breakfast just one day after his acquittal, the President was surrounded by evangelical supporters and articulated his disapproval of Romney (Fea, 2020). Later, the President continued his criticism in an East Room event: "And then you had some that used religion as a crutch. They never used it before," Trump said. "But you know, it's a failed presidential candidate, so things can happen when you fail so badly running for president." Four days after his impeachment trial, Trump retweeted that Romney "stabbed Trump in the back," by joining Democrats in an attempt to overturn the outcome of the 2016 election.

Questioning and attacking Romney's faith and his loyalty were certainly not new. As a religious minority politician, Romney still has not been able to use his formidable credentials, not to mention as the GOP nominee for president in 2012, to at least take the issue of his faith out of politics. Romney's religious connection with The Church of Jesus Christ of Latter-day Saints—a truly "American religion" initiated, developed, and matured entirely inside the United States—could still trigger political resentment, as he fully realized in his 2008 and 2012 presidential elections. And, ironical perhaps for their similarities, Romney's family roots crossed borders much like that of Obama's forebears. Romney's ancestors came to the United States for religious freedom but within one generation had to flee to Mexico (where his great-grandfather established roots in Colonia Juarez) because of federal persecution and threats of criminal prosecution for the practice of polygamy.

As discussed in chapters 9 and 10, the end of WASP-dominant group status has led to the atomic structure being reconfigured. Now the core is all whites of European origin, not just WASPs. Of course, as the ethnicity of an original European ancestry became increasingly less relevant in contemporary U.S. politics, the new core of all whites became much more diverse, and those previously peripheral white religious groups have become more assertive in the electoral arena. In this chapter, we will examine closely the political aspiration for the presidency by a predominantly white religious minority. We will show why a major reason for the volatility of U.S. politics after the end of WASP-dominant group status is the increasing diversity of candidate pools and the necessity for white voters to think strategically about the contexts in which various candidates run. A strategically conscious voter evaluates the implications of primaries and general elections carefully and finding a viable candidate to support so that the perceived threats can be minimized is a priority.

Many studies have examined the conditions upon which a racial minority candidate can win the support of white voters in the U.S. presidential elections. Little has been learned, however, about the factors that may impact the political fate of a religious minority candidate in such elections. This chapter focuses on the historical candidacy of Romney who, as a Latter-day Saint candidate, won the Republican nomination and went on to compete in the 2012 election. The theories of rational choice, group positions, and social psychology are used to propose hypotheses regarding religious group support for Romney's candidacy. Overall, the findings presented in this chapter suggest that a theoretical model of the strategic religious voter, as derived from the atomic structure introduced throughout the book, is necessary to explain the political change in the Obama era. Moreover, this chapter emphasizes a key implication of the atomic structure. Namely, the political fate of religious minority candidates is a result of not only their own campaign strategies but also, more importantly, the candidate pool and the levels of perceived threats to the traditionally dominant group, as observed in specific elections.

THE MINORITY CANDIDATES

As a religious minority, members of The Church of Jesus Christ of Latter-day Saints had made notable impacts on U.S. national politics before Romney's campaigns in 2008 and 2012. Their assimilation into the white electorate as a whole, especially as a reliable Republican bloc, had become an asset in GOP's presidential elections of recent decades, but the controversy concerning their religious beliefs also continued. This is especially clear in the electoral arena. The religious problem, for example, was an issue for Romney in his two presidential campaigns, but John Kerry, a white Catholic who was nominated by the Democratic Party and ran for the presidency in 2004, never encountered any religious problem in his campaign. Indeed, the distance principle (the second axiom, A2) of this book offers a good explanation for why Romney's church is still perceived as a threat. But its amplitude is not as great as the Black threat represented by the Obama presidency.

More importantly, the clash between Romney and Obama in 2012 symbolized one clear trend since the end of WASP-dominant group status, namely, the increase in minority candidacies while homogeneous WASP-only electoral races are becoming less common. When a white religious-minority candidate is running against a Black candidate, how will white voters respond? I will introduce the existing literature first, and then use the ADVICE principles that govern the atomic structure to derive a strategic voting hypothesis.

THEORIES AND HYPOTHESES: SOLVING THE CHAPTER 1 PUZZLE

Many prominent political scientists have emphasized the central role of social groups in the democratic processes (Dahl, 1961; Putnam, 2000). The importance of social groups in the American electoral politics has been extensively documented by political scientists. There are two conditions on which minority candidates may challenge the domination of a majority group in U.S. elections (recall our discussion in chapters 4 and 5 about concrete threat): the first is the population growth of minority groups and sustained demographic changes (Schmidt et al., 2013) and the second is the electoral coalition built by minority candidates (Barreto, 2012; Liu, 2010; Hajnal, 2006; Sonenshein, 1993). The success of a multiracial electoral coalition depends on the effective campaign strategies of racial minority candidates, which often take the form of deracialized campaign style to appeal to white voters (Barreto, 2007; Liu and Vanderleeuw, 2006; Hajnal, 2007), as well as the shared values and liberal ideologies (Sonenshein, 1993; Browning et al., 2003).

For religious-minority candidates to build a successful electoral coalition, though the co-religionists may be especially mobilized to support their campaigns, the key is to win enough support from the dominant group (e.g., Protestants in the U.S.). In addition, building the coalition with other minority groups (e.g., Catholics) can also be critical to winning in the American First-Past-the-Post electoral system which does not provide the opportunity of winning through proportional representation. Thus, the ability to identify the potential voter groups that may or may not support the religious-minority candidates is the necessary step toward a successful presidential campaign. We introduce the following four theses concerning religious groups that may or may not support Romney in 2012, as based on the existing literature.

The "Deprivatization of Disbelief" Thesis

In terms of the impact of religion on a voter's daily life, a voter may be religiously committed, somewhat religious, or not religious. We focus on the last category first. In comparison, the not-religious voters are likely against the religious establishment, especially when they perceive a religious threat to their preferred secular beliefs (Ribberink et al., 2013, 101–120; Adkins et al., 2013, 235–263). In their study of fourteen western European countries, Ribberink et al. (2013) propose the deprivatization hypothesis: "[D]isbelievers in countries with low levels of religiosity are less anti-religion than disbelievers in countries like the United States, where religion is virtually omnipresent" (106). The not-religious voters are especially sensitive to those politicians who appear to be religiously threatening in such contexts as the U.S. presidential election. As discussed earlier, Romney was portrayed as a religious, prominent Latter-day Saint, his experiences in Boston church leadership and his controversial position on women's rights issues were widely reported by the media during his 2008 and 2012 campaigns. Thus, our first hypothesis is:

> Hypothesis 1 (H1): The anti-Romney vote was cast more likely by the not-religious voter group than by religious voters.

The Religious Commitment Thesis

In comparison, the religiously committed are more likely to be influenced by the religious cues than are less committed (Adkins et al., 2013, 239–240). Religious commitment has been suggested as a key factor in fostering partisanship where religious voters are more likely to be identified as Republicans (Putnam and Campbell, 2010). Furthermore, the most religiously committed voters understand the theological differences between and among religious groups and may have strong religious opinions from "top of the head" (Zaller, 1992). Mainline Protestants are less religiously committed than are born-again Protestants (Wilcox and Robinson, 2011). With respect to the 2012 election, it is reasonable to regard born-again evangelical Protestants as the most religiously committed group. They were more likely than other religious voters to discern theological differences between Protestant beliefs and Latter-day Saints' doctrines. Thus, the second hypothesis is:

Hypothesis 2 (H2): The anti-Romney vote was more likely to be cast by born-again Protestants than by other religious voters.

The Group Position thesis

As introduced in chapter 4, Herbert Blumer (1958) offers a theoretical proposition based on the positions of social groups. Our atomic structure thesis also draws from this position theory, as we differentiate the position of the core of the atomic structure from its peripheries. The group position theory stresses that there are similarities and differences between voters based on their group identities and membership (Smith, 2013). Groups are located in the fixed positions in a social and political structure, which was initiated and politicized by the dominant group (Williams, 1998; Blumer, 1958; Dawson, 1994). Power and threat are perceived based on the respective group positions (Key, 1949). Thus, due to the same marginalized group position shared by Catholics and Latter-day Saints, which are two religious minority groups historically discriminated against by the dominant WASPs, the third hypothesis, therefore, is:

Hypothesis 3 (H3): Catholics are more likely to vote for Romney than WASPs, because of the traditional minority and periphery status for both Catholics and Latter-day Saints in U.S. history.

The "Strategic Religious Voter" Thesis (as derived from the Atomic Structure)

As a starting point for testing our hypotheses, we will use the framework of atomic structure developed throughout this book. First, we reiterate Axiom 1 about the attraction principle. As with previous theories, we assume that religious beliefs (or nonbelief), commitment, and group positions provide voters with important predispositions and preferences (Kinder and Sanders, 1996), which serve as setting the goal for these voters to reach an electoral outcome consistent with these predispositions and preferences (see the discussion of de Mesquita et al., 2005 on affinity, p. 61). But, by only using the attraction principle, we cannot derive a hypothesis about voting behavior when a particular group is perceiving multiple threats from external groups. Thus, we need to revisit the ADVICE principles collectively governing the atomic structure.

The distance principle (Axiom 2) suggests that Blacks would constitute the greatest threat perceived by white voters, especially WASPs. The volatility principle (Axiom 3) suggests that groups such as Latter-day Saints can experience volatility within even a short period of time. But it is Blacks who receive the highest level of hostility from the white electorate in the core of the atomic structure. The internal-threat principle (Axiom 4) suggests that some whites may regard Black threat as a concrete threat while other whites will not, and it is usually the white subgroups who perceive the threat to their status and interests (in this case, WASPs) that are more hostile to Blacks. Finally, the competitive-election principle (Axiom 5) forces all voters to evaluate their choices and make the decision to maximize their chance to succeed. It occurs because of this principle, which sometimes is necessary to effect strategic voting, given the volatility of the electoral candidate pool.

The strategic religious model presupposes that religious voters want to be on the side of a winning coalition (Riker, 1962; de Mesquita et al., 2005; Liu, 2010), and the electoral means used by the religious voters will maximize their opportunity to reach their goal based on their religious predispositions. This is particularly true for those religious voters such as born-again evangelicals who are committed religiously. They have a deeper level of understanding of the differences between their religion and minority counterparts, such as Mormonism, than those who are less religiously committed voters. Put differently, their knowledge and predisposition encourage them to consider voting decisions consistent with their knowledge and predispositions (Zaller, 1992; Lau and Redlawsk, 2006). The religious knowledge allows these voters to use memory-based information processing, beyond the less cognitively challenging online-based information processing (Kim and Garrett, 2012), which we discussed in part I of the book.

Religious voters are also strategic, which suggests that they need to evaluate the candidate pool that defines the choice set in a given election, and then vote based on the best available option. Another way to examine the strategic religious voter thesis is to regard the candidate pool as the supply and the voters' predispositions as the demand (Stark and Finke, 1996, 1999). The task for the strategic voter is, first of all, to classify the candidates in the choice set. There are three types of candidates for a rational/strategic voter, which we develop a set of hypotheses to examine empirically, as follows:

H4(a): A congruent candidate (CC) is a candidate who shares the critical group identities with the rational voter of a given social group, and a CC thus can be regarded as a political agent for the strategic voter.

H4(b): An unacceptable candidate (UC) is a candidate who does not share the critical group identities with the rational voter, and, furthermore, this candidate can be regarded as the threat to the strategic voter's identities. An UC is thus the candidate whose victory is exactly what the voter wishes to avoid.

H4(c): An acceptable candidate (AC) is a candidate that the strategic voter accepts in an attempt to minimize the chance of an unacceptable candidate's (UC) victory.

Based on the availability of these three types of candidates, a strategic voter can decide accordingly the choice in an election. First, in an ideal election where there is at least one congruent candidate (CC) who is also viable, the voter would then provide strong support for this candidate as the agent of his/her religious group (H4a). We will see Trump as this type of ideal candidate for the white evangelicals (see chapter 13). But some elections can only be dealt with a strategic decision by the voter. In particular, if there is not a single congruent and viable candidate available (CC), but there is at least one acceptable candidate (AC), the rational voter then decides strategically for the acceptable candidate to defeat the unacceptable candidate (UC) (H4b). Finally, there is also a crisis election, in which neither congruent nor acceptable candidate is available. Under this circumstance, the voter would cast no vote (H4c).

Of course, our strategic religious voter thesis suggests that the ranking of candidates varies for different religious groups because of their respective religious predispositions, and their vote choices therefore are different. Romney was not a congruent candidate for white Protestants in the Republican primaries, because of his religious connection, as evangelical pastor Robert Jeffrey reminded his congregation. But Romney was a viable candidate because of his professional portfolio, name recognition, campaign funding, and organizational achievements. Thus, as stated in H4a, the goal for the religiously committed voters, especially the born-again Christians, in the GOP primaries, was to find the candidate to defeat Romney.

Obviously, the set of choices for the 2012 general election differed from the GOP primaries: Romney and Obama. Romney became the acceptable candidate (AC) for the religiously committed white voters in an attempt to defeat Obama, the unacceptable candidate (UC). For many white Christian voters, especially highly committed evangelicals, Obama was not only Black, but also unacceptable because he was regarded as hostile to Christian values, perhaps even secretly a Muslim, as some persistently claimed without evidence.

On January 15, 2008, during the Democratic presidential debate in Las Vegas, moderator Brian Williams asked Obama about the accusation that he was "trying to hide the fact that [he is] a Muslim." Obama responded, "The facts are: I am a Christian. I have been sworn in with a Bible . . . in the Internet age, there are going to be lies that are spread all over the place. I have been victimized by these lies." Obama later added: "I'm a Christian by choice," and concluded, "I think my public service is part of that effort to express my Christian faith."

Public opinion surveys, however, show that a sizable population was not convinced by Obama's defense and clarification of his religion. For example, a survey conducted by Pew Research Center in March 2008 found 10 percent of respondents believed Obama to be Muslim. Another Pew research poll conducted in August 2010 discovered that 18 percent of Americans and 30 percent of Republicans believed Obama to be Muslim. This misperception was actually a growing trend among Republicans, which continued through Obama's first term (Grieve, 2010).

As noted in chapter 4 in a *Fox News* interview, white Southern evangelical leader Robert Jeffress was asked who he would vote for as an evangelic leader in the general election if the GOP primaries had his favorite choice Rick Perry (who later became the U.S. Energy Secretary in the first term of the Trump Administration) defeated, he responded that picking Romney over Obama would be the right choice in the general election because Romney "embraces [biblical] principles [better] than Obama." In short, as stated in H4b, our strategic religious voter hypothesis predicts that white Protestants, especially born-again evangelicals, would cast their strategic vote for Romney in the general election rather than in the GOP primaries due to a different set of choices. Before presenting empirical findings from the 2012 election, it is necessary to introduce the data and the method for testing these hypotheses.

DATA AND METHOD

To test the hypotheses, this chapter uses the data from both the 2012 Republican primaries and the general election. The primary data were obtained from CNN.com, which posted the aggregated exit poll results in key states throughout the primaries. The advantages of using the aggregate primary data are twofold: First, the American primary elections are sequential, which allows researchers to examine whether or not voting patterns concerning religious groups change over time and across different states. Given that momentum is a measurable predictor of the eventual winner in a primary election, one can examine whether or not Romney generated any momentum from religious groups (Mutz, 1997; Tolbert and Squire, 2009; Donavan and Hunsaker, 2009). Second, the primary data also allow researcher to not only compare Romney's support from multiple groups at a given time, such as his support from the born-again religious group versus that from the not-born-again group, but also examine the support of a given religious group (e.g., Catholics) for Romney with the support of the same group for other candidates, such as Rick Santorum (a Catholic). The groups can be compared when the factor of partisanship is excluded or minimized, unlike the general election when all voters, regardless of parties, can participate.

To test the hypotheses, we also examine data from the general election. We use the 2012 National Election Study (NES), which collected data from 5,914 respondents through both face-to-face interviews and web surveys. The individual-level data from the 2012 NES provide a valuable source to evaluate whether or not the pattern discovered in the GOP primaries still held in the general election. This is especially important for testing our hypothesis (H4), which asserts that different candidate pools lead to different strategic voting decisions of religious voters.

In testing the hypotheses, we also control for other possible factors that may explain the vote for Romney. These factors include traditional Social-economic-status (SES) and demographic variables such as income, age, and gender. Party identification is also entered into the empirical model. Furthermore, we also control for affective measures of the Latter-day Saints as a group (the standard thermometer score) and cognitive evaluation of the religion (i.e., whether or not the doctrine of Latter-day Saints can be regarded as a faith of Christianity and whether or not the respondent's belief system has anything in common with that religion). Finally, based on the findings from another study (Campbell et al., 2012, 2014) which suggests that it is the voters with a modest amount of interaction with Latter-day Saints that were more likely to vote against him, our model also takes into consideration the effect of social contact with Latter-day Saints on the probability of voting for Romney.

FINDINGS ON THE 2012 GOP PRIMARIES

With main rivals including Santorum and Newt Gingrich, Romney endured the long primary season and finally clinched the Republican presidential nomination on May 29, 2012. In addition to his well-developed ground organization and solid financial backing, non-religious voters kept Romney in the game long enough to end up eventually as the nominee. Using the average percentages of group support as measured on a given primary date, it turns out that the not-religious voter group consistently supported Romney at a higher level (about 40% or more) than did the religious voter group (about 10 to 30%) in the 2012 GOP primaries. This finding rejects the first hypothesis (H1), which is derived from the deprivatization of disbelief thesis.

But why did religious voters cast ballots against Romney in the primaries? Was it because, as suggested in one study (Campbell et al., 2012), they perceived his religious affiliation—The Church of Jesus Christ of Latter-day Saints—as a main threat to Christianity, in general, and Protestantism, in particular? Consistent with the second hypothesis (H2), Romney received a lower level of support from the born-again religious voter group than from the non-born-again voter group in the primaries. While the born-again religious vote was never more than 40 percent, the not-born-again Republicans, in most cases, supported Romney with more than 50 percent of their votes. This finding suggests that a high level of commitment to one's religion did translate to an enhanced level of hostility toward the candidate from a minority group. Indeed, the majority of born-again Protestant voters echoed Robert Jeffress' strong words against the Latter-day Saints religion when they cast their votes in the 2012 Republican primaries.

Many of the not-born-again religious voters reported themselves as Catholics. We can compare Romney's Catholic support with that of Santorum in the primaries. A Catholic, Santorum was a former U.S. senator from Pennsylvania, and he had been defeated even in his own state as an incumbent for re-election and had minimal, if any, national name recognition early in the primaries. But Santorum became popular among Catholics and even beat Romney in some later primary states. This finding suggests that Catholic voters in the GOP primaries were strategic, in that they first cast more votes for Romney because he was regarded as a better candidate than other Protestant candidates. When they discovered that a candidate from their own faith, Santorum, had become more competitive, these GOP Catholics added their support, giving him the necessary momentum to stay in the race. The third hypothesis (H3) derived from the group position thesis is partially confirmed by our empirical findings.

Compared to the born-again religious voter group, Catholics favored Romney more than his Protestant opponents. Despite Romney's religious affiliation not being shared by Catholic voters, they cast their ballots for him, arguably perhaps for the shared experience of Catholics as a religious minority. There is empirical evidence to suggest that like racial minorities who formed the racial coalition for Obama during the 2008 presidential election, the religious minorities supported Romney in the 2012 GOP primaries. But would they vote in the same way in the general election as they did in the primaries? The fourth hypothesis (H4) predicted a change in the voter's choice in the general election, given the makeup of the general election candidates. We now turn to the findings regarding the general election.

THE 2012 GENERAL ELECTION

Immediately after the 2012 primaries, Romney's lack of support from religious Republicans, especially evangelical Protestants, raised concerns about his chance of winning the general election. For one thing, the Protestants, especially the born-again religious right, had been an integral part of GOP victories in past presidential elections (Wilcox and Robinson, 2011). The election outcomes of the primaries had shown that the religious group did respond to Protestant leaders' views on the danger of electing a Latter-day Saint as president. Nearly seven out of ten Republican born-again Protestants voted against Romney consistently throughout the primaries. Without the backing of this critical voting bloc, the Republican candidate's chance of winning the general election would be improbable.

Romney did end up winning 47.2 percent of the popular vote, but 4 percent less than President Obama. Romney blamed Hurricane Sandy, a late season storm that was the second costliest hurricane on record in U.S. history, and the advantages of Obama's incumbency as reasons for his defeat. In 2016, Trump mocked Romney as incompetent for not going after Obama harder. Romney responded by urging Republican voters to reconsider their support for Trump in 2016. In that speech, of course, Romney did not mention why he had lost to Obama in 2012. Regardless, white evangelical antagonism against Romney's religion was never used as a reason for his defeat.

Romney's post-election silence on the vote of the religious right was not because he wanted to avoid fresh controversies surrounding his deep connection with the church. For Romney, there did not appear to be any substantial white Protestant antagonism against his church in the 2012 general election at all. As introduced in the chapter 1 puzzle, non-Christian voters supported Romney at comparably lower levels, regardless of the race of survey respondents. White mainline Protestants (many of whom were WASPs) gave more than 60 percent of their votes to Romney, which was the highest among all groups with the only exception coming from non-mainline white Protestants/Christians (i.e., the religious right such as evangelical born-again Protestants). White Protestants from the religious right gave 71 percent of their votes to Romney. In comparison, Catholics, regardless of race, offered modest and less than majority support for Romney, while Black Americans, regardless of their religious affiliation, offered at best nominal support for Romney. Only about 5.7 percent of Black born-again Protestants cast their votes for Romney, which was 65 percent less than his white Protestant support from the same religious group.

Romney's lack of support from racial minority groups, especially Black Americans, can be explained by the fact that he was running against Obama, the nation's first Black president, who happened to be the incumbent. But what were the driving forces behind this change of heart on the part of white Protestants? We return to the fourth hypothesis (H4) derived from the strategic religious voter thesis. According to H4, religious voters are rational, in that they want to use electoral means to maximize the opportunity to protect interests that reflect their religious identification. They decide to vote strategically for the acceptable candidate (AC) to defeat the unacceptable candidate (UC; see H4a and H4b) given the candidate pool.

Regardless of the extent to which white Protestants cast votes against Romney in the primaries because of their concern of a religious threat from the LDS Church, this concern faded in the general election in which Obama, notably a Protestant, shared the same religious affiliation with white Protestants. But Obama's Protestantism did not matter to these white Protestant voters. The true religion of Obama (even his American citizenship and birthplace) was questioned by a significant segment of white Protestants (including Trump) who asserted that Obama was actually a Muslim (Grieve, 2010). The Black threat that Obama posed to these white Protestants was perceived as much more serious than the Mormon threat.

Table 12.1 provides three logistical equation models concerning the probability of voting for Romney, as based on the full 2012 NES dataset including both online survey and face-to-face interviews. The demographic variables indicate that Romney voters tended to be older, richer, and less educated. Note that the contact with Latter-day Saints variable designed to test the effect of social contact/capital on the probability of voting for Romney did not turn out to be statistically significant, and the finding casts doubts about the earlier findings on the importance of social contact (Campbell et al., 2012, 2014; Huckfeldt and Sprague, 1995). We also examined the possible curvilinear relationship between social contact with Latter-day Saints and the voter's choice (Campbell et al., 2012) and the polynomial term was not significant (results not shown in table 12.1).

The other control variables concerning voters' affective and cognitive information processing demonstrated that, indeed, voters' decisions were rooted in the political psychological factors identified in the literature about critical referents, which emphasize the power of social group on the affect of voters (Zschirnt, 2011, 687). The thermometer reading about Latter-day Saints as an affective group referent is a powerful predictor. Those who were warmer toward Latter-day Saints as a group were more likely to vote for Romney in the 2012 general election. Cognitively, as indicated by H4b and H4c, the voters who believed that the religious belief of Latter-day Saints had a great deal or a lot in common with their own were more likely to vote for Romney than those who thought that the religion had little or nothing at all in common with their own beliefs. This finding suggests that religious beliefs can serve as a potent predisposition for voters to set their goal in elections to

Racial Minority versus Religious Minority 175

Table 12.1 Logistic Regression for the Romney Vote in the 2012 General Election

	Equation 1 β (s.e.)	Equation 2 β (s.e.)	Equation 3 β (s.e.)
Age	.07 (.02)***	.07 (.02)***	.07 (.02)***
Income	.02 (.01)**	.03 (.01)**	.03 (.01)**
Education	-.27(.06)***	-.24 (.06)***	-.23 (.06)***
Gender	-.06 (.12)	-.01 (.13)	.01 (.13)
Mormon Thermometer	.01 (.00)***	.01 (.00)***	.01 (.00)***
Mormon Belief	-.30 (.06)	-.19 (.08)*	-.19 (.08)*
Mormon Christian	-.16 (.12)	-.24 (.15)	-.25 (.15)
Mormon Contact	-.00 (.00)	-.00 (.00)	-.00 (.00)
Republican	4.67 (.19)***	4.70 (.20)***	4.69 (.21)***
Independent	2.21 (.15)***	2.27 (.16)***	2.26 (.16)***
Other Party	2.61 (.30)***	2.64 (.35)***	2.68 (.35)***
Protestant	.35 (.15)*	---	---
Other Religion	-.02 (.37)	---	---
Not Religious	-.41 (.16)*	---	---
Non-Hisp White	.36 (.23)	.42 (.27)	.07 (.30)
Non-Hisp Black	-.2.67 (.39)***	-2.68 (.41)***	-2.55 (.42)***
Hispanic	-.42 (.27)	-.45 (.31)	-.46 (.30)
Born Again	---	.62 (.14)***	.04 (.26)
Born Again x Non-Hisp White	---	---	.80 (.30)**
Intercept	-1.66 (.56)**	-2.37 (.63)***	-2.10 (.64)**
Pseudo R-Squared	.62	.70	.70
N	2936	2434	2434

Note: Two-tailed test. *p<.05, **p<.01, p<.001.
Source: Created by the author with the data source from American National Election Study (ANES), 2012.

maximize their opportunity to protect their own belief against the threat from other belief systems.

We also use the Democratic Party affiliation as the base category to examine the effect of party identification on the probability of voting for Romney. As all three of the H4 sub propositions show in the model's three equations, all comparison groups (i.e., Republicans, independents, and other party identifiers) were more likely to vote for Romney than were Democrats in the 2012 Presidential election. This finding illustrates the robustness of the hypothesis testing with respect to other important predictors of candidate choice of religious voters.

To test the hypotheses concerning the specific religious groups, we use Catholics as the base group. Equation 1, as applied in table 12.1, shows how Protestants, voters with non-Christian religious affiliation, and not-religious voters compared to Catholics in their voting choice. This indicates that Protestants were more likely to vote for Romney than Catholics, while the not-religious voters were less likely to vote for him than Catholics. These findings reverse what we found in the GOP primaries, indicating that the first three hypotheses in this chapter (H1, H2, and H3) cannot be supported or rejected based on just the ballots cast in the primaries. As proposed in the strategic religious voter model (H4a, b, and c), a change in the candidate pool can lead to a corresponding change in the voting choice.

To further examine the first three hypotheses and demonstrate that H4 has more predictive power in the context of the 2012 general election, the logistical model incorporates variables for race variables and the dichotomous variable concerning whether or not a voter was a born-again Christian (Equation 2). The findings reveal that born-again religious voters, contrary to the pattern discovered in the GOP primaries, supported Romney in the general election, as predicted by the fourth hypothesis (H4). Equation 3 adds another interactive term between born-again and the non-Hispanic white racial group. This interactive term is positive and statistically significant (at the $p<.01$ level). Plainly, white born-again religious voters, after we control for demographics, affective and cognitive predispositions and party affiliation, became the voting bloc for Romney in the 2012 general election.

A closer examination of the three equations in table 12.1 also shows the strategic consideration of different racial and religious groups. There are three dichotomous racial variables in table 12.1 measuring non-Hispanic whites, non-Hispanic Blacks, and Hispanics. The base group includes Asians and other minority racial categories (e.g., Native Americans and Pacific Islanders, etc.). Thus, those voters in the base group (i.e., Asians and other racial groups) did not have any co-racial candidates in the field in 2012, unlike the voters in the three comparison groups. Note that some Hispanics regard themselves as white, so therefore Hispanics were listed as a comparison group in table 12.1.

As shown in Equations 1 and 2, Blacks were much more likely to vote against Romney than the base group voters in 2012, which demonstrated the goal of Black voters was to defeat Romney (an unacceptable candidate) and elect Obama (a congruent candidate). Non-Hispanic whites were not necessarily more likely to vote for Romney than base group voters, as indicated by the statistical insignificance of this variable in Equations 1 and 2. This is because Romney was not the congruent candidate for most white voters. As noted above, the affective and cognitive predispositions of many whites did not lead them to display a greater tendency to vote for Romney than the base group (note that the non-Hispanic white variable is not statistically significant). But, for the white born-again racial group, Obama became the unacceptable candidate whom they needed to defeat, and they chose to vote for Romney as an acceptable candidate for them to maximize the chance to defeat Obama. Given the voting choice available to them in the general election, the decision of the white born-again to vote for Romney was a strategic one, and their true preference was not him to begin with, as demonstrated by their choice in the GOP primaries.

CONCLUSION

The end of WASP domination in the atomic structure has led to unprecedented volatility in the composition of candidate pools in the contemporary era. The 2012 presidential elections featured two minority candidates (Romney and Obama). This is an important election to analyze because it provides a unique opportunity to examine how white voters, in the core of the atomic structure, and various religious groups respond to minority candidates: Did Obama's race and Romney's religion matter to them?

Obama's first term witnessed a surge of political activism from the white electorate. The quickly emerging prominence of Tea Party to challenge Obama's landmark policies, such as the *Affordable Care Act* and the bailouts of major corporations and industries during the recovery of economic recession, served to rev up the engine for the Republican Party in 2012 (Skocpol and Williamson, 2012). The goal of the Tea Partiers was not only to defeat Obama in 2012 but also to remake the Republican Party itself. For Romney in the 2012 general election, attacking Obama's "failed policy," as he claimed it, on economic recovery could have been a winning strategy, but it was a message compromised by his inconsistency on policy. This included a leaked video that suggested Romney was out of touch with the economic realities of voters, who might have supported him, and contradicting figures and data in his proposals. Had he been able to craft the message more precisely, he could have convinced voters to see the difference from Obama, especially his own impressive portfolio as an economic turnaround expert, rather than religion. Faced with attacks from evangelical leaders such as Robert Jeffress and Bill Keller, Romney calmly reminded voters that they "should remember that decency and civility are values, too" and his faith reinforced his belief in finding the common ground.

Romney's cautious response showed the recognition of the potential damage his faith might inflict on his campaign to become president. From this perspective, one can see how minority groups face an uphill battle as they try to move to the nation's top political prize. For minority groups, how they can reduce, if not completely remove, the perception of their group's threat to the powerful majority is a high political order. To a large extent, the political experience of minority groups depends upon how the majority decides to respond politically to the perception of minority threat, which is a major argument in the atomic structure thesis.

Why do majority voters, such as WASPs, need to be concerned with a minority threat, given the relatively small size of Romney's religious community, which is only about 2 percent of the U.S. population? What kind of a political threat can it actually form? More puzzling is why the religious threat, if it did exist, cause white Protestants to vote against Romney only in the primaries, but not in the general election in 2012? To answer these questions, one must solve two problems theoretically. The first is the rationality behind the majority-group's decision-making process. The second is to find the underlying factors that may lead to the perception of minority group threat to the majority.

This chapter examined the voting choices of religious groups in the 2012 presidential election. To understand the extent to which religion played a role in social groups' decision-making process, I analyzed voting patterns in both GOP primaries, in which the party identification was not a factor, as well as the general election, which determined the eventual election outcome of the presidential election. Three main hypotheses were derived suggesting that the role of religion is grounded on religiosity, commitment, and group positions. The most striking finding is that all three hypotheses have some empirical support, but none of the hypotheses alone or in combination can be used to explain the voting choices of all groups throughout the primaries and the general election. Thus, the atomic structure theory is used to propose a strategic religious voter theory, which suggests that minority candidates on certain occasions win substantial support from the majority voters, but such support also does not mean that a vote for the minority candidate is the true preference of the traditionally dominant group. To understand group choices, one must rely on existing theories to derive the predispositions and preferences of the groups.

More importantly, the religious voters, just like their non-religious counterparts, also are strategic, in that they must evaluate the candidate pool based on the choice set and vote based on the best available option. The main reason for the necessity of this strategic decision on the part of WASPs (or white Protestants, in general), the nation's most enduring dominant group for much of U.S. history, was that the end of the WASP-dominant group status had led to increasing volatility in national elections. Previous minority groups, such as Blacks and Latter-day Saints, have become much more assertive, and the size and power of WASPs no long can control outcomes in these volatile elections.

The findings also shed an important light on the long-term political strategy of the white evangelical voter group. Recent empirical work on the role of white evangelicals suggests that their support for Trump in 2016 had its root in white Christian nationalism (e.g., Rozell and Wilcox, 2018; Whitehead et al., 2018; Wong, 2018; Deckman et al., 2016). This chapter adds yet more empirical evidence about the 2012 election, which reveals the deep-seated racial and religious predispositions of Christian nationalism.

The other contribution of this chapter is an empirically confirmed hypothesis derived from the atomic structure theory. It shows the strategic consideration of the white evangelical voters, especially those white born-again religious voters, when faced with rapid demographic changes in the nation and the increasing likelihood of racial and religious minority candidacies emerging in the American electoral arena.

If some white voters, especially white born-again religious voters, made their strategical decision to vote for Romney in the 2012 general election, it also would be natural for them to become even more enthusiastic toward a congruent candidate sharing the same racial (white) and (protestant) religious identities. Their desire for finding such a candidate who can better represent the traditional WASP identity and have a viable chance to beat the Democratic opponent became more urgent after the 2012 election failure to elect a Republican candidate. To their excitement, this viable candidate would come to the national frontlines quickly, and both political parties were shocked by Trump's rapid ascendancy. The success of Trump in 2016 would deliver to his enthusiastic supporters what Rick Perry later called "the chosen one" (Martin, 2020). White evangelicals in particular would become the most loyal supporters of Trump throughout his first term. The next chapter will take a closer look at the "unexpected" victory of Trump in his 2016 campaign.

Chapter 13

The Surge of White Nationalism in the Trump Era

The previous chapter showed that facing the threat of Obama's re-election as the nation's first Black president, white Protestants, especially white evangelical voters, strategically decided to vote for Romney in the general election, despite their reluctance and prior attacks in the GOP primaries on Romney surrounding his religious connection with the Church of Jesus Christ of Latter-day Saints. The decision had its roots, as we have seen so far in this book, in the most significant political development in the atomic structure—the end of the WASP-dominant group status at the core.

As explained previously, the new core of this atomic structure since the 1960s has included all whites of European origins. The process of this political incorporation has enlarged the size as well as the diversity of the core. The increasing heterogeneity and the fragmentation of the white electorate have enhanced the level of internal threats inside the atomic core. Previously peripheral groups, such as white Catholics and Latter-day Saints, now have become politically empowered and are willing to run and are, indeed, winning elections at the federal and state levels. On the other hand, the question of whether or not to stay in the Democratic Party for these previously peripheral white groups, especially white Catholics who once composed the major part of the New Deal coalition, has become a significant question.

Their response to this question has contributed to the volatility of the atomic structure in recent times. As political scientists Mark Rozell and Clyde Wilcox (2018) indicate, one of the key reasons for Trump's success in the 2016 presidential election was that "he won the Catholic vote, which, unlike several of the latest previous presidential elections, broke more strongly in favor of the GOP nominee," and most importantly, "Trump's 60-37 percent margin among white Catholics over Hillary Clinton anchored his 52-45 percent margin among all Catholics" (5). Trump's performance among white Catholics surprised shrewd political scientists such as Rozell and Wilcox, as they acknowledge the fact that Trump openly criticized Pope Francis as "very political" and "naïve" about the immigration issue. "Given the enormous worldwide popularity of the pope . . . [the pope's] disapproval of the Republican presidential candidate would potentially discourage some Catholics from voting for Trump. Nonetheless, the frequently touted 'Francis effect' on U.S. politics simply did not materialized" in 2016 (Rozell and Wilcox, 2018, 8). What happened to make Trump the choice of these white Catholics, many of whom resided in the key battleground states of Michigan, Wisconsin, and Pennsylvania? In addition, why was Trump able to receive as much as 81 percent of the white evangelical vote, outperforming the two immediately preceding GOP nominees, Romney and Bush. This occurred despite the highly publicized image of Trump on the cover of *Playboy* magazine, accusations of sexual harassment, and instances of predatory sexual language, as caught on tape and featured in a widely shared report on *Access Hollywood.*

To understand Trump's success at winning white voter support, this chapter suggests examining the new configuration of the atomic structure since the end of the WASP-dominant group status. The association to "whiteness," rather than WASP identity, constitutes the new dominant political cleavage in reconfiguring the atomic structure. How to find issue politics for the Republican Party to build a successful electoral coalition, as we have seen throughout this book, has always been a political priority. But to completely shape this party around the vitality of a distinct white identity appears to have become a greater political necessity. In this new era, the WASPs, the members of the original dominant core, cannot succeed politically by claiming that they alone are the victim of the new configuration of the atomic structure. Instead, they have to incorporate all whites of European origins to make a case that they collectively have become victims of political correctness. The political skill of building the image of GOP as the party to save all whites from the victimhood of new politics that has gathered stream since the Civil Rights Movement Era is essential to defeating the political left that is exemplified by the Obama electoral coalition. Trump succeeded because of his highly charged rhetorical appeal to whiteness and its preservation in the status quo of the core.

FINDING THE "RIGHT" STRATEGY
TO WIN THE WHITE VOTE

In the heat of the 2016 campaign, Trump spoke at a rally in San Diego in which he accused U.S. District Judge Gonzalo Curiel, who presided over a class-action lawsuit against Trump University, as a "hater of Donald Trump" and "a total disgrace." Trump said that Judge Curiel was "very hostile" and had "railroaded" him." He added, "I think Judge Curiel should be ashamed of himself. I think it's a disgrace that he's doing this . . .The judge, who happens to be, we believe, Mexican" said Trump (Kendall, 2016).

Trump's remarks about Judge Curiel's Mexican ethnicity quickly drew national attention. Hillary Clinton, the Democratic nominee, called it a racist attack on the federal judge. John Dickerson, the host of CBS's *Face the Nation*, asked Trump on June 5, 2016 why the Mexican heritage of the judge had anything to do with the Trump University case. Trump responded that it had "a lot to do with it" and "he [the Judge] is a member of a club or society, very strongly pro-Mexican, which is all fine. But I say he's got bias. I want to build a wall. I'm going to build a wall" (Johnson and Rucker, 2016).

Dickerson pressed Trump by asking, "Isn't there sort of a tradition, though, in America that we don't judge people by who their parents were and where they came from?" Trump said that he was not talking about tradition but about common sense. He explained, "You know, we have to stop being so politically correct in this country. And we need a little more common sense, John. And I'm not blaming. I'm proud of my heritage, we're all proud of our heritage. But I want to build a wall" (Kertscher, 2016).

Trump's response to Dickerson's questions certainly did not resonate well with Mexican Americans, though he insisted in the interview that Hispanics would eventually love and vote for him. It turned out that only 28 percent of Hispanics voted for him in 2016. But 57 percent of whites did vote for him, and Trump's comments about the judge, who was born in Indiana, did not prevent him from winning the presidency, along with comments on other groups during the campaign.

A poll conducted in early June 2016 showed that 81 percent of Democrats thought that Trump's comments were racist while only 22 percent of Republicans and 43 percent of whites believed so (Moore, YouGov, 2016). Polarization between Democrats and Republicans, and also between whites and minorities, on racial issues has been well-documented in political science literature (King and Smith, 2011; Frymer, 1999; Kinder and Sanders, 1995; Dawson, 1994). Trump's comments should not simply be dismissed as racist. A more profound question is why the country has remained divided on racial issues, and what Trump said connected with some voters but not others, beyond the obvious distinctions.

It is important to note that Trump's defense of his comments about Judge Curiel's alleged biases was centered on how his Mexican heritage was the reason why Trump was mistreated in a lawsuit hearing. Trump depicted himself as a victim because of race, and he certainly was not the first one who felt this way. As early as 2011, economist Michael Norton and psychologist

Samuel Sommers examined longitudinal data to show that "whites see anti-white bias as more prevalent than anti-black bias" in the 2000s (Norton and Sommers, 2011, 216). Norton and Sommers call this view a "zero-sum" approach to racial relations (i.e., the progress made for Blacks is at the expense of whites). This study was based on a correlation analysis that did not address why whites have held this view of a zero-sum game, but the researchers speculate that "affirmative action policies designed to increase minority representation may focus whites' attention on the impact of quota-like procedures on their own access to education and employment, in effect threatening their resources (Norton and Sommers)." Certainly not all whites compete directly with minorities for the access to education and employment. Norton and Sommers offer another possible explanation: "Whites may fear that minorities' imposition of their cultural values represent an attack on White cultural values and norms, as evidenced by Whites' resentment of norms of political correctness . . . and the belief of many whites in a 'War on Christmas'" (Norton and Sommers, 2011, 217).

THE THREAT ENVIRONMENT
BEHIND THE RISE OF TRUMP

In the 2012 general election, though Romney's LDS religious affiliation cost him some primary votes, especially those from white Protestants in the South, white voters finally voted for him by an approximate 6:4 ratio. To be clear, many white voters were not happy about the Obama administration's performance. As Obama entered his second term, he understood that his white support had eroded. Furthermore, despite the 93 percent Black support for him in 2012, Black voters' patience also was being tested. They were not satisfied with the status quo, and they wanted real change, echoing the president's campaign message. Some Black voters brought their frustration to the streets. Starting in 2013 and throughout Obama's second term, the Black Lives Matter (BLM) movement campaigned against violence and what they criticized as systematic racism directed toward the Black American community.

The movement grew to more than thirty local chapters by 2016 and organized protests and demonstrations in many cities, especially in Ferguson, Missouri, and New York City where police shootings resulted in the loss of Black lives. The movement also expanded to college campuses across the country. Reactions to the movement differed dramatically along racial lines. According to a 2015 PBS NewsHour/Marist Poll, about two-thirds of Blacks mostly agreed with the movement's objectives. On the other hand, nearly six out of every ten whites believed Black Lives Matter distracted attention from real issues of discrimination (Miringoff, Carvalho, and Griffith, 2015). The criticism toward BLM led to a spinoff campaign under the slogan of All Lives Matter, a phrase even used by Clinton in 2015. To understand the racial differences in reactions to the movement, it is essential to examine the contemporary atomic structure, as discussed previously. As illustrated in chapter 8, individuals inside the dominant core look at the American democratic system from a different perspective than the one shared by minority groups in the peripheries. The operations of the atomic structure are subject to the five axioms, which determine how the dominant core orders and responds to the perceived multiple threats from the minority groups in the peripheries.

In this chapter, we will focus on how the reordering of multiple threats was completed by Trump's rise as a candidate. The five axioms will be applied to contemporary racial and religious relations. The chapter will explain how the Trump campaign rank ordered the threats from Blacks, Mexicans, and Muslims and how this ordering has affected American politics and continues to this day.

THE REORDERING OF MULTIPLE THREATS IN THE TRUMP ERA

Having a Black president did not improve much of the nation's resolve to reconcile its entrenched racial divides. Both whites and Blacks agree that race relations had deteriorated during Obama's second term (Miringoff et al., 2015). Blacks and whites, however, look at the role of race differently. The 2015 PBS NewsHour/Marist Poll showed that the majority of whites believe that a middle-class lifestyle is equally attainable, regardless of race while 60 percent of Black Americans believe that they have fewer opportunities to achieve this objective. The crucial question to ask is which racial group's view means more as far as American politics is concerned. This book has argued that it is the dominant core of the atomic structure that ranks the multiple threats from the minorities, as based on the attraction principle (A1) and distance principle (A2). Chapter 11 demonstrates that the members of the dominant core include whites with European origins.

Two critical factors contribute to the formation of this dominant core. First, both political parties need white voters to win federal elections. Second, minorities such as Blacks can only be "attached to" white voters to have a chance to be on the winning side of electoral coalitions, which would contribute to their future political status (which is represented in the fifth axiom). Blacks, in particular, have been always loyal to the Democratic Party, especially since the Civil Rights Movement Era. But even when the Democrats win federal elections, white liberals still comprise the largest voting bloc inside the Democratic Party by absolute numbers. Thus, the location of Black Americans in the atomic structure is still at the periphery (despite their over-whelming majority percentages in casting ballots for Democratic candidates), and it is still the white group view that dominates how the federal government should operate. Therefore, it is important to focus on white voters' percep-tions of multiple threats.

To understand their perceptions of multiple threats, it is necessary to review the demographic changes in recent decades. One of the most vis-ible demographic changes is the growth of the Latino population. V.O. Key (1949) in his classic study of southern politics in the 1940s documents how the increasing presence of Blacks enhanced the white perception of (concrete) Black threats. In the twenty-first century, the growing presence of Hispanics and immigrants, in general, has enhanced the perceived threat, augmented by the rise of Trump. But before we dig deeper into Trump's presidential cam-paign in 2016, it is instructive to examine how the wave of anti-immigration opinion among white voters had already helped reconstruct the Republican Party leadership before Trump's win.

In the 2014 mid-term elections, Eric Cantor, then the Republican majority leader in the U.S. House of Representatives who had won nearly 80 percent of the 2012 primary votes in Virginia's Seventh Congressional District, faced an unexpected challenge. Voters were angry in his home district because Cantor and other Republican leaders had discussed the possibility of immi-gration policy reform, though no action had ever been taken in the U.S. House. Cantor was booed by angry voters, especially Tea Party activists, at the district's convention. His primary opponent, Dave Brat, used the immi-gration policy, as the main target:

> 'Why does big business want amnesty? Why does The Chamber [of Commerce] want amnesty? Because it's cheap labor. Big business gets cheap labor and what do you get?' Brat asked his audience in Henrico, Virginia.
> 'The shaft!' responded the audience. Brat continued,
> 'Who's going to pay for the unintended costs that's going to come with amnesty? Who's going to pay for the education, Medicare, food stamps, Medicaid? Is big business going to pay those bills, or are you? You're going to pay those bills'. (Fuerherd, 2014)

In this exchange, Brat, a professor of economics and ethics at Randolph-Macon College in Ashland, Virginia, portrayed himself as an anti-estab-lishment candidate and won support from the conservative movement's national media personalities, including Laura Ingraham, Mark Levin, and Ann Coulter. Brat defeated Cantor by 12 percentage points in the primary and went on to win the general election with 61 percent of the votes.

Brat's success in the 2014 congressional election rattled the Republican Party. No one had ever defeated a sitting U.S. House Majority Leader since the position was created in 1899. What was more revealing was how he won the election. Brat put the anti-immigration message front and center. This was a popular message, as the 2012 NES data showed that 14 percent of the Americans wanted to see levels of immigration increased, while 43 percent wanted the levels to remain the same and another 43 percent wanted them to be decreased. Brat called immigration reform proposals that might give undocumented workers a pathway to citizenship as amnesty. He emphasized that the losers would be ordinary American workers if such a policy were enacted by Congress. He also remarked that illegal immigrants would cost the voters' money to pay for education and higher welfare expenses in programs, such as Medicare, food stamps, and Medicaid. In short, immigration reform would be a threat to the financial well-being of American voters.

To state that illegal immigrants are taking jobs away and adding financial burden on the taxpayers injects the perception of an abstract threat. It is necessary to visualize such a threat to make it concrete, as indicated by the internal threat principle (the fourth axiom). Who are the undocumented immigrants? Which racial groups see immigration as the threat to their well-being? According to Pew Research Center, in 2012, 78.8 percent of the total unauthorized immigrants were from Latin America, and among them 52.4 percent were from Mexico (Passel and Cohn, 2014). But, those numbers have changed significantly in recent years. According to Pew survey research, "in 2017, about 4.95 million of the 10.5 million undocumented population were from Mexico, 1.9 million from Central America, and 1.45 million from Asia. About two-thirds of undocumented immigrants have been in the U.S. for 10 years or longer. In 2017, just 20% of undocumented, adult immigrants had lived in the U.S. for 5 years or less" (Kamarck and Stenglein, 2019).

The visualization of Hispanics, in general, and Mexicans, in particular, as a threat to white voters came to fruition when Trump officially announced his candidacy on June 16, 2015. "When Mexico sends its people, they're not sending the best. They're not sending you, they're sending people that have lots of problems and they're bringing those problems," Trump said in his speech at Trump Tower in New York City. Trump's target was not just illegal immigrants, and he started his attack by generalizing that Mexico sends the people who are not their best, and they have "lots of problems." Trump reminded his American audience that "they're not sending you," a clear indication that Mexicans are different from the Americans. Recall Axioms 1 and 2 which state that the formation of the perception of threat is based on how the threatener is similar (first axiom) and distant from the threatened (second axiom). Trump specified the "problems" of Mexicans in this way: "They're bringing drugs, they're bringing crime. They're rapists and some, I assume, are good

people, but I speak to border guards and they're telling us what we're getting."
Trump then made his signature proposal to respond to the Mexican threat, as
the third axiom (the volatility principle) would suggest: "I would build a Great
Wall, and nobody builds walls better than me, believe me, and I'll build them
very inexpensively. I will build a great, great wall on our southern border and
I will have Mexico pay for that wall, mark my words."

Trump's promise to build a Great Wall along the U.S.-Mexico border
would later become the mantra of his countless campaign rallies. Trump's
rallies drew big crowds not only in the south with a heavy presence of white
evangelical voters but also in the Midwest where the white working class
was an essential voting bloc for any effective presidential campaign. Despite
several missteps, including his remarks about women and disabled individuals, the size of his white audience grew with each rally. In many instances,
the crowds were homogeneously white. The whiteness of his campaign rallies
became such a norm that when occasionally a Black individual was spotted in
the crowd, he was regarded as a protestor, rather than a supporter.

Trump also remarked on Black American lives on the campaign trail.
His messages about Black Americans showed less hostility compared to his
messages on Mexicans. In responding to the Black Lives Matter movement,
he urged Black voters to give him "a chance." His reason was that Blacks
already gave Democrats a chance and had not seen the positive changes they
wanted. Trump especially described Black lives in the urban areas as danger-
ous and poor, and he would be a "law-and-order" president. Also he openly
attacked protestors who demanded greater control and punishment over racial
profiling and white police brutality against mainly Black citizens. Moreover,
Trump's involvement in the birther movement which believed Obama was a
foreign-born national, and his own controversial history as a business leader
showing hostility toward Black residents in New York City contributed to a
deep racial division throughout his 2016 campaign.

Trump's campaign displayed the highest levels of hostility toward another
group: Muslims. Compared to Hispanics, Muslims are a much smaller minority group inside the United States, about 1 percent of the total population in
2016, according to a Pew Research Center report. But the recent growth of
Muslim immigrants has drawn attention from the native population. In 2009
alone, more than 115,000 Muslims became legal residents of the United
States, according to the Pew Research Center. It was in this context that
Trump made his anti-Islam remarks. Trump said that Muslim immigrants
in the West were killing innocents at nightclubs, offices, and churches and
extreme measures were needed. In the wake of the San Bernardino terrorist
attack in December 2015, Trump called "for a total and complete shutdown
of Muslims entering the United States until our country's representatives
figure out what is going on." While Trump's anti-Muslim position reflected
the public anxiety about the refugee crisis in the Middle East and Europe,

he repeatedly articulated a vision in which the Western countries stood firm against the "hateful ideology of radical Islam."

To win the white evangelical votes, Trump made efforts to connect with white Christian leaders. He visited Liberty University on January 18, 2016 and received the endorsement from Jerry Falwell Jr., the school's president. He told the university students that he was a Protestant, and he was "very proud of it". He also warned the students (CNN, 2016):

> And we've got to protect because bad things are happening, very bad things are happening, and we don't—I don't know what it is. We don't band together, maybe. Other religions, frankly, they're banding together . . . You've banded together. You created one of the great universities, colleges, anywhere in the country, anywhere in the world, and that's what the country has to do that around Christianity.

Through the message of unity in Christianity, Trump effectively described Islam as a threat to American lives and Muslims as the "others" (i.e., the most "distant" group from white Christians) who would endanger America's national identity. It is important to note that Trump did not just describe Muslims outside of the United States as a threat. He grouped all Muslims including American Muslims. On March 10, 2016 in an interview with Anderson Cooper of CNN, Trump stated, "I think Islam hates us." Thus, in the group ordering of multiple threats, Muslims are ranked as the highest level of threat. The response range toward such a threat should also be the largest, as Axiom 3 (the volatility principle) indicates. A total Muslim ban means exclusion among the possible responses by the dominant group to a peripheral group threat.

We use figure 13.1 to depict the group ordering in the new atomic structure, as observed in the Trump era. The figure shows the layers of group threats to whites, who constitute the core in the atomic structure. Based on the attraction principle (first axiom) and the distance principle (second axiom), Blacks form the lowest level of threat to whites; Muslims, the highest, and Mexicans (Hispanics) are in between. In order to test whether or not the new atomic structure based on this group ordering indeed affected public opinions and the results of the 2016 presidential election, we turn to an empirical analysis.

ANTI-IMMIGRATION PUBLIC
OPINION AND PUBLIC POLICY

Before testing empirically how the atomic structure affects the public opinion on immigration policy, it is useful to survey the historical public opinion data and significant public policies on immigration. As we have shown in previous

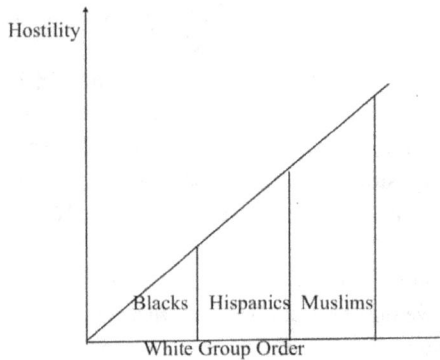

Figure 13.1   White Group Order and Hostility in Trump Campaign. Created by the author.

chapters, throughout U.S. history, immigrants often were the political target of the dominant core of the atomic structure. The WASP anti-immigration sentiment can be traced to as early as the time of the pre-Revolutionary Era when Benjamin Franklin designed policies to assimilate German immigrants. The anti-Catholic movement helped elect the Know-Nothing Party in the 1840–1850s. During the 1870s and 1880s, the target was switched to the Chinese immigrants who were brought to the United States to build the continental railroads. The Irish-American workers, for example, viewed the Chinese immigrants as "taking jobs away from native-born whites" (Espenshade and Hempstead, 1996, 537). In 1882, the U.S. Congress passed the *Chinese Exclusion Act*, the only legislation in U.S. history enacted to stop immigrants from a particular country. For a short period after the Exclusion Act, Japanese immigrants were welcomed to fill in the cheap labor gap left by the absence of the Chinese. But, anti-Japanese sentiment quickly developed, and the so-called 1905 *Gentlemen's Agreement* was passed to halt the immigration levels from Japan for fifty years.

The resurgence of the Ku Klux Klan and the fascination with eugenics led the nation to another wave of anti-immigration in the 1920s. Southern and eastern Europeans as well as Jews were looked at as inferior to WASPs. The *1921 Emergency Quota Act* was put together shortly after the influenza pandemic of 1918, which reduced the immigration levels from Europe to less than 3 percent of what it was before World War I. In 1924, *the Johnson-Reed Act* restricted the immigration level even further, on the ground that "the time has arrived when we should shut the door, otherwise, unchecked immigration will lead to war over resources, or that such immigrants will melt the pot in place of us being the melting pot" (Kusow and Delisi, 2016, 1). The level of immigration permitted depended upon the country of origin, and the quota system favored primarily western European immigrants who were considered by some to be superior to other races and non-WASP ethnicities.

Throughout World War II, anti-immigration sentiment was captured by some public opinion surveys. In one poll dating to May 1938, as many as 68 percent of the respondents were opposed to allowing mainly Jewish refugees from Germany and Austria to enter the country (Harwood, 1986). In 1939, that result rose to a stunning 83 percent. In June 1944, FDR informed Congress that nearly 1,000 refugees from Italy, most of whom were Jewish, would be returned to their homelands when the war was over. Earlier on February 19, 1942, FDR also issued the Executive Order 9066 to move Japanese Americans to internment camps.

During the 1950s and 1960s, coinciding with the Civil Rights Movement, the perception of minority threat to the atomic structure was centered around Black Americans rather than immigrants. Public opinion shifted to a pro-immigration position. This more liberal and welcoming view toward immigrants helped the U.S. Congress pass the 1965 landmark *Immigration and Nationality Act*, eliminating the allocation of immigrant visas based upon country of origin (i.e., the quota system). The act resulted in unprecedented levels of immigration from non-European countries (Fetzer, 2000).

The pro-immigration sentiment proved to be short-lived, however. The waves of immigrations from Latin America led to the rise of the "Hispanic threat" along with the steady increase in negative portrayals of Hispanics in the mass media (Massey and Pren, 2012). During the late 1970s and early 1980s, already roughly two-thirds of Americans wanted immigration cut back, and only 4 percent wanted an increase in immigration (Harwood, 1986). Meanwhile, waves of refugees came to the United States in the midst of the Cold War, which also enhanced the perception of immigrant threat. According to a Gallup poll in 1979, less than one-third of respondents supported refugees from the former South Vietnam and other southeastern Asian countries to emigrate to the United States (Hardwood, 1986).

As anti-immigration sentiment rose to a new high, the U.S. Congress in President Reagan's second term passed the *Immigration Reform and Control Act* (IRCA), which added hurdles to slow the momentum of immigration. In particular, the IRCA required immigrants to provide evidence of knowledge of American history and some level of proficiency in English, and for immigrants to apply for U.S. citizenship, the cost was raised to levels that potentially would reduce immigration flows, especially from Latin America (Dustmann, 2015). Moreover, the IRCA also placed an annual limit on the numbers of legal immigration and family reunification visas.

Democratic administrations also had to deal with the pressure from public opinions and the anti-immigration voice represented in Washington. The restriction on family reunification was further specified in the *1996 Illegal*

Immigration Reform and Immigrant Responsibility Act during the Clinton Administration. Protocols for a deportation procedure also were implemented by the *1996 Anti-Terrorism and Effective Death Penalty Act*, which states that any non-citizen who had committed a crime, regardless of date of the crime, could be immediately deported (Dustmann, 2015). The *USA Patriot Act* provided the federal government with the most far-reaching authority, in the wake of September 11, 2001 terrorist attacks, through which the U.S. Attorney General had the power to deport immigrants (temporary or permanent residents) without hearings or a presentation of evidence.

A STATISTICAL ANALYSIS OF
ANTI-IMMIGRATION PUBLIC OPINION

As discussed above, Trump ran his presidential campaign largely based on the platform of stopping immigrants, especially Mexicans and Muslims, from coming into the United States, while demanding more immigration from "good countries," such as Norway. It is worth reiterating that Trump's campaign rallies were mainly composed of white voters, and his messages were designed to convince white voters that Mexicans are not "the best" and they bring in problems, and Muslims also should be banned because America's Christian identity is at stake. Thus, in terms of group threats to white voters, the level is raised in the order of Blacks, Hispanics, and Muslims. We empirically test how this configuration in atomic structure affected voters' anti-immigration opinions shifting between 2012 and 2016 by using the NES data. Note the dependent variable represents how the respondents would like to see the level of immigration in the U.S. shift in the future: increase a lot (coded as 1), increase a little (coded as 2), leave the same as it is now (coded as 3), decrease a little (coded as 4), and decrease a lot (coded as 5).

As shown in table 13.1, the atomic structure, which features whites in the core of the atomic structure, and Blacks, Hispanics, and other minorities (especially, Muslims) in the peripheries, contributed positively to anti-immigration sentiment shifts between 2008 and 2016. To characterize the atomic structure as discussed, we have assigned the most political power to white respondents (coded as 4), followed by Blacks (coded as 3), Hispanics (coded as 2), and others (coded as 1). Given there is no particular category in the NES data to show Muslim respondents, they are included in the "others" category. One more reason for coding atomic structure in the manner, as explained above, is that it also shows how a racial group is politically incorporated into the political system. Clearly whites have the largest advantage in terms of their elected politicians; African Americans are the second most

Table 13.1   Ordinal Logistic Regressions for Anti-immigration Opinion, National Election Studies, 2008–2016

	2008 β (s.e.)	2012 β (s.e.)	2016 β (s.e.)
Atomic Structure	.33 (.05)***	.17 (.03)***	.15 (.03)***
Partisanship	-.02 (.02)	.14 (.01)***	.33 (.02)***
Age	.10 (.03)***	.10 (.02)***	.14 (.02)***
Education	-.22 (.04)***	-.24 (.03)***	-.23 (.03)***
Income	.00 (.03)	-.06 (.02)***	-.08 (.02)***
Female	.03 (.08)	.18 (.05)***	.18 (.07)**
N	1860	5147	3363
Pseudo R-Squared	.02	.03	.07

**p<.01; ***p<.001.
Source: Created by the author with the data source from American National Election Study (ANES), 2016.

successful group by the same measure; Hispanics are the third most successful and the remainder are the least successful. Within this atomic structure, whites are most likely to take an anti-immigration position.

Table 13.1 reveals that anti-immigration opinion is also related to age and education. The older the age, the greater the probability of taking an anti-immigration position; the higher the level of education, the smaller the probability of having an anti-immigration opinion. Furthermore, female voters were more likely to take anti-immigration position than were male voters in 2012 and 2016.

To investigate whether or not the probability of having an anti-immigration opinion was also attributed to partisanship, table 13.1 includes party identification in the model. The variable measures how the survey respondents positioned themselves on the 7-point scale ranging from strong Democratic to strong Republican. In 2008, party identification had no effect on the anti-immigration view. But, in 2012 and 2016, Republican voters were much more likely to take anti-immigration position than Democratic voters. This finding indicates that immigration has increasingly become a partisan issue.

As we discussed in chapter 8, the perceptions of minority threats are not shared by all members of the dominant group (the internal threat principle). While whites, in general, are more likely to take an anti-immigration position than minorities, partisanship also plays a major role. Mexican undocumented immigrants, on average, make white Republicans much more concerned than they affect white Democrats. The political fate of Mexican undocumented immigrants, according to the competitive-election principle (the fifth axiom), is dependent on which political party eventually wins the federal elections. We turn to the 2016 presidential election and examine whether or not partisanship and race both contributed to Trump's win.

THE EFFECT OF THE ATOMIC STRUCTURE
ON THE 2016 PRESIDENTIAL ELECTION

The divergent views on immigration and different perceptions of multiple threats among white voters in 2016 led to a unique electoral dynamic in history. Trump, a billionaire businessman, presented himself as an anti-establishment candidate. Clinton was the first female candidate who had won the nomination of a major political party. Trump accused the Obama administration, in which Clinton served as the U.S. Secretary of State, of failing to curb illegal and legal immigration. He also blamed Black Lives Matter leaders for endangering police forces around the nation. He promised to help the white working class, especially those in Midwest states, to recoup jobs from countries like Mexico and China. His main targets were Mexicans and Muslims as the major threat to his view of Make America Great Again (MAGA).

Trump received endorsements from major right-wing organizations including the KKK, Breitbart, and many others. But his electoral victory also relied on the voters beyond the right-wing organizations. He needed to convince the majority of whites that his platform was in their best interest. His "Make America Great Again" agenda would effectively deal with the major threats facing his voters.

Table 13.2 examines the anti-immigration positions and the Trump supporters, and it shows that, indeed, Trump was able to mobilize Republicans to vote for him while the Democrats voted against him, which confirms expectations based on the internal-threat principle (the fourth axiom), and why two major parties mattered even with such unique candidate circumstances. Trump's supporters cast votes for him because they believed that the government agendas and policies would be made in their favor.

The logistic regression model also shows that Trump supporters were mainly whites (the base group in the table), the core of the atomic structure, even when controlling for other variables, while Hispanics and Blacks were more likely to vote for Clinton. Trump's voters also were characterized as authoritarians who valued order, authority, and norms (MacWilliams, 2018; Hetherington and Weiler, 2009; Stenner, 2005). Two other control variables were also statistically significant: women and voters with higher levels of education were more likely to vote for Clinton, rather than Trump. It is also evident that those who have very "cold" Muslim thermometer scores would be more likely to favor immigration restriction and vote for Trump—a clear indication that Trump's campaign had effectively engendered the concrete threat of Muslims.

The overall finding of table 13.2 supports the main theme of this book— that is, the atomic structure is the enduring feature of American democracy.

Table 13.2   Anti-Immigration Position and Trump Vote, 2016 NES

	Equation 1 (Ordered Logit) Anti-Immigration Position B (s.e.)	Equation 2 (Logit) Trump Vote B (s.e.)
Party Identification	.07 (.02)***	.18 (.02)***
Populism	.09 (.03)***	-.01 (.05)
Income	-.00 (.03)	.01 (.04)
Education	-.18 (.03)***	-.08 (.06)
Gender	.23 (.07)***	-.26 (.10)*
Muslim Thermometer	-.03 (.00)***	-.03 (.00)***
Authoritarianism	.38 (.04)***	.25 (.06)***
Black	-.48 (.12)***	-3.28 (.35)***
Asian	-.94 (.18)***	-.73 (.32)*
Native American	-.41 (.39)	-1.04 (.79)
Hispanic	-.73 (.11)***	-1.38 (.22)***
Other Race	-.18 (.18)	-.53 (.27)*
Anti-Immigration Position		.77 (.06)***
Pseudo R Squared	.47	.62
N	3165	2422

Note: Two-tailed Test, *p<.05, **p<.01, ***p<.001.
Source: Created by the author with the data source from American National Election Study (ANES), 2016.

The ADVICE principles worked in the time of Thomas Jefferson, and they have operated similarly in the Trump Era, even though the perceptions of multiple threats may change over time, and the configuration of the atomic structure may be different. Trump was able to take advantage of the atomic structure he forcefully pushed in his "Make America Great Again" message. Winning competitive election matters, as the fifth axiom indicates. Trump's win in 2016, based on the ADVICE principles, suggests that minorities, especially Hispanics and Muslims, would see public policies enacted against their group interests. Indeed, the executive order travel ban issued against citizens from seven Muslim-majority nations received strong support from white evangelical Christians (Rozell and Wilcox, 2018, 11), and his political fight with the Democratic-majority U.S. House of Representatives after the midterm elections of 2018 was often centered on his request to erect a border wall between Mexico and the U.S. Countless separated families (including infants and toddlers appearing in court hearings) who were detained on the U.S.-Mexico border, the crackdown of Immigration and Customs Enforcement (ICE) forces against undocumented immigrants and the protests of Dreamers, protected by the policy of Deferred Action for Childhood Arrivals (DACA), have become the indelible images of the Trump presidency. Once again, we see the modern actualization of the volatility principle (the third axiom).

CONCLUSION

As we have seen so far in this book, the end of the WASP-dominant group status in the American political atomic structure has led to profound political changes. The new atomic core includes all whites, rather than just WASPs. This new core became much more heterogeneous than ever before, as those prior white ethnic groups who had been marginalized by the old WASP monopoly of power found themselves now occupying the center of the political universe. The end of WASP domination did not end racial tensions, and there has never been a true "post-racial" America (see Tesler, 2016; Harris and Liberman, 2013). On the contrary, the identity of whiteness, in fact, became even more relevant. The rise of Trump, to a great extent, has been the rediscovery and reconfirmation of the white identity for many individual white voters—being WASPs, Catholics, working-class, southerners, Midwesterners, for example. For these white voters, the shared identity of being white became the most potent call for political action, regardless of their differences in religion, geographic location, social class, and ethnicity.

The dominant question of the atomic structure in the twenty-first century is how whites perceive their differences from other racial minorities, and who represent the most urgent threat to their white identity. This perception can become politically potent when whiteness is intrinsically linked to "Western civilization." Heather MacDonald, a *New York Times* bestselling author and conservative thinker, summarizes the intellectual context in how Western civilization has been under attack by the political agenda of multiculturalism, which she calls "the diversity delusion" (MacDonald, 2018). According to MacDonald, the drive to seek more equality and diversity has transformed American universities and colleges where "multiculturalism's cover for unblemished ignorance of the past—the reflexive 'dead, white male' taunt—is being used to further rationalize formal and informal censorship [of Western cannon by the political left]" (5). MacDonald's list of the Western canon contained authors of familiar names from Europe, and not just prominent WASP figures such as "Chaucer, Spenser, Milton, and Wordsworth" (1). According to MacDonald, students educated at the American universities nowadays no longer read the works of such non-Anglo European giants as Plato, Aristotle, Kant, Rousseau, or listen to Mozart and Beethoven because the multiculturalists call them "racist" or "sexist" (29). The agenda of the left in the name of multiculturalism is to end Western civilization itself, she contends. MacDonald, in particular, cites one incident on the campus of Emory University where the students "drew on *The Communist Manifesto*" to protest and call Trump "fascist, racist" in 2016 (26–27). "Campus intolerance," asserts MacDonald, "is at root not a psychological phenomenon, but an ideological one. At its center is a worldview that sees Western culture as endemically racist and sexist" (29).

Many community voters, based on decades of empirical studies, do not form their political opinions based on systematic, deeply rooted ideology (Kinder and Kalmoe, 2017; Zaller, 1992). In the early 1990s, political scientists Paul Sniderman and Thomas Piazza (1993) in *The Scar of Race*, discover that white voters' opinions about minority groups can change quickly, dependent upon external stimuli. They believe that through education more whites will become more tolerant in terms of their views on racial relations. Their argument offers an optimistic outlook toward the future, as whites are becoming more educated over time. Other scholars dispute if this optimist view has come true. They especially question whether whites' deeply held views, such as Protestant individualism, may have in fact played a negative role in their attitude about minorities, especially Black Americans (Kinder and Sears, 1981, 1996).

This book suggests that whites may change their view about minorities, but the extent of the change also is dependent upon how they perceive threats from the minorities. It is the political elites, especially candidates such as Trump, who play the leadership role in materializing the perception of voters concerning how the minority threats should be ranked ordered and how a particular minority-group become the faces of imminent concrete threats to whites. To fully understand whether or not a campaign strategy can succeed in mobilizing white electorate to respond to such minority threats, one needs to examine the atomic structure and its governing ADVICE principles.

This chapter adopts the atomic structure to explain group relations in the Trump era. In doing so, we focus on how Trump has articulated a threat environment in which whites are the threatened, and Hispanics and Muslims are the two main sources of threats. We also focus on how Trump articulates the threat contents that these two groups have brought to white Christians. As shown by the statistical findings presented in this chapter, Trump's articulation about why the greatness of America was threatened by certain groups (e.g., Mexicans and Muslims) had a major impact on white opinions about immigration and the outcome of the 2016 presidential election. We now turn to the conclusion to put the Trump era in the broad context of American history and develop a normative claim regarding the trajectory of the constitutional democratic republic.

Conclusion

On January 8, 2019, at 9 p.m. Eastern Standard Time, President Trump used a prime-time nationally televised address to urge the U.S. Congress to cooperate with him on dealing with a "growing humanitarian and security crisis" at the nation's southern border. Trump asked Congress to approve his request for $5.7 billion in border wall funding, along with millions for additional detention beds and new screening technology, designed to counteract the flow of new immigrants into the country. Minutes after Trump completed his address, Nancy Pelosi, U.S. Speaker of the House, joined her Democratic colleague, Senate Minority Leader Chuck Schumer to respond to Trump's remarks. Pelosi accused Trump of holding federal workers and the government hostage "over his obsession with forcing American taxpayers to waste billions of dollars on an expensive and ineffective wall—a wall he always promised Mexico would pay for."

As the nation watched the two parties fighting against each other on a nationally televised broadcast about the future of protecting the nation's southern border, nine federal agencies, including the U.S. Department of Agriculture, had been shut down for eighteen days since December 21, 2018, which affected more than 800,000 federal employees, and, as some reports quoted, "millions of America's most vulnerable citizens are in danger of being left to go hungry" (Golshan, 2019). Trump's speech would not resolve the matter at that point, as the government shutdown already had become the second longest in U.S. history and the second time in his presidency that federal workers had been furloughed. "What will happen to these federal employees and millions of Americans who need paycheck from the federal government?" Americans went to bed with this question on January 8, 2019. For sure, it was also the question President Trump and the Democratic leaders in Congress wanted to know the answer to that night.

Of course, politics deal with unpredictability and uncertainty. And, even when the root cause of the crisis is apolitical, such as the COVID-19 pandemic in 2020, unpredictability is poised to undo and make new political dynamics for success. Arguably, one of government's most important functions should be to provide predictability and stability in people's lives. But what if the government itself is responsible for why unpredictability and uncertainty disrupt people's lives? More importantly, to what extent should people expect the government to ensure predictability and stability in their lives, especially as services have a direct impact at home, in their schools and in their workplaces? What about democracy? Are we seeing the American democracy—the most mature and highly developed political system of its kind in modern history—become perpetually mired in problems of unpredictability and instability?

The day after Trump's speech, a White House meeting with Congressional leaders ended abruptly, as the president slammed his fist on the table and left the room after Pelosi again rejected his request to fund the construction of a southern border wall. Meanwhile, Republican Congressional leaders claimed that such a dramatic end to the meeting did not occur, adding the president was cordial. Two days after his speech, the president held a rally in McAllen, Texas, not denying the speculation that he would declare a national emergency to build the wall. Meanwhile, Pelosi dismissed such threats as a calculated distraction from other problems. On January 12, 2019, the shutdown became the longest in the modern era, as the president went to Twitter with the following: "Democrats should come back to Washington and work to end the Shutdown, while at the same time ending the horrible humanitarian crisis at our Southern Border. I am in the White House waiting for you!" Several days later, Pelosi wrote to the president, recommending that he postpone the State of the Union address, scheduled for January 29, until after the shutdown was resolved. On January 17, the president pulled security funds and military air access for a previously secret Congressional delegation visit to Brussels and Afghanistan. On January 19, Trump announced he would offer a limited period extending the Deferred Action for Child Arrivals (DACA) program in exchange for funding the border. Democrats quickly rejected the offer. The shutdown ended finally on January 25 when Trump agreed to a three-week stopgap appropriations bill. Despite polls showing most Americans did not consider the border wall a sufficient reason to shut the government for so long, on February 15, the president declared a national emergency, bypassing the Congress to secure allocations for the wall. The episode epitomized the confrontational nature of national politics.

The election of Trump in 2016 took many observers of democracies, including veteran political scientists, by surprise. Harvard University scholars Levitsky and Ziblatt (2018) published their *New York Times* bestseller, *How*

Democracies Die, after the 2016 election. The book was based on a comparative study of how democracies ended in different nation-state contexts, but it also had a clear aim of reminding American people of the potential danger of electing Trump. Throughout the history of political science, however, most scholars have agreed that the American democracy, especially its electoral feature of "First-Past-the-Post," produced greater stability than various proportional representation systems developed in European democratic arrangements (see Milnor, 1969). A closer look at American history, nonetheless, reveals instability as well. This instability is not all bad, and the volatility engendered by the American democracy, in fact, sometimes has helped racial and religious minorities, while at other times has hurt their most critical interests.

This book proposes a theoretical model—an atomic structure to address the unpredictability and uncertainty that have touched all major political groups, including major ethnic and religious subgroups from the white electorate, namely, Germans, Catholics, Latter-day Saints, and Jews, etc. The book also has discussed how the political fates of racial minorities (Blacks, Native Americans, Hispanics and Asians) have fluctuated throughout history. Even the WASPs, the dominant political group that founded the Republic, did not escape the political fate of volatility, and their dominant status now is in the history book with a finite ending. This book points to the underlying structure that has contributed to the unpredictability and instability of American democracy in the first place.

The book uses the term "volatility," because volatility entails both unpredictability and instability. Imagine this analogy from the economic world: When investors use the term "volatility," they most likely stress their inability to forecast the performance of financial markets, especially stock prices. This inability usually exhibits two unusual conditions in which investors find themselves. First, their previously useful forecast model loses its power to predict. The theory, which was used to build the model, seems like a poor fit in a new situation. Second, the speed of changes has increased in a digital environment where events break and unfold instantaneously, which reminds investors that the time dimension has become much more crucial, and the stake of making quick and the best decisions is raised accordingly. In politics, to say that the system has become volatile, we should also examine whether or not the unpredictability satisfies two tests. That is, an existing insufficient predictive power and the heightened decision-making pressure that must be reconciled within an ever-narrowing interval.

It is in this sense that this book contributes to rethinking and remodeling the idea of political volatility, which becomes instructive for future political leaders who are sensitive to reconciling that volatility with effective impact addressing the groups comprising the atomic structure of American politics.

As indicated above, volatility also implies instability, which is an important and necessary feature. Just because one cannot predict what will happen to stock prices does not mean necessarily that the stock market is unstable. It may turn out that the actual prices of stocks become stable at the end. Therefore, we cannot call this scenario a volatile market. To be volatile, the stock prices must exhibit instability, which, in effect, requires the upward and downward movements in price changes in one fashion or another. One important corollary of this instability (i.e., because it can go up, or down) is that the outcome of volatility does not have to be a worsening process. Some investors may, in fact, become the winners of a volatile stock market. Put differently, volatility does not always harm the actors in the market.

For the same reason, when we discuss the volatility in the American democratic political system, it is possible that the political outcomes may favor some political groups. Throughout history, we see that racial and religious minorities occasionally become political winners in spite of their peripheral positions in the atomic structure, which does not stop white voters, still comprising the super majority of the electorate in the United States today, from occupying the center stage of power structure. Minorities can become winners occasionally, but they also cannot accomplish any political success without significant support from a key subset of the white electorate.

Though it is difficult to examine a democratic political system to make a judgment about unpredictability and instability, political scientists fortunately can use at least two important political indicators to gauge the political unpredictability and instability affecting government's ability to govern. The first such indicator points to the changes in policies which include laws, administrative decisions, court decisions, and judicial opinions, etc., which can be collectively called the changes in policy output. If the changes in policy output indeed reveal unpredictability and instability, then we can say that the political system is volatile. In this book, we have shown how social groups in history, especially based on race and religion, have faced volatility in terms of the unexpected changes in policy outputs. The second useful indicator for political volatility points to political changes in elected officials. If one sees a greater turnover in U.S. Congress within a short period, for example, it is a clear sign of volatility. If the presidency switches hands between the two major political parties within a short time, it is another sign of volatility. Moreover, if the types of politicians elected or nominated to powerful positions differ significantly from the conventional nature or portfolio of politicians, it also is a sign of volatility.

For example, Obama, the first Black American was elected in 2008, and he was re-elected in 2012 by defeating Romney, the first Latter-day Saint politician ever nominated by a major political party. Trump, the first elected president without any prior political or military experience, defeated Clinton, the first woman nominee for a major political party, in 2016. This new class of precedent-setting politicians competed and succeeded for the highest elected office of the land within a period of just eight years, which demonstrates political volatility in the American electoral system today. The most important task certainly is to find out why there has been political volatility in American democracy. This book suggests that to investigate the causes of political volatility in the United States, it is imperative to pay attention to structural factors. A political system is volatile because it is structured to act in such a manner. This book explains why the atomic structure is essential to political volatility.

SOLVING THE POLITICAL PUZZLES

In the first two chapters of this book, we raised a fundamental question: Can a politically cohesive social group experience any significant change in its group status within the American democratic framework? The answer to this question, as previous chapters have demonstrated, is clearly yes. To explain why political changes are inevitable for all major social groups, we examined why between the 2012 primary and general presidential election that year white Protestants, the traditionally dominant religious group in the United States, changed their attitude toward Romney, a prominent candidate from a religious minority group. In addition, the book focused on why racial minority groups throughout history, such as African Americans, have experienced political changes in their group status—sometimes for better, sometimes for worse. Another political puzzle was what led to the end of the WASP-dominant group status.

These puzzles can be solved by the theory of atomic structure, as proposed in this book, which suggests that to study any political change related to a social group in the atomic structure the most important objectives are, first, to identify the threat environment in which the dominant group reacts to the perceptions of multiple threats from the peripheral groups; and, second, to identify the competing views within the dominant group that lead to the success of one electoral coalition against another.

With respect to the first task, the three elements of a threat environment—the threatener, the threatened, and threat content—are governed by two axioms: the attraction principle (A1) which states that in a political system the dominant group (DG) ranks, orders, and positions the subordinate groups (SGs), based on how similar they are, and the distance principle (A2), which states that the extent of threat from a particular SG is based on the distance between the DG and this SG. The reactions to multiple threats by the DG and the consequences of such reactions follow the volatility principle (A3):

the higher the perception of a SG threat, the greater the range of possible DG responses to such a threat, and thus the higher the political volatility this SG experiences. Obama's two elections showed that the dominant white group perceived and ordered multiple threats from minority groups (e.g., from Blacks and Latter-day Saints) and reacted accordingly.

With respect to the second task, it is important to remember that though the members of the DG may collectively perceive multiple threats from SGs, this perception sometimes only remains at the abstract threat level that may not necessarily lead to similar political actions, such as voting in a way that is anti-minority either on a candidate or an issue. In fact, individual DG members may act differently toward minority groups because of various concrete threats they perceive from the minority groups versus the perceived threat from other whites who happen to be in the opposing electoral coalition. We refer to the internally different reactions from the white electorate as the internal-threat principle (A4). Thus, to understand the temporary political status of a SG at a given time, it is necessary to know which electoral coalition wins competitive elections, especially in presidential years, because the winner now has the chance to enact institutional decisions toward the SG (A5). These five axioms comprise the ADVICE principles in this book.

Certainly, it always is important to ask which social group(s) are permitted to enter the dominant core of the atomic structure. Obviously in a democratic system, demographic changes always have a profound impact on the formation and change of the dominant core and political fate of minorities (see chapter 11). But it also is equally important, if not more so, to examine the institutional decisions that either incorporate or marginalize minority groups. In chapter 7, we discussed seven possible responses that the dominant core may institutionally act upon regarding the minority groups. These responses include assimilation, negotiation, discrimination, disfranchisement, exclusion, removal, and enslavement.

It is clear that different minority groups may experience different institutional treatments that take the form of one or more of the aforementioned responses. To be incorporated into the dominant core, however, a minority group must go through the assimilation process. This book, especially in chapters 9, 10 and 11, shows that German Americans, white Catholics, and eventually all whites of European origin were gradually assimilated to the modern-day group of whites, who now occupy the core of the current atomic structure. One consequence of transforming the core of the atomic structure was the end of the WASP-dominant group status. The implications of ending this status were magnified in the Trump era, both in terms of emboldened self-confidence among minority groups, as well as the backlash of some segments of the white electorate against the political agenda carried out during the Obama Administration.

In sum, this book offers a unified theory to explain the remarkable changes in the political statuses of major social groups, including WASPs, German and other western Europeans, white Catholics, Blacks, Hispanics, Asians, American Indians, and other minority groups. They contribute to an ever-diversifying demographic portrait of the United States. It is worth noting that while these political changes are inevitable in the long run for all social groups, the underlying atomic structure and the five axioms upon which the atomic structure operates likely will continue to endure.

THE ATOMIC STRUCTURE IS NOT A HIERARCHICAL/CASTE SYSTEM

Given the "stickiness" of race (Harris and Liberman, 2013), it is tempting to conclude that the American political system is a hierarchical one. This claim, surprisingly, has been made by both liberal thinkers on the political left (e.g., Winant, 2004) and conservative scholars on the right (e.g., MacDonald, 2018). Winant (2004), for example, wrote, "Once, U.S. society was a nearly monolithic racial hierarchy, in which everyone knew 'his' place" (4). The Civil Rights Movement, according to Winant, only achieved a symbolic success, as white supremacy now goes "hidden" behind the new "confused" and "anxiety-ridden" morality of whites (4). Conservative scholars, even those who do not directly claim an intellectual allegiance to conservatism, believe that whites are now at the bottom of the racial hierarchy because of the successful political agenda advocating for multiculturalism (Kaufmann, 2004; MacDonald, 2018).

On the 2016 presidential campaign trail and during his term, Trump often invoked the phrase of "politically correct" to talk about how the country had been dominated by liberal ideologues and that white voters like himself had long been victimized in American liberal politics. Trump was speaking to his white-voter base, especially his white evangelical stronghold. As discussed in chapter 13, one study (Norton and Sommers, 2011) contends that white racial attitude is deeply rooted in the perception of how whites are threatened, either through a concrete threat such as affirmative action policies or through an abstract threat to white (European) values in general. But, Norton and Sommers's study also failed to explain why 43 percent of white voters voted against Trump in the 2016 general election (42 percent of whites rejected him in 2020). This study also cannot explain why 43 percent of whites did not share Trump's racially charged views about Judge Curiel (a Mexican American), who presided over a class-action lawsuit against Trump University.

To be sure, a theory of racial relations must be able to account for not only what divides racial groups (i.e., intergroup differences) but also what divides the people of the same race (i.e., intragroup divergence). To modify the prevailing approach used in many previous studies of racial politics, namely focusing on either intergroup differences or intragroup divergence, this book has filled the gap by studying both intergroup and intragroup differences simultaneously. The atomic structure, therefore, represents an integrated approach of examining intergroup and intragroup differences.

The intragroup differences, more specifically as represented by the internal-threat principle of this book (A4), is important because it invites researchers to focus on how internal differences occur and are manifested. The inner division, which is rooted in disagreements among white elites and voters concerning whether or not they should treat minorities as a concrete threat, makes the whole atomic structure capable of generating and adapting to changes in the political environment including demographic changes and immigration patterns. Moreover, despite the potent attraction principle, which is empirically supported by the NES data as analyzed in this book, the competing opinions inside the dominant white group at the core of the atomic structure about how the political system should treat minorities differentiates the atomic structure from its hierarchical counterparts elsewhere, such as the caste system in India, which operated between 1860 and 1920 when there was a homogeneous ruling class.

Even at the founding of the American republic, there already was the rivalry between pro- and anti-slavery alliances (King and Smith, 2011). As Rogers Smith reminds us, even among the Founding Fathers, there was a major difference between those (e.g., Thomas Paine), who cherished the idea of brotherly love of all Europeans, and those who wanted the door closed to non-Anglos. For Thomas Jefferson, even "'Scotch and foreign mercenaries' did not share 'our common blood'" (Smith, 2015, 151). Furthermore, though the Founding Fathers delayed the slavery problem for future debates, the division about slavery in the post-constitutional era was a key driving force for the eventual positive and dramatic change for Black political status in the 1860s. A hierarchical, static, and closed caste-like political system would not have been able to produce this change. Furthermore, the atomic structure in the U.S. history was reconfigured periodically—for example, the new racial alliances of pro-Jim Crow versus anti-Jim Crow after 1896 would replace the old rivalry of pro-slavery versus anti-slavery alliances, and the contemporary rivalry took its form after the 1960s between the color-blind and race-conscious alliances (King and Smith, 2011). In each historical era, there has been a racial alliance that has fought politically for more constitutional and legal protections of minority groups.

As an eyewitness to the horrors imposed on the Blacks in the South in 1831, the young French aristocrat, Alexis de Tocqueville wrote, as translated here, "If one refuses freedom to Negros in the South, they will in the end seize it violently themselves" (Tocqueville, 2000, 348). Tocqueville's prediction at least was wrong, in that the freedom of Blacks was not achieved by Black violence. He certainly could not have predicted the eventual success of the atomic structure, as presented in this book, in electing the nation's first Black president. His pessimism was certainly not due to him underestimating the human desire for equality. In fact, he forcefully argued that between the goal of liberty and the desire for equality, the former cannot match the power of the latter in human history. Tocqueville published his masterpiece, *Democracy in America*, to appeal to European audiences to embrace democracy, as he had observed in the young republic in North America. But why did he fail to anticipate the American progress and equality for non-Europeans including the Black slaves about whom he had written so compassionately? The answer comes from his failure to notice the whole picture of the atomic structure in the American constitutional democracy, which already had taken its enduring form.

VOLATILITY AND POLITICAL PROGRESS

All social groups demand political changes to achieve favorable outcomes in a constitutional democracy. Changes may take many forms, and they can be forward looking (e.g., "change we can believe in" slogan, as coined by the Obama campaign), or nostalgic (e.g., "make America great again," as coined by the Trump campaign). But all changes often lead to unintended consequences, and thus political volatility becomes inevitable. Obama's successful campaigns in 2008 and 2012, for example, led to greater white resentment manifested by the Tea Party movement and the subsequent election of Trump in 2016. This book addresses the empirical question of why political volatility occurs, and the normative question of whether or not social justice is achievable over time, given seemingly ubiquitous political volatility.

The attraction and distance-threat principles (A1 and A2) receive empirical support, as based on our survey data and electoral analyses. This book indicates that members of religious and racial groups always are capable of having greater affections for themselves, as suggested by intuitionists, such as David Hume. But, in-group favoritism also did not disempower Americans and led to greater inequality over time at the group level. Greater degrees of equality at the group level can be measured by rights, legal protections, and the expanding political representation of traditionally marginal groups. For example, the access to a ballot is protected constitutionally today for minorities much more so than in the distant past. The right of citizenship once was granted to only free white persons, and it is now available to qualified legal immigrants from all over the world. The U.S. Congress today has lawmakers who represent various racial and religious groups including Muslims. All these measures of progress have been achieved because of collective forces— namely, the atomic structure of politics.

Inside the atomic structure, political groups interact with each other and form particular threat environments between and among themselves. The political fate of a particular group, whether it is the dominant core or the secondary periphery, is determined by multiple environmental factors. As we have seen from the empirical analysis of the 2012 presidential election, voters and politicians do calculate strategically in order to defeat their perceived most threatening candidate in volatile environments. A minority group (such as Latter-day Saints) may be the beneficiary of these strategic calculations of risk aversion, as shown in chapter 12 of this book.

More equality among racial and religious groups does not suggest, nonetheless, that there is always a monotonic increase toward equality. In fact, religious and racial minority groups often receive worse treatments just after they gain more rights, political status, and benefits from the political system. For example, we saw the backlash during the Jim Crow South after the Reconstruction Era, and immediately following Obama's administration we have witnessed the hostility of the Trump administration toward legal and undocumented immigrants, most notably from Latin America. Despite the volatility facing minority groups, this book explains the fundamental reason for the existence of inequality between and among groups, as well as the positive political changes in the long run, influenced by various electoral majorities to reduce such inequality.

The 2020 election outcomes, once again, demonstrated the volatile political era the country has experienced. While 81 million votes were cast for Joe Biden, the second Catholic candidate winning a presidential election, Trump gathered more than 74 million votes, the second largest number of votes cast for a candidate in the U.S. history. Despite the Democratic victory in the presidential race, the Republican Party gained more seats in the House of Representatives and state legislatures across the country. As Morris Fiorina (2017) commented at the end of his book regarding the 2016 election:

"For now, at least, an era of unstable majorities continues" (223).

Bibliography

Acharya, Avidit, Matthew Blackwell, and Maya Sen. 2018. *Deep Roots: How Slavery Still Shapes Southern Politics.* Princeton, NJ: Princeton University Press.

Adkins, Todd, Geoffrey C. Layman, David E. Campbell, and John C. Green. 2013. "Religious Group Cues and Citizen Policy Attitudes in the United States." *Politics and Religion*, 6(2), 235–263.

Adorno, T., E. Frenkel-Brunswik, D. Levinson, and R. Sanford. 1950. *The Authoritarian Personality.* New York: Norton.

AP Reporting. 2019. "Candidate: Marysville Should Be as White as Possible." https://www.wxyz.com/news/candidate-marysville-should-be-as-white-as-possible. Accessed December 1, 2019.

Ayres, I., F. E. Vars, and N. Zakariya. 2005. "To Insure Prejudice: Racial Disparities in Taxicab Tipping." *Yale Law Journal*, 114, 1613–1674.

Barreto, Matt. 2007. "Si Se Puede! Latino Candidates and the Mobilization of Latino Voters." *American Political Science Review*, 101(3, August), 425–441.

Barreto, Matt. 2011. *Ethnic Cues: The Roles of Shared Ethnicity in Latino Political Participation.* Ann Arbor, MI: The University of Michigan Press.

Barrett, Devlin, Nick Miroff, and Marissa J. Lang. 2020. "More Federal Agents Dispatched to Portland as Protests Rise in Other Cities." *The Washington Post.* https://www.washingtonpost.com/politics/more-federal-agents-dispatched-to-portland-as-protests-rise-in-other-cities/2020/07/27/20a717be-d03c-11ea-8d32-1ebf4e9d8e0d_story.html. Accessed July 27, 2020.

Bartels, Larry M. 2008. *Unequal Democracy.* Princeton, NJ: Princeton University Press.

Beck, Paul Allen, and Frank J. Sorauf. 1992. *Party Politics in America.* New York, NY: Harper Collins Publishers.

Bennett, Lerone. 2000. *Forced into Glory: Abraham Lincoln's White Dream.* Johnson Publishing Co.

Billig, Michael, and Henri Tajfel. 1973. "Social Categorization and Similarity in Intergroup Behaviour." *European Journal of Social Psychology*, 3, 27–52.

Black, Earl, and Merle Black. 2002. *The Rise of Southern Republicans*. Cambridge, MA: Harvard University Press.

Blumer, Herbert. 1958. "Racial Prejudice as a Sense of Group Position." *The Pacific Sociological Review*, 1(1), 3–7.

Brigham, Carl C. 1923. *A Study of American Intelligence*. Princeton, NJ: Princeton University Press.

Brown, Robert. 2005. "Minority Politics in the 2004 Presidential Election." In Larry J. Sabato, ed. *Get in the Booth: A Citizen's Guild to the 2004 Election*. New York: Pearson Education, Inc. pp. 107–118.

Browning, Rufus, Dale Rogers Marshall, and David H. Tabb. 2003. *Racial Politics in American Cities*. New York: Longman.

Bruce, Steve. 2004. "The Strange Death of Protestant Britain." In Eric P. Kaufmann, ed. *Rethinking Ethnicity: Majority Groups and Dominant Minorities*. London and New York: Routledge. pp. 61–83.

Byrne, D. 1961. "Interpersonal Attraction and Attitude Similarity." *The Journal of Abnormal and Social Psychology*, 62, 713–715. doi:10.1037/ h0044721.

Cain, Bruce. 1995. "Racial and Ethnic Politics." In Gillian Peele, Christopher J. Bailey, Bruce Cain and B. Guy Peters, ed. *Developments in American Politics*. Chatham, NJ: Chatham House Publishers, Inc. pp. 45–66.

Campbell, Angus, Philip E. Converse, Warren E. Miller, and Donald E. Stokes. 1960. *The American Voter*. New York: John Wiley & Sons, Inc.

Campbell, David E., John C. Green, and J. Quin Monson. 2012. "The Stained Glass Ceiling: Social Contact and Mitt Romney's 'Religion Problem'." *Political Behavior*, 34(2), 277–299.

Campbell, David E., John C. Green, and J. Quin Monson. 2014. *Seeking the Promised Land: Mormons and American Politics*. New York: Cambridge University Press.

Carmines, Edward G., and James A. Stimson. 1989. *Issue Evolution: Race and the Transformation of American Politics*. Princeton, NJ: Princeton University Press.

Carsey, Thomas M. 1995. "The Contextual Effects of Race on White Voter Behavior: The 1989 New York City Mayoral Election." *The Journal of Politics*, 57, 221–228.

Ceaser, James W., Andrew E. Busch, and John J. Pitney, Jr. 2009. *Epic Journey: The 2008 Elections and American Politics*. Lanham: Rowman & Littlefield Publishers, Inc.

Christakis, Nicholas A. 2019. *Blueprint: The Evolutionary Origins of a Good Society*. New York: Little, Brown Spark.

Chua, Amy, and Jed Rubenfeld. 2014. *The Triple Package: How Three Unlikely Traits Explain the Rise and Fall of Cultural Groups in America*. New York: The Penguin Press.

Clayton, Dewey. 2010. *The Presidential Campaign of Barrack Obama: A Critical Analysis of a Radically Transcendent Strategy*. New York, NY: Routledge.

Clymer, Adam. 2002. "Republican Party's 40 Years of Juggling on Race." *New York Times*, December 13, 2002.

CNN. "Donald Trump Speech at Liberty University; Democratic Rivals Clash over Health Care at Debate." January 18, 2016. http://transcripts.cnn.com/ TRANSCRIPTS/1601/18/ath.01.html.

Coates, Ta-Nehisi. 2004. "Running from Race." *The Village Voice*, February 11–17, 2004.

Coates, Ta-Nehisi. 2013. "The Unromantic Slaughter of the Civil War." *The Atlantic.* https://www.theatlantic.com/national/archive/2013/06/the-unromantic-slaughter-of-the-civil-war/277051/. Accessed March 20, 2020.

Coleman, Steve. 2012. "Robert Jeffress, Southern Baptist Pastor Who Called Mormonism a 'Cult,' Endorses Mitt Romney." *Huffington Post.* http://www.huffingtonpost.com/2012/04/17/robert-jeffress-mitt-romney- endorsement_n_1433215.html. Accessed April 17, 2012.

Crotty, William, ed. 2012. *The Obama Presidency: Promise and Performance.* Lanham, MD: Lexington Books.

Culter, Lloyd N. 1986. "To Form a Government." In Robert A. Goldwin and Art Kaufman, ed. *Separation of Powers: Does It Still Work?.* Washington, DC: American Enterprise Institute. pp. 1–17.

Dahl, Robert. 1962. *Who Governs? Democracy and Power in American City.* New Haven, CT: Yale University Press.

Davidson, Chandler. 1972. *Biracial Politics: Conflict and Coalition in the Metropolitan South.* Baton Rouge: Louisiana State University Press.

Davidson, Chandler. 1994. "The Recent Evolution of Voting Rights Law Affecting Racial and Language Minorities." In Chandler Davidson and Bernard Grofman, ed. *Quiet Revolution in the South: The Impact of the Voting Rights Act, 1965–1990.* Princeton, NJ: Princeton University Press. pp. 21–37.

Davidson, Chandler and Bernard Grofman, ed. 1994. *Quiet Revolution in the South: The Impact of the Voting Rights Act, 1965–1990.* Princeton, NJ: Princeton University Press. pp. 21–37.

Dawson, Michael C. 1994. *Behind the Mule: Race and Class in African-American Politics.* Princeton, NJ: Princeton University Press.

De Mesquita, Bruce Bueno, Alastair Smith, Randolph M. Siverson, and James D. Morrow. 2005. *The Logic of Political Survival.* Cambridge, MA: The MIT Press.

Do, Mai N. 2020. "In 2018, 70 Percent of Asian American Candidates Won State Legislative Office." *AAPI Data.* http://aapidata.com/blog/aa-state-leg-elections-2018/. Accessed March 20, 2020.

Donovan, T. 2010. "Obama and the White Vote." *Political Research Quarterly,* 63(4), 863–874.

Donavan, Todd, and Rob Hunsaker. 2009. "Beyond Expectations: Effects of Early Elections in U.S. Presidential Nomination Contests." *PS: Political Science and Politics,* 42(1, January), 45–52.

Dovere, Edward-Issac. 2012. "Romney's Mormon Faith in Spotlight." *Politico.* http://www.politico.com/news/stories/0512/76776.html. Accessed May 28, 2012.

Downs, Anthony. 1957. *An Economic Theory of Democracy.* New York, NY: Harper and Row.

Doyle, John (Jack). 2014. "Measuring 'Problems of Human Behavior': The Eugenic Origins of Yale's Institute of Psychology, 1921–1929." Unpublished manuscript. p. 27.

Dustmann, C. 2015. *Migration: Economic Change, Social Challenge.* Oxford: Oxford University Press.

Easley, Jason. 2013. "Mitt Romney Blames The IRS and Hurricane Sandy For His Loss to Obama." *Politics USA*. http://www.politicususa.com/2013/06/06/mitt-romney-blames-irs-hurricane-sandy-loss-obama.html. Accessed June 6, 2013.

Elazar, Daniel. J. 1984. *American Federalism: A View from the States*. New York: Crowell.

Espenshade, T. J., and Hempstead, K. 1996. "Contemporary American Attitudes toward U.S. Immigration." *International Migration Review*, 30(2), 535.

Fea, John. 2020. "After Impeachment Acquittal, Trump Uses Prayer Breakfast for Political Target Practice." *USA Today*. https://www.usatoday.com/story/opinion/2020/02/06/trump-attacks-pelosi-and-romney-national-prayer-breakfast-column/4679150002/. Accessed February 10, 2020.

Fetzer, J. S. 2000. *Public Attitudes toward Immigration in the United States, France, and Germany*. Cambridge: Cambridge University Press.

Finnegan, Michael. 2004 May 3. "Kerry's Low Profile May Cost Crucial Latino Votes." *Los Angeles Times*. https://www.latimes.com/archives/la-xpm-2004-may-03-na-latinovotes3-story.html.

Fiorina, Morris. 1989. *Congress: Keystone of the Washington Establishment*. Yale University Press.

Fiorina, Morris. 1996. *Divided Government*. 2nd ed. Boston: Allyn and Bacon.

Fiorina, Morris. 2017. *Unstable Majorities: Polarization, Party Sorting and Political Stalemate*. Stanford, CA: Hoover Institution Press.

Foner, Eric. 1970. *Free Soil, Free Labor, Free Men: The Ideology of the Republican Party before the Civil War*. New York: Oxford University Press.

Foster, Graig L. 2008. *A Different God? Mitt Romney, the Religious Right, and the Mormon Question*. Salt Lake City, UT: Greg Kofford Books.

Fox News Reporting. 2011. "Baptist Pastor Defends 'Cult' Description of Mormonism, Still Backs Romney over Obama." http://www.foxnews.com/politics/2011/10/09/baptist-pastor-defends-cult-description-mormonism-still-backs-romney-over-obama/. Accessed October 9, 2011.

Friedman, Thomas L. 2020. "Whatever Trump Is Hiding Is Hurting All of Us Now." *The New York Times*. https://www.nytimes.com/2018/02/18/opinion/trump-russia-putin.html. Accessed February 20, 2018.

Frymer, Paul. 1999. *Uneasy Alliances: Race and Party Competition in America*. Princeton, NJ: Princeton University Press.

Feuerherd, Ben. 2014. "Dave Brat: The Anti-Immigrant Thorn In Eric Cantor's Side." http://www.nationalmemo.com/dave-brat-anti-immigrant-thorn-eric-cantors-side/. Accessed May 9, 2017.

Gaertner, S. L., and Bickman, L. 1971. "Effects of Race on the Elicitation of Helping Behavior: The Wrong Number Technique." *Journal of Personality and Social Psychology*, 20, 218–222. doi:10.1037/h0031681.

Garrison, William Lloyd. [1868–1879] 1981. *The Letters of William Lloyd Garrison, Vol. VI: To Rouse the Slumbering Land, 1868–1879*. Edited by Walter M. Merril and Louis Ruchames. Cambridge, MA and London: Belknap Press.

Genovese, Eugene D. 1974. *Roll, Jordan, Roll: The World the Slaves Made*. New York, NY: Pantheon Books.

Giles, M. W., and M. A. Buckner. 1993. "David Duke and Black Threat: An Old Hypothesis Revisited." *Journal of Politics*, 55(3), 702–713.

Giles, M., and K. Hertz. 1994. "Racial Threat and Partisan Identification." *American Political Science Review,* 88(2), 317–326.

Gillespie, Andra, ed. 2012. *Whose Black Politics? Cases in Post-Racial Black Leadership.* New York, NY: Routledge.

Gillespie, Andra. 2012. *The New Black Politician: Cory Booker, Newark, and Post-Racial America.* New York, NY: New York University Press.

Gillion, Daniel Q. 2016. *Governing with Words: The Political Dialogue on Race, Public Policy, and Inequality in America.* New York, NY: Cambridge University Press.

Gimpel, James G. 1999. *Separate Destinations: Migration, Immigration, and the Politics of Places.* Ann Arbor: The University of Michigan Press.

Glaser, J. M. 1994. "Back to the Black Belt: Racial Environment and White Racial Attitudes in the South." *Journal of Politics,* 56(1), 21–41.

Gleason, Philip. 1992. *Speaking of Diversity: Language and Ethnicity in Twentieth-Century America.* Baltimore and London: John Hopkins University Press.

Golshan, Tara. 2019. "More than 38 Million People Are on Food Stamps. The Government Shutdown Could Hit Them Hard." *Vox.* https://www.vox.com/2019 /1/7/18172198/government-shutdown-snap-food-stamps. Accessed January 10, 2019.

Green, Donald P., and Ian Shapiro. 1994. *Pathologies of Rational Choice Theory.* New Haven, CT: Yale University Press.

Greenwald, A. G., and T. F. Pettigrew. 2014. "With Malice toward None and Charity for Some: Ingroup Favoritism Enables Discrimination." *American Psychologist.* Advance online publication. doi:10.1037/a0036056.

Grieve, Tim. 2010. "31% of Republicans Believe Barack Obama Is Muslim." *Politico.* http://www.politico.com/news/stories/0810/41248.html. Accessed August 19, 2010.

Griffin, John D., and Brian Newman. 2008. *Minority Report.* Chicago: The University of Chicago Press.

Guadagnoli, E., Velicer, W. F., et al. 1988. "Relation of Sample Size to the Stability of Component Patterns." *Psychological Bulletin,* 103(2), 265–275.

Haidt, Jonathon. 2012. *The Righteous Mind: Why Good People Are Divided by Politics and Religion.* New York: Vintage Books.

Haines, Pavielle E., Tali Mendelberg, and Bennett Butler. 2019. "'I'm Not the President of Black America': Rhetorical versus Policy Representation." *Perspective on Politics,* 17(4), 1038–1058.

Hajnal, Zoltan L. 2006. *Changing White Attitudes toward Black Political Leadership.* New York, NY: Cambridge University Press.

Harper, Richard Conant. 1980. *The Course of the Melting Pot Idea to 1910.* New York: Arno Press.

Harris, Fredrick C. 2012. *The Price of the Ticket: Barack Obama and the Rise and Decline of Black Politics.* New York, NY: Oxford University Press.

Harris, Fredrick C., and Robert C. Lieberman, eds. 2013. *Beyond Discrimination: Racial Inequality in a Post Racial Era*. New York, NY: Russell Sage Foundation.

Harwood, E. 1986. "American Public Opinion and U.S. Immigration Policy." *The Annals of the American Academy*, 484: 201–212.

Hatemi, Peter K., and Rose McDermott, ed. 2011. *Man Is by Nature a Political Animal: Evolution, Biology, and Politics*. Chicago, IL: University of Chicago Press.

Hawthorne, Thomas. 2019. "'It's Real. It's Violent:' After El Paso, Latinos across America Live in Fear." *USA Today*. https://apple.news/A7BziU18LQzastp TCX4hdsQ. Accessed November 1, 2019.

Hayes, Christal. 2019. "Alabama Republicans Are Urging Rep. Ilhan Omar's Expulsion from Congress." *USA Today*. https://apple.news/Ap6z2eC4rQGKXqP qRhWFPhQ. Accessed December 1, 2019.

Henry, Charles P., Robert L. Allen, and Robert Chrisman, eds. 2011. *The Obama Phenomenon: Toward a Multiracial Democracy*. Chicago, IL: University of Illinois Press.

Hero, R. E. 2007. *Racial Diversity and Social Capital: Equality and Community in America*. New York, NY: Cambridge University Press.

Hero, Rodney E. 1992. *Latinos and the U.S. Political System: Two-Tiered Pluralism*. Philadelphia, PA: Temple University Press.

Hetherington, Marc J., and Jonathan D. Weiler. 2009. *Authoritarianism and Polarization in American Politics*. New York: Cambridge University Press.

Higham, John. 1988. *Strangers in the Land: Patterns of American Nativism, 1860–1925*. New Brunswick: Rutgers University Press.

Hobson, Charles F. 1996. *The Great Chief Justice: John Marshall and the Rule of Law*. Lawrence, KS: University Press of Kansas.

Horowitz, Jason. 2012. "Is Mormonism Fair Game?" *The Washington Post*. http://www.washingtonpost.com/opinions/is-mitt-romneys-mormonism-fair-game/2012/06/01/gJQAhDo56U_story.html. Accessed June 1, 2012.

Howell, Susan E. 1994. "Racism, Cynicism, Economics, and David Duke." *American Politics Quarterly*, 22, 190–207.

Huckfeldt, R. R. 1986. *Politics in Context: Assimilation and Conflict in Urban Neighborhoods*. New York, NY: Agathon Press, Inc.

Huckfeldt, Robert, and John Sprague. 1995. *Citizens, Politics, and Social Communication: Information and Influence in an Election Campaign*. New York, NY: Cambridge University Press.

Hudson, Winthrop S. 1961. *American Protestantism*. Chicago: The University of Chicago Press.

Hume, David. 1978. *A Treatise of Huma Nature*. Oxford: Oxford University Press.

Inazu, John D. 2016. *Confident Pluralism: Surviving and Thriving through Deep Difference*. Chicago: The University of Chicago Press.

Ingraham, Christopher. 2014. "White People Are Winning the War on Whites." *The Washington Post*. https://www.washingtonpost.com/news/wonk/wp/2014/08/07/white-people-are-winning-the-war-on-whites/. Accessed December 1, 2019.

Jacobson, Gary C. 1997. *The Politics of Congressional Elections*. 4th ed. New York: Longman.

Jacobson, Gary C. 2000. *The Politics of Congressional Elections.* 5th ed. Pacific Grove, CA: Brooks/Cole Publishing Company.

Jennings, James. 1994. "Conclusion: Racial Hierarchy and Ethnic Conflict in the United States." In James Jennings, ed. *Blacks, Hispanics, and Asians in Urban America.* Westport, CT: Praeger. pp. 143–158.

John C. Calhoun, Senate Speech of January 4, 1848. Cited from Steinfield, 1970, p.75.

Johnson, Jenna, and Philip Rucker. 2016. "In San Diego, Trump Shames Local 'Mexican' Judge as Protesters Storm Streets." *The Washington Post.* https://www.washingtonpost.com/news/post-politics/wp/2016/05/27/in-san-diego-trump -shames-local-mexican-judge-as-protesters-storm-streets/?utm_term=.adfb-1b8852ad. Accessed May 20, 2017.

Jost, Kenneth. 2005. "School Desegregation." In Issues in Race, Ethnicity and Gender, 2nd edition. CQ Press. pp. 173–197.

Kamarck, Elaine, and Christine Stenglein. 2019. "How Many Undocumented Immigrants Are in the United States and Who Are They?" *Brookings Institute.* https://www.brookings.edu/policy2020/votervital/how-many-undocumented -immigrants-are-in-the-united-states-and-who-are-they/. Accessed March 20, 2020.

Kantor, Jodi. 2012. "Romney's Faith, Silent but Deep." *The New York Times.* http://www.nytimes.com/2012/05/20/us/politics/how-the-mormon-church-shaped-mitt -romney.html?pagewanted=all&_r=1&. Accessed May 20, 2012.

Katznelson, Ira. 2005. *When Affirmative Action Was White: An Untold History of Racial Inequality in Twentieth-Century America.* New York: W. W. Norton & Company.

Kaufmann, Eric P. 2004a. *The Rise and Fall of Anglo-America.* Cambridge, MA: Harvard University Press.

Kaufmann, Eric P. 2004b. "The Decline of the WASP in the United States and Canada." in Rethinking Ethnicity: Majority Groups and Dominant Minorities. New York Routledge. Edited by Eric P. Kaufman. pp. 54–73.

Kendall, Brent. 2016. "Trump Says Judge's Mexican Heritage Presents 'Absolute Conflict'." *The Wall Street Journal.* https://www.wsj.com/articles/donald-trump -keeps-up-attacks-on-judge-gonzalo-curiel-1464911442. Accessed May 20, 2017.

Kersch, Ken I. 2004. *Constructing Civil Liberties: Discontinuity in the Development of American Constitutional Law.* New York, NY: Cambridge University Press.

Kertscher, Tom. 2016. "Donald Trump's Racial Comments about Hispanic Judge in Trump University Case." *Politifact.* http://www.politifact.com/wisconsin/article /2016/jun/08/donald-trumps- racial-comments-about-judge-trump-un/. Accessed May 20, 2017.

Kesler, Charles R. 2012. *I Am the Change: Barack Obama and the Crisis of Liberalism.* New York, NY: Broadside Books.

Key Jr., V.O. 1949. *Southern Politics in State and Nation.* New York: Alfred A. Knopf, Inc.

Kim, Thomas P. 2007. *The Racial Logic of Politics: Asian Americans and Party Competition.* Philadelphia, PA: Temple University Press.

Kim, Young Mie, and Kelly Garrett. 2012. "On-line *and* Memory-based: Revisiting the Relationship Between Candidate Evaluation Processing Models." *Political Behavior,* 34(2), 345–368.

Kinder, Donald R., and Cindy Kam. 2010. *Us Against Them: Ethnocentric Foundation of American Opinion*. Chicago: The University of Chicago Press.

Kinder, Donald R., and David O. Sears. 1981. "Prejudice and Politics: Symbolic Racism versus Racial Threats to the Good Life." *Journal of Personality and Social Psychology*, 40, 414–431.

Kinder, Donald R., and Lynn M. Sanders. 1996. *Divided by Color: Racial Politics and Democratic Ideas*. Chicago: University of Chicago Press.

Kinder, Donald R., and Nathan P. Kalmoe. 2017. *Neither Liberal Nor Conservative: Ideological Innocence in the American Republic*. Chicago: The University of Chicago Press.

King, Desmond, and Rogers Smith. 2011. *Still a House Divided: Race and Politics in Obama's America*. Princeton, NJ: Princeton University Press.

King, Desmond S., and Rogers M. Smith 2005. "Racial Orders in American Political Development." American Political Science Review 99 (1), 75–92.

King, G., R. O. Keohane, and S. Verba. 1994. *Designing Social Inquiry: Scientific Inference in Qualitative Research*. Princeton University Press.

King, Ryan D., and Melissa F. Weiner. 2007. "Group Position, Collective Threat, and American Anti-Semitism." *Social Problems*, 54(1), 47–77.

Kousser, Morgan J. 1999. *Colorblind Injustice: Minority Voting Rights and the Undoing of the Second Reconstruction*. Capel Hill, NC: The University of North Carolina Press.

Kranish, Michael, and Scott Helman. 2012. *The Real Romney*. New York, NY: HarperCollins Books.

Kusow, A. M., and M. Delisi. 2016. "Conceptualizing American Attitudes toward Immigrants Dual Loyalty." *Socius: Sociological Research for a Dynamic World*, 2(0), 1–12.

Ladd, Jr., Everett C., and Charles D. Hadley. 1975. *Transformation of the American Party System: Political Coalitions from the New Deal to the 1970s*. New York, NY: W.W. Norton & Company, Inc.

Lasswell, Harold. 1936. *Politics: Who Gets What, When, How*. New York: Whittlesey House.

Lau, Richard R., and David P. Redlawsk. 2006. *How Voters Decide*. Cambridge University Press.

Levistsky, Steven, and Daniel Ziblatt. 2018. *How Democracies Die*. New York: Crown.

Lewis-Beck, Michael S., William G. Jacoby, Helmut Norpoth, and Herbert F. Weisberg. 2008. *American Voters Revisited*. Ann Arbor, MI: The University of Michigan Press.

Lichtman, Alan J. 2008. *White Protestant Nation: The Rise of the American Conservative Movement*. New York, NY: Atlantic Monthly Press.

Lincoln, Abraham. 1855. "Letter to Joshua Speed." Abraham Lincoln Online: Speeches and Writings. http://www.abrahamlincolnonline.org/lincoln/speeches/speed.htm. Accessed July 14, 2017.

Lissak, Rivka Shpak. 1989. *Pluralism and Progressives: Hull House and the New Immigrants, 1890–1919*. Chicago, IL: University of Chicago Press.

Liu, Baodong. 2003. "Deracialization and Urban Racial Contexts." *Urban Affairs Review*, 38(4), 572–591.

Liu, Baodong. 2010. *The Election of Barack Obama: How He Won*. New York: Palgrave Macmillan.

Liu, Baodong. 2014. "Post-Racial Politics? Counterevidence from the Presidential Elections, 2004–2012." *Du Bois Review: Social Science Research on Race*, 11(2), 443–463.

Liu, Baodong, and James M. Vanderleeuw. 2007. *Race Rules: Electoral Politics in New Orleans, 1965–2006*. Lan Ham: Lexington Books.

Liu, Baodong, Zachary Stickney, and Nicole Batt. 2020. "Authoritarianism for and Against Trump." *Journal of Behavioral and Social Sciences*, 7(3), 218–238.

Longoria, T. 1999. "The Impact of Office on Cross-Racial Voting Evidence from the 1996 Milwaukee Mayoral Election." *Urban Affairs Review*, 34(4), 596–603.

Lynn, M., M. Sturman, C. Ganley, E. Adams, M. Douglas, and J. McNeil. 2008. "Consumer Racial Discrimination in Tipping: A Replication and Extension." *Journal of Applied Social Psychology*, 38, 1045–1060. doi:10.1111/j.1559-1816.2008.00338.x.

MacCallum, R. C., K. F. Widaman, K. J. Preacher, and S. Hong. 2001. "Sample Size in Factor Analysis: The Role of Model Error." *Multivariate Behavioral Research*, 36(4), 611–637.

Mac Donald, Heather. 2018. *The Diversity Delusion: How Race and Gender Pandering Corrupt the University and Undermine Our Culture*. New York: St. Martin's Press.

Machiavelli, Niccolo. 1977. *The Prince: A Norton Critical Edition*. (English translation by Robert M. Adams). New York: W.W. Norton & Company.

MacWilliams, Matthew C. 2016. "Who Decides When The Party Doesn't? Authoritarian Voters and the Rise of Donald Trump." *PS: Political Science & Politics*, 49(4), 716–721.

Mansfield, Harvey C. 1978. *The Spirit of Liberalism*. Cambridge, MA: Harvard University Press.

Martin, Stephanie. 2020. "The Danger of Nikki Haley and Rick Perry Saying Trump's Presidency was Ordained by God." *USA Today*. https://www.usatoday.com/story/opinion/2019/12/20/danger-nikki-haley-rick-perry-trumps-presidency-ordained-god-column/2667947001/. Accessed January 5, 2020.

Marx, G. T. 1971. *Racial Conflict*. Little, Brown.

Mason, Lilliana. 2018. *Uncivil Agreement: How Politics Became Our Identity*. Chicago: The University of Chicago Press.

Massey, D. S., and K. A. Pren. 2012. "Unintended Consequences of US Immigration Policy: Explaining the Post-1965 Surge from Latin America." *Population and Development Review*, 38(1), 1–29.

McClain, Paula D., and Joseph Stewart Jr. 2002. *"Can We All Get Along?" Racial and Ethnic Minorities in American Politics*. Denver, CO: Westview Press.

McClain, Paula D., Monique L. Lyle, Jeffrey D. Grynaviski, and Shayla C. Nunnally. 2008. "Black Elites and Latino Immigrant Relations in a Southern City: Do Black Elites and the Black Masses Agree?" In Jane Junn and Kerry L. Haynie, ed. *New*

Race Politics in America. Cambridge and New York: Cambridge University Press. pp. 145–165.

McCormick, Joseph, and Charles E. Jones. 1993. "The Conceptualization of Deracialization: Thinking Through the Dilemma." In Georgia A. Persons, ed. *Dilemma of Black Politics: Issues of Leadership and Strategy*. New York: Harper Collins College Publishers. pp. 66–84.

McDonald, Michael. 2020. "United States Elections Study Project." http://www.electproject.org/home/voter-turnout/demographics. Accessed June 1, 2020.

McRae, Elizabeth Gillespie. 2018. *Mothers of Massive Resistance: White Women and the Politics of White Supremacy*. New York: Oxford University Press.

Mellow, N. 2014. "The Elections of 2012." In M. Nelson, ed., *Voting Behavior: How the Democrats Rejuvenated Their Coalition*. CQ Press. pp.73–97.

Mendelberg, Tali. 2001. *The Race Card: Campaign Strategy, Implicit Messages, and the Norm of Equality*. Princeton University Press.

Miller, David. 1999. *Principle of Social Justice*. Cambridge, MA: Harvard University Press.

Milnor, A. J. 1969. *Elections and Political Stability*. Boston, MA: Little, Brown and Company.

Miringoff, Lee M., Babara L. Carvalho, and Mary E. Griffith. 2015. "Summary of National Survey Findings." *PBS NewsHour/Marist Poll*.

Moore, Leonard Joseph. 1985. *White Protestant Nationalism in the 1920's: The Ku Klux Klan in Indiana*. Unpublished doctoral dissertation, University of California at Los Angeles.

Moore, Peter. 2016. "Most Americans Say that Trump's Comments about Gonzalo Curiel Were Racist, But Most Republicans Disagree." *YouGov*. https://today.yougov.com/news/2016/06/08/slim-majority-americans-trump-comments-racist/ . Accessed May 20, 2017.

Mulcare, D. M. 2008. "Restricted Authority Slavery Politics, Internal Improvements, and the Limitation of National Administrative Capacity." *Political Research Quarterly*, 61(4), 671–685.

Mutz, Dianna C. 1997. "Mechanisms of Momentum: Does Thinking Make It So?" *Journal of Politics*, 59, 104–125.

Nackenoff, Carol. 2014. "Borrowing and Building State Capacity: The Immigrants' Protective League's "Friendly and Sympathetic Touch," 1908–1924." *American Political Development*, 28(02), 129–160.

Nakanishi, Don T., and James S. Lai, ed. 2003. *Asian American Politics: Law, Participation, and Policy*. Rowman and Littlefield Publishers, Inc. see especially, Part I, the four Supreme Court Decisions concerning Asian Americans: pp. 47–88.

Nelson, M. 2014. *The Elections of 2012*. CQ Press.

Norton, Michael I., and Samuel R. Sommers. 2011. "Whites See Racism as a Zero-Sum Game that They Are Now Losing." *Perspectives on Psychological Science*, 6, 215–218.

Novkov, J. 2008. "Rethinking Race in American Politics." *Political Research Quarterly*, 61(4), 649–659.

Olson, Laura R., and John C. Green. 2006. "The Religious Gap." *PS: Political Science and Politics*, 39, 455–459.

Orey, Byron D'Andra, L. Marvin Overby, Pete Hatemi, and Baodong Liu. 2011. "White Support for Racial Referenda in the Deep-South." *Politics & Policy*, 39(4), 539–558.

Passel, Jefferey, and D'Vera Cohn. 2014. "Pew Research Center, Chapter 2: Birthplaces of U.S. Unauthorized Immigrants." *Pew Hispanic.* http://www.pewhispanic.org/2014/11/18/chapter-2-birthplaces-of-u-s-unauthorized-immigrants/. Accessed May 9, 2017.

Perdue, Theda, and Michael D. Green. 1995. *The Cherokee Removal: A Brief History with Documents.* Boston, MA: Bedford Books of St. Martin's Press. pp. 73–74.

Persons, G. A. 1993. *Dilemmas of Black Politics: Issues of Leadership and Strategy.* New York, NY: Harper Collins Publishers.

Petracca, Mark P. 1991. "Divided Government and the Risks of Constitutional Reform." *PS: Political Science & Politics XXIV*, 4, 634–637.

Pettigrew, Thomas. 1972. "When a Black Candidate Runs for Mayor: Race and Voting Behavior." In Harlan Hahn, ed. *People and Politics in Urban Society.* Beverly Hills: Sage. pp.99–105.

Phillips, Kevin P. 1969. *The Emerging Republican Majority.* New Rochelle, NY: Arlington.

Polybius. 1991. "The Histories." In William Ebenstein and Alan O. Ebenstein, ed. Great *Political Thinkers: Plato to the Present.* New York: Harcourt Brace Jovanovich College Publishers. p. 138.

Putnam, Robert. 2000. *Bowling Alone: The Collapse and Revival of American Community.* New York, NY: Simon and Schuster.

Putnam, Robert, and David Campbell. 2010. *American Grace: How Religion Divides and Unites Us.* New York, NY: Simon and Schuster.

Rawls, John. 1971. *A Theory of Justice.* Cambridge: Harvard University Press.

Reilly, Shauna. 2020. *The Trifecta in Voting Barrier Causation: Economics, Politics, and Race.* Lanham, MD: Lexington Books.

Rethinking Ethnicity: Majority Groups and Dominant Minorities. London and New York: Routledge. pp. 116–135.

Ribberink, Egbert, Peter Achterberg, and Dick Houtman. 2013. "Deprivatization of Disbelief?: Non-Religiosity and Anti-Religiosity in 14 Western European Countries." *Politics and Religion*, 6(1), 101–120.

Rieselback, Leroy. 1994. *Congressional Reform.* Washington, DC: CQ Press.

Riker, William H. 1962. *The Theory of Political Coalition.* New Haven, CT: Yale University Press.

Ripley, Randall B., and Grace A. Franklin. 1992. *Congress: The Bureaucracy, and Public Policy.* Chicago, IL: Dorsey Press.

Rosen, Jay. 1996. *Getting the Connections Right: Public Journalism and the Troubles in the Press.* New York: Twentieth Century Fund.

Rozell, Mark, and Clyde Wilcox, ed. 2016. *God at the Grassroots 2016.* Lanham, MD: Roman and Littlefield.

Samson, Frank L. 2013. "Multiple Group Threat and Malleable White Attitudes toward Academic Merit." *Du Bois Review*, 10(1), 233–260.

Sanders, Elizabeth. 1999. *Roots of Reform: Farmers, Workers, and the American State, 1877–1917.* Chicago, IL: University of Chicago Press.

Satori, Giovanni. 1987. *The Theory of Democracy Revisited*. Chatham, NJ: Chatham House Publishers.

Schaeffer, Katherine. 2019. "Democrats Far More Likely Than Republicans to See Discrimination Against Blacks, Not Whites." *Pew Research Center*. https://www.pewresearch.org/fact-tank/2019/11/20/in-a-rising-number-of-u-s-counties-hispanic-and-black-americans-are-the-majority/

Scherer, Michael. 2007. "A Vote for Romney Is a Vote for Satan." *Salon*. http://www.salon.com/2007/11/06/mormons_2/. Accessed November 6, 2007.

Schilken, Chuck. 2017. "Protests: LeBron James' Remarks Take on Trump." *Los Angeles Times*. http://www.latimes.com/sports/nba/la-sp-lebron-james-trump-20170925-story.html. Accessed February 20, 2018.

Schmidt Sr., Ronald, Yvette M. Alex-Assensoh, Andrew L. Aoki, and Rodney E. Hero. 2009. *Newcomers, Outsiders, and Insiders: Immigrants and American Racial Politics in the Early Twenty-First Century*. Ann Arbor, MI: The University of Michigan Press.

Schrag, Peter. 1971. *The Decline of the Wasp*. New York: Simon & Schuster.

Schreiber, Darren. 2011. "From SCAN to Neuropolitics." In Peter K. Hatemi, and Rose McDermott, ed. *Man Is by Nature a Political Animal: Evolution, Biology, and Politics*. Chicago, IL: University of Chicago Press. pp. 273–299.

Skocpol, Theda. 2012. *Obama and America's Political Future*. Cambridge, MA: Harvard University Press.

Smith, Kevin B., and John R. Hibbing. 2011. "The Mind-Body Connection: Psychophysiology as an Approach to Studying Political Attitudes and Behaviors." In Peter K. Hatemi and Rose McDermott, ed. *Man Is by Nature a Political Animal: Evolution, Biology, and Politics*. Chicago, IL: University of Chicago Press. pp. 224–246.

Smith, Rogers. 2015. *Political Peoplehood: The Roles of Values, Interests, and Identities*. Chicago, IL: The University of Chicago Press.

Sonenshein, Raphael. 1993. *Politics in Black and White: Race and Power in Los Angeles*. Princeton, NJ: Princeton University Press.

Stark, Rodney, and Roger Finke. 1999. *Act of Faith: Explaining the Human Side of Religion*. Los Angeles, CA: University of California Press.

Stark, Rodney, Laurence R. Iannaccone, and Roger Finke. 1996. "Religion, Science, and Rationality." *American Economic Review*, 86, 433–437.

Steele, Shelby. 2008. *A Bound Man: Why We Are Excited about Obama and Why He Can't Win*. New York: Free Press.

Steinfield, Melvin. 1970. *Cracks in the Melting Pot: Racism and Discrimination in American History*. Beverly Hills, CA: Glencoe Press.

Stenner, Karen. 2005. *The Authoritarian Dynamic*. New York: Cambridge University Press.

Stevens, J. P. 2002. *Applied Multivariate Statistics for the Social Sciences*. Hillsdale, NJ: Erlbaum.

Sundquist, James L. 1992. *Constitutional Reform and Effective Government*. Rev. ed. Washington: Brookings Institute.

Swain, Carol M. 2002. *The New White Nationalism in America: Its Challenge to Integration*. New York: Cambridge University Press.

Takaki, Ronald. 1998. *Strangers from a Different Shore*. Boston, MA: Back Bay Books.

Tamir, Yael. 1993. *Liberal Nationalism.* Princeton, NJ: Princeton University Press. Cited from Kaufmann, Eric P. 2004b. *The Rise and Fall of Anglo- America.* Cambridge, MA: Harvard University Press. p. 285.

Tate, Katherine. 2014. *Concordance: Black Lawmaking in the U.S. Congress from Cater to Obama.* University of Michigan Press.

Taylor, M. C. 1998. "How White Attitudes Vary with the Racial Composition of Local Populations: Numbers Count." *American Sociological Review*, 63(4): 512–535.

Tesler, Michael. 2016. *Post-Racial or Most-Racial: Race and Politics in the Obama Era.* Chicago, IL: University of Chicago Press.

The New York Evening Post editorial published on December 24, 1847. From Steinfield, Melvin. 1970. *Cracks in the Melting Pot: Racism and Discrimination in American History.* Beverly Hills, CA: Glencoe Press. p. 74.

Thernstrom, S., and A. Thernstrom. 1999. *America in Black and White: One Nation, Indivisible.* Touchstone Books.

Thinkers: Plato to the Present. New York: Harcourt Brace Jovanovich College Publishers., 1991. p. 138.

Tocqueville, de Alexis. 2000. *Democracy in America.* Translated by Harvey C. Mansfield and Delba Winthrop. Chicago: The University of Chicago Press.

Tolbert, Caroline and Peverill Squire. 2009. "Reforming the Presidential Nomination Process." *PS: Political Science and Politics*, 42(1, January), 27–31.

Uenuma, Francine. "During the Mexican-American War, Irish-Americans Fought for Mexico in the 'Saint Patrick's Battalion'." *Smithsonian Magazine.* https://www.smithsonianmag.com/history/mexican-american-war-irish-immigrants-deserted-us-army-fight-against-america-180971713/. Accessed March 20, 2020.

U.S. Department of Justice. 2020. https://www.justice.gov/crt/search-cases-and-matters. Accessed June 1, 2020.

"'Vote for Romney Is Vote for Satan': Christian Leader Follows Up Sharpton Attack on Mormons." *WND.* http://www.wnd.com/2007/05/41546/#ZgRrLvPSV4PgtEHk.99. Accessed May 10, 2007.

Wald, Kenneth D., and Allison Calhoun-Brown. 2011. *Religion and Politics in the United States.* Lanham, MD: Rowman and Littlefield Publishers, Inc.

Walzer, Michael. 1984. *Spheres of Justice.* New York, NY: Basic Books.

Wasserman, David. 2020. "Who's behind Trump's Big Polling Deficit? Two Key Groups Defecting to Biden." *The Cook Political Report.* https://cookpolitical.com/analysis/national/national-politics/whos-behind-trumps-big-deficit-college-educated-whites-and/. Accessed July 24, 2020.

Welna, David. 2020. "Citing Election Delay Tweet, Influential Trump Ally Now Demands His Re-Impeachment." *NPR.* https://www.npr.org/2020/07/31/897724197/citing-election-delay-tweet-influential-trump-ally-now-demands-his-re-impeachmen. Accessed July 30, 2020.

West, Darrell M. 2010. *Air Wars: Television Advertising in Election Campaigns, 1952–2008.* Washington, DC: CQ Press. p. 31.

Whitehead, Andrew L., Samuel L. Perry, and Joseph O. Baker. 2018. "Make America Christian Again: Christian Nationalism and Voting for Donald Trump in the 2016

Presidential Election." *Sociology of Religion: A Quarterly Review*, 79(2), 1–25. doi:10.1093/socrel/srx070.

Wilcox, Clyde and Carin Robinson. 2011. *Onward Christian Soldiers? The Religious Right in American Politics*. Boulder, CO: Westview Press.

Williams, Melissa S. 1998. *Voice, Trust, and Memory: Marginalized Groups and the Failings of Liberal Representation*. Princeton, NJ: Princeton University Press.

Wilson, David C., and Darren W. Davis. 2011. "Reexamining Racial Resentment: Conceptualization and Content." *The Annals of the American Academy*, 634(March), 117–133.

Wilson, Woodrow. 1902. *A History of the American People*. New York: Harper & Brothers. Volume 5. p. 58.

Winant, Howard. 2004. "Behind Blue Eyes: Whiteness and Contemporary U.S. Racial Politics." In Michelle Fine, Lois Weis, Linda Powell Pruitt, April Burns, ed. *Off White: Readings on Power, Privilege, and Resistance*. New York and London: Routledge. pp. 3–16.

Winkler, Adam. 2013. "Are Polygamy Bans Unconstitutional?" *Huffington Post*. http://www.huffingtonpost.com/adam-winkler/are-polygamy-bans- unconst_b _4454076.html. Accessed December 16, 2013.

Wong, Janelle. 2018. "The Evangelical Vote and Race in the 2016 Presidential Election." *Journal of Race, Ethnicity and Politics*, 1–26. doi:10.1017/rep.2017.32.

Wright, Sharon D., and Richard Middleton. 2001. "The 2001 Los Angeles Mayoral Election: Implications for Deracialization and Biracial Coalition Theories." *Politics and Policy*, 29(4), 692–707.

Wright, Theodore P. 2004. "The Identity and Changing Status of Former Elite Minorities: The Contrasting Cases of North Indian Muslims and American WASPs." In Eric P. Kaufmann, eds. *Rethinking Ethnicity: Majority Groups and Dominant Minorities*. London and New York: Routledge. pp. 40–58.

Yinger, J. Milton. 1985. "Assimilation in the United States: the Mexican- Americans." In Walker Connor, ed. *Mexican-Americans in Comparative Perspective*, Washington, DC: Urban Institute Press. pp. 29–55.

Zaballos-Rolg, Joseph. 2020. "Warren Tore into Bloomberg at the Democratic Debate for Linking the End of Discriminatory Housing Practice to the 2008 Financial Crisis." *Markets Insider*. https://markets.businessinsider.com/news/stocks/war-ren-tears-bloomberg-redlining-financial-crash-democratic-debate-discriminatory-housing-2020-2-1028924265. Accessed April 20, 2020.

Zaller, John R. 1992. *The Nature and Origins of Mass Opinion*. Cambridge University Press.

Zhou, Min. 2009. "Rethinking Assimilation: The Paradox of "Model Minority" and "Perpetual Foreigner." In *Contemporary Chinese America: Immigration, Ethnicity, and Community Transformation*. Temple University Press. pp. 221–236.

Zschirnt, Simon. 2011. "The Origins & Meaning of Liberal/Conservative Self-Identifications Revisited." *Political Behavior*, 33(4), 685–701.

Index

About the Author

Baodong Liu is a professor of political science and ethnic studies at The University of Utah. His many books include *The Election of Barack Obama: How He Won*; *Race Rules: Electoral Politics in New Orleans, 1965–2006*; *Solving the Mystery of the Model Minority: the Journey of Asian Americans in America*; and *Social Research: Integrating Mathematical Foundations and Modern Statistical Computing*.

www.ingramcontent.com/pod-product-compliance
Lightning Source LLC
Chambersburg PA
CBHW050641280326
41932CB00015B/2741